A Woman's Framework for a Successful
Career and Life

A Woman's Framework for a Successful Career and Life

James Hamerstone and Lindsay Musser Hough

palgrave
macmillan

A WOMAN'S FRAMEWORK FOR A SUCCESSFUL CAREER AND LIFE

First published in 2013 by
PALGRAVE MACMILLAN®
in the United States—a division of St. Martin's Press LLC,
175 Fifth Avenue, New York, NY 10010.

Where this book is distributed in the UK, Europe and the rest of the world,
this is by Palgrave Macmillan, a division of Macmillan Publishers Limited,
registered in England, company number 785998, of Houndmills,
Basingstoke, Hampshire RG21 6XS.

Palgrave Macmillan is the global academic imprint of the above companies
and has companies and representatives throughout the world.

Palgrave® and Macmillan® are registered trademarks in the United States,
the United Kingdom, Europe and other countries.

ISBN: 978–1–137–29318–3 (hc)
ISBN: 978–1–137–29319–0 (pbk)

Library of Congress Cataloging-in-Publication Data

Hamerstone, James, 1942–
    A woman's framework for a successful career and life / James
Hamerstone and Lindsay Musser Hough.
        pages cm
    Includes bibliographical references and index.
    ISBN 978–1–137–29319–0 (alk. paper)—
    ISBN 978–1–137–29318–3 (alk. paper)
    1. Women—Employment. 2. Career development. 3. Women
professional employees. I. Musser Hough, Lindsay, 1976– II. Title.

HD6053.H2596 2013
650.1082—dc23   2013000422

A catalogue record of the book is available from the British Library.

Design by Newgen Imaging Systems (P) Ltd., Chennai, India.

First edition: July 2013

10 9 8 7 6 5 4 3 2 1

Transferred to Digital Printing in 2013

From James Hamerstone

To my mother, wife, daughter, daughters-in-law, and my granddaughter, who helped me to understand women and allowed me to give them advice

To my students, whose enthusiasm for the topic and helpful insights motivated me to write this book

From Lindsay Musser Hough

To my parents, Sandy and Tim, who taught me as a child that I really could do anything I wanted to and continue to support me in that effort today

To my husband Adam, whose support of me continues to be unwavering

And to Amelia and Cole, who inspire me to leave the world a little better than how I found it

Contents

List of Figures and Tables   ix

Acknowledgments   xi

Chapter 1   Introduction   1

Part I   What Women Need to Build in Order to Have a Successful Career

Chapter 2   Build Your... Board   7

Chapter 3   Build Your... Brand   27

Chapter 4   Build Your... Communication Skills   45

Chapter 5   Build Your... Negotiation Skills   65

Part II   What Women Need to Consider throughout a Successful Career

Chapter 6   Consider ... Ambition   89

Chapter 7   Consider ... Leadership   103

Chapter 8   Consider ... Work-Life Fit   125

Chapter 9   Consider ... Career-Path Navigation   141

Chapter 10   Consider ... Working in a Global Environment   157

Chapter 11   Do ... Put It All Together   175

Notes   179

Bibliography   191

Index   203

Figures and Tables

Figures

2.1	Personal board of advisors	10
2.2	Phases of mentoring	14
2.3	Network components	19
2.4	Network rings	21
2.5	Integrated network	24
3.1	Your personal brand	30
3.2	Brand SWOT analysis	33
3.3	Job interview process	39
4.1	Power poses	62
5.1	Locus of Control	67
5.2	Integrated approach to negotiation	73
7.1	Management style of transformational leader	110
7.2	Strategic planning process	115
7.3	Your personal leadership style	122
8.1	Factors influencing your perspective on work-life balance	130

Tables

2.1	Managing your board	13
2.2	Maintaining connections with your network	23
3.1	Sample brand SWOT analysis	34
4.1	Actions requiring an apology	52
4.2	Situations that do not require an apology	53
4.3	Peggy Klaus's bragging myths	56
4.4	Your elevator speech	58
4.5	How to punch up your value statement	59
4.6	Cheat sheet for professional dress	64
5.1	Impact of negotiating a starting salary	79

5.2	Answering common compensation questions	81
8.1	US work and family historical trends	128
9.1	Flexible work arrangement options	145
9.2	Sample conversation flow when requesting a flexible work arrangement	148
10.1	Trompenaars's seven fundamentals of culture	169
10.2	Individualism versus collectivism	171

Acknowledgments

Many people have given us support for this book, and we thank them sincerely for their contributions.

The book grew out of a course Jim taught at Gettysburg College, where Lindsay was a frequent guest speaker. As such, we are grateful to the young women who enrolled in the course for sharing their perspectives on these issues through conversations and research papers. The course was shaped over time through their input. We particularly appreciated the insights from women who, after graduation, reported back to us about the useful aspects of the course as they began their professional careers. Additionally, the accomplished and candid guest speakers who participated in the course added practical experience to bolster the concepts being studied in class.

Elizabeth Richardson-Viti, a French professor at Gettysburg College with a strong interest in women's studies, originally encouraged Jim to develop and teach a course for young women who are about to leave academia and join the workforce. Her input regarding course content was extremely helpful and her ongoing support for the class has been appreciated.

Clare Hartigan, Chelsea Wendlinger, and Shannon McWilliams were student assistants for the course and were exceptionally helpful in early courses. Their suggestions and enthusiasm for the topic led Jim to continue teaching the class and to write this book. Kelsey McCormick and particularly, Stephanie Gulden, both college seniors, provided research assistance, organizational support, and candid advice for the book.

Sarah Clayville supported us through all the early drafts of the manuscript with specific and gentle editing. Sarah is an accomplished author, respected teacher, and fun-loving mother of two whose encouragement and quick turn-around on reviews was very helpful in keeping the momentum going in our writing process. Cynthia Graeff did a terrific job of bringing our thoughts alive through the creation of the figures and illustrations and Jennifer Baish was patient enough to do photography work for us.

Lindsay could not have written this book without the support of her employer, and is grateful for the encouragement she received for her participation in this effort.

Numerous women shared their stories with us and provided feedback on early versions of chapters. Meredith Bove, Maia Comeau, and Diane Cramer all provided thoughtful feedback that was incorporated into the book.

We can't quite recall how we were first connected, but it's likely that Charlie Scott, a fellow Gettysburg alum and accomplished leader in the field of talent consulting, introduced us to each other. Charlie's workshop on interviewing skills provided the basis for the content on that topic in this book. If it wasn't Charlie who first introduced us to each other then, it most likely was Kathy Williams, the director of the Gettysburg College Center for Career Development. Kathy and her team were always willing to help connect course activity with related efforts at the Center for Career Development.

As any parent knows, there is nothing more important than the care of your children. Lindsay continues to be extremely grateful to Denise Pion and Sandy Musser for their loving care of Amelia and Cole. If she didn't have that support, neither her career, nor this book would be possible.

Jim is grateful to his daughter, Sarah, for her perspective on the topics in this book, as well as his daughters-in-law Ann and Brandi, for sharing their thoughts. Finally, we thank our spouses. Lindsay's husband Adam rarely blinks anymore when she comes up with a new idea or project and knowing that he'll be supportive enables her to grow professionally and personally. Jim's wife Lisa provided early and ongoing encouragement for the book, without which, this idea may never have come to fruition.

CHAPTER 1

Introduction

Over the last two decades, opportunities for women have increased dramatically. Women commonly hold US cabinet positions. They lead large corporations and global nongovernmental organizations. Women make up about 58 percent of college graduates and 50 percent of professional workers.[1] They account for a third of lawyers and doctors,[2] up from less than 10 percent in 1970.[3] Still, the proportion of women in leadership positions continues to hover below 15 percent,[4] and in a recent survey of Gen-Y women, a whopping 77 percent indicated they believe gender discrimination is still an issue in the workplace.[5] Reports like these have led some to suggest that perhaps women's progress in the workplace has stalled.[6]

There is no one reason that explains why more women aren't in leadership roles; and even if we were able to identify it, addressing one issue alone wouldn't be a silver bullet for success. Building a satisfying career isn't easy for women or men, and unfortunately hard work alone won't make it happen. Women who successfully manage work do so intentionally and take responsibility for nurturing their careers on an ongoing basis. They create options for their work and family life; they take steps to see that they are compensated appropriately; and they engage others as advisors throughout their careers.

Why We Wrote This Book

There are a slew of great books with guidance on how women can move forward in their careers. Unfortunately, we find that because these books tend to be targeted at women closer to the midpoints of their careers, younger women aren't being exposed to many of these important concepts early enough in their career. As a result, those fresh to the workforce are hitting roadblocks that could have been avoided in the first place. Young women may also be missing out on opportunities unique to women early in their careers. Formulating a perspective on work-life fit early in your career will influence the little decisions you make along the way, ensuring that they are consistent with your own perspective. Understanding how to build your own board of advisors enables you to pick up the best supporters along the way, instead of finding yourself stuck as a middle manager without the support base necessary to move to the leadership level. Fine-tuning a personal leadership style throughout your early career is preferable to trying to establish a leadership presence after you have already been in the workforce without one. In short, if you establish positive practices at the start of your career, you are setting yourself up for long-term success.

How to Use This Book

While the chapters are loosely connected and build on one another, for the most part, you may chose to read through the topics in whatever order you choose; each one is essentially a stand-alone discussion of the issue. These topics each include a summary of key research and leading thought on these issues. The chapters are infused with examples and commentary from successful women of all ages, gathered through conversations and interviews with women in business, government, and not-for-profit organizations. These real examples (though names and identifying details have been changed in each story) illustrate the points we make. We also recommend additional reading if you have the need or interest to explore any of the topics further.

Why Books Like This Are Needed

The idea for this book grew out of a popular class Jim was teaching at Gettysburg College centered on women in organizations. Lindsay, a regular guest speaker in the class, was not only impressed with both the intensity and engagement of the students in the class, but also concerned about what she identified as a real lack of readiness by the students to be successful in the early years of their careers. Women clearly demonstrated the technical competency to move forward in their chosen careers, but often exposed a hesitancy or ambivalence when it came to discussions around career paths, negotiation, ambition, and leadership. It is for this reason we decided to write this book.

At times we engage in conversation with people who question whether books like this are still necessary. We offer two reasons:

1. The data about the disproportionate number of women in leadership roles is compelling. The reasons for this issue are complex—discrimination, conflicting expectations around gender roles, and persistent organizational cultures of inflexibility are just a few reasons commonly identified.

2. There are often core stylistic differences between men and women that impact how they can operate most successfully at work. Both men and women perform better when they understand how these differences may impact their own approaches to work as well as perceptions of them by others.

Throughout this book, we strive to take a positive, balanced approach to these issues. It is not our intent to operate from a "deficit" model. Such a perspective suggests that the male way—which is often still the basis for organizational, particularly corporate, norms in the United States and globally—is the "right" way, and that women need to be "fixed." We are not supportive of this kind of approach to addressing gender differences in the workplace. However, at its core, this is an advice book, and it is our intent to make suggestions that move you toward your career goal. Sometimes those suggestions may involve acknowledging that discrimination and bias exist, and implementing strategies to minimize these factors. You can't control what others think about you or how they treat you; but you can always benefit from advice and information on how to achieve your desired result. Our approach isn't meant to take the place of legal, political, or cultural changes that may still be needed in some situations. Rather, we offer practical approaches that can be used by women now in any type of organization.

Continued Shifts in the Environment for Working Women

While women still face bias and discrimination, they experience less of it now than in past years. Now, women have female role models in all fields and, increasingly, in their own offices. Many employers offer career development programs for all employees focused on mentoring and improving business skills.

Additionally, for many women, how and where they perform work is changing due to technology. New and exciting tools have paved the way for working in a different way. Such changes enable some women and men to work from home, stay in touch when they may be engaged with a family commitment during business hours, and keep connected with caregivers and family who need support during the workday. Organizations are increasingly offering benefits that appeal to working parents, such as parental leave, part-time policies, and flexible work arrangements.

Chapter Topics

The first part of the book is more skills focused, while the second half offers perspectives for you to consider while navigating your career.

- Part I: What Women Need to Build in Order to Have a Successful Career

  - Build Your...Board: Introduces the concept of a personal board of advisors and discusses how you can develop the mentor and sponsor relationships you need
  - Build Your...Brand: Articulates the definition of a personal brand and guides you through the process of creating your own
  - Build Your...Communication Skills: Explains the differences in how men and women communicate and suggests approaches to strengthening your own skills
  - Build Your...Negotiation Skills: Illustrates how critical it is to negotiate early and often throughout your career

- Part II: What Women Need to *Consider* throughout a Successful Career

  - Consider...Ambition: Tackles the sensitive subject of women's ambition and offers some perspectives for you to consider regarding your own ambition
  - Consider...Leadership: Uses a historical lens, with input from current approaches to management and employee involvement, to explain perceptions and challenges for women leaders
  - Consider ... Work-Life Fit: Addresses what continues to be one of the toughest aspects for early–mid-career women
  - Consider...Career-Path Navigation: Offers some new metaphors for careers that are more consistent with the realities of successful working women and makes suggestions on how to navigate your own
  - Consider...Working Globally: Discusses both working globally and working on global teams, which are experiences increasingly required for career growth

The book closes with advice on bringing all the insights together and building *a framework for a successful career and life* in "Do...Put It All Together."

PART I

What Women Need to Build in Order to Have a Successful Career

CHAPTER 2

Build Your ... Board

The school principal tells Aliyah, a third-year teacher in the school, to come to his office. He informs her that she is being offered a position in the school district's unit that is focused on helping other teachers incorporate technology into their classroom. Aliyah, excited about the offer, asks for a few days to think about it. On her way home she starts making calls to people for advice. Her first call is to the teacher who mentored her during her initial year of teaching, the second to teacher who used to work in the same unit, and the third to a friend from graduate school who took a similar role in another district.

Liz is on the train, on her way to Washington, DC, for a professional conference. She is excited about the event—her department chair approved the payment of the fee and travel by the hospital. But as she looks over the detailed schedule, she sees many long breaks and pre-/post-dinner socials. She knows they will likely be filled with sales representatives from pharmaceutical and other life sciences product companies. "Ugh," she thinks, "I hate those events with all the small talk. I think I'll use that time to get some exercise at the hotel gym."

When Aliyah left the principal's office, she knew who she wanted to call before she got into her car. Although she may not have known the term, the individuals she was calling were members of her unofficial "board of advisors." Typically, a board of advisors (or directors) is a group of elected or appointed members who jointly oversee the activities of a company or organization. And believe it or not, you need your very own personalized board. Your life—including your career—will present choices, decisions, and options—and you will find yourself seeking advice. In these situations, having a personal board already in place means that there are a group of advisors prepared to help you navigate the next opportunity or potential turn in your career.

This personalized board is a core component of your broader network, which includes individuals with whom you have some kind of common connection. In the example above, Liz is faced with an opportunity to grow her network but is reluctant to engage in what she finds to be exhausting and somewhat painful social exchanges. Unfortunately, she is missing a valuable opportunity. On the other hand, Aliyah's previous work establishing her board of advisors enables her to quickly tap them for advice as she considers the offer for the new position.

The Issue

A board of advisors is your own group of mentors and sponsors, and it's critical that you have this team in place. In both the ambition and leadership chapters, we report on the gender gap in leadership positions. At Fortune 500 companies, women hold only 16 percent of corporate office positions[1] and only 4 percent of CEOs of Fortune 500 companies are women.[2] Of all the programs and approaches proposed to shift these numbers, most agree that mentoring is one of the most important and effective tools.[3] For women, particularly those in male-dominated fields, sponsorship (a very focused form of mentoring where someone more senior personally promotes your career and helps you to navigate obstacles) provides legitimacy that is critical to upward mobility in the organization. Although much of the research is focused on the impacts of mentoring on women and minorities, there is clear evidence that all individuals benefit from mentoring. Across genders, individuals with mentors have higher salaries and advance more quickly than those without mentors. In fact, a 2010 report by Catalyst included research that demonstrated men may actually benefit more than women from mentoring; the reasons though are ones from which we can all learn.[4] It turned out that men selected mentors who tended to be more senior in the organization, presumably with more power to promote and back their mentee. Essentially the men's mentors were serving as full-fledged sponsors. This sponsorship concept is one we explore in this chapter.

Making It Work

Mentor, sponsor, buddies—think of these as essential roles on your personal board. All the roles must be filled for you to be positioned well for long-term success, just like any commercial or nonprofit organization's board must be well staffed. It is important to consider who should fill those roles, what your commitment to and relationship is with those individuals, and finally, how you yourself are paying it forward and serving as a mentor to others.

The Board Concept

Why More Is Better

The idea of a personal board of advisors has been promoted for years. In a 2010 *Harvard Business Review* collection on mentoring, Priscilla Claman, president of Career Strategies, makes a powerful case for the creation of a board versus one mentor.[5] She highlights the following benefits of assembling such a team:

- Today a midlevel or senior manager is just as likely to leave or be laid off as more junior staff. If you have just one mentor, and that mentor leaves, you may find yourself unsupported and unconnected in your organization.
- Claman also points out that "no one person could possibly give you all the guidance and nurturing you'll need to reach your potential." In other words, the job is just too big for one person. You'll benefit from the advice of many.

In their book *Break Your Own Rules,*[6] the partners of Flynn Heath Holt Leadership suggest that a "board of directors" be comprised as many as six sponsors. They propose a team model as a way of building advocates for your career to help you advance to the next level. Another benefit of a board model is that it encompasses more nontraditional mentoring relationships, such as peer mentoring. A mentoring relationship with a person at your level, but perhaps with longer history in the organization, or in a different business unit, can be a valuable relationship. Harvard Business School Press's book *Coaching and Mentoring: How to Development Top Talent and Achieve Stronger Performance* includes an entire chapter on peer mentoring, citing studies that have demonstrated that relationships with professional peers can be as or more important than those with superiors.[7]

Positions on Your Board

"Mentor" is the word most often used to describe a more experienced person providing guidance to a less experienced individual. However, there are many other important positions on one's personal board of advisors as illustrated in figure 2.1.

Mentor
Mentor is the name of a character in the epic Greek poem *Odyssey*. The Goddess Athene disguises herself as a mentor in order to serve as both guide and advisor to Telemachus. The use of the word has changed over time; the current definition according to the *Oxford English Dictionary* is, "The action

Figure 2.1   Personal board of advisors. A robust personal board of advisors comprises a variety of individuals who are willing to support you in the achievement of you career goals.

of advising or training another person, especially one who is younger and less experienced."[8] Today, most women (and men) know they need to have a mentor and typically seek one out, formally and/or informally. People typically look to a mentor to provide advice and feedback, and guide them through an organization or industry. A mentor can be assigned through a formal mentoring program or the relationship may develop organically, based on a natural connection made with a more senior person.

Sponsor
A sponsor takes on responsibility for a person's career and as a result, overtly or quietly takes action on his or her behalf. Sponsors advocate for the individual and support them. In *The Sponsor Effect: Breaking through the Last Glass Ceiling*, a study coordinated by the Center for Talent Innovation, research revealed that qualified women were held back because they didn't have the backing to inspire, propel, and protect themselves on their journey through upper management. The study essentially disclosed that too many women lacked *sponsorship*.[9] The concept of a sponsor goes beyond that of a mentor. A sponsor is a clear supporter; someone who wants you to do well and is willing to be a "table pounder" as an advocate for you and your career. A sponsor is someone who actively promotes you in your organization and is willing to do more than just give you advice and teach you the ropes.

A similar 2012 study by the same organization but of women in the United Kingdom,[10] indicated highly qualified British women were not breaking through to leadership positions. The researchers concluded that it wasn't because there aren't enough work-life balance programs; instead the reason for the lack of progression into leadership roles was because women tended not to have sponsors. The authors defined sponsors as "powerful champions willing to take a bet on a young talent, go out on a limb for him/her and advocate for the next promotion. Sponsors are the people that propel and protect high performing employees through the treacherous shoals of upper management." The study found that men with sponsors are 40 percent more likely to be promoted than men without, while women with a sponsor are 52 percent more likely to be promoted.

Peer Mentoring: A Buddy
A "buddy" is a peer mentor—an individual at your own level in the organization's hierarchy, but who has been with the organization longer than you and can help guide you through some of the more mundane and personal aspects of succeeding in a new position. A buddy can answer general questions about the organization's rules, written and unwritten. Lindsay developed a buddy relationship at one of her first jobs—essentially a friendly peer in the cubicle next to her—who, among other things, was kind enough to explain the complicated parking hierarchy in the office parking garage. A peer relationship such as this is extremely helpful for questions that are important, but inappropriate for a senior mentor—because they are too trivial, too personal, or even too embarrassing. Examples would include questions about dress code, how late people are really expected to stay on Friday, or whether spouses usually participate in corporate social events. Additionally, smart employees have much they can learn from each other— they can share experiences and solutions to common issues. They also serve as a source of emotional support when needed. Buddies or peer mentors may or may not be a core part of your personal "board" but they should be part of your extended network.

Your Board Composition

Your board should consist of a small group of people who care about you and are in a position to provide sound counsel on your career. Mentors, sponsors, and sometimes buddies, should serve on your board. Given the significant value that a true sponsor has for a woman's career, you should seek to have a multiple sponsors on your personal board. The benefit to you is twofold: you benefit from richer advice with a wider pool of people and your position is enhanced through a wider base of support.

The downside of a larger board is that you are likely (in fact, pretty much guaranteed) to receive conflicting advice. Because of the career path options available today, there is no longer just one way to the top. For example, if your board includes individuals who followed a more traditional, hierarchal career ladder, they may try to dissuade you from taking lateral positions. If you do find yourself getting too much conflicting advice from your board (after all, we call it a board, but there won't really be meetings and a gavel!), then it may be time to trim down the group to just a few mentors and sponsors.

Developing the Relationships

Gaining this level of support is not as simple as just asking someone to be your sponsor. A true sponsor relationship must be earned and cultivated. A mentor relationship is one that at least initially, can begin as more transactional; meaning, it is generally acceptable to seek out a mentor and ask that person if he or she would be willing to mentor you in a particular area. For example, it is very common for a new sales agent to ask a more experienced agent to serve as a mentor in order to help guide the new agent through his or her first months. Over time, to be most fruitful, a mentoring relationship needs to be reciprocal, though that reciprocity can manifest in various forms. In fact, the vast majority of mentors indicated that they too learn from the experience just through serving as a mentor.

Seeking Breadth

It can be extremely valuable to acquire members for your board who work outside your current organization. While such a person may not be a particularly effective sponsor, since he or she would likely lack the organizational stature typical of a sponsor, a person outside your organization can be an extremely helpful resource. Such an individual can offer a broader perspective relative to the larger industry. Additionally, sometimes a mentor relationship is more powerful when it is based on common experiences outside of work. At Gettysburg College, the Garthwait Center for Leadership initiated an alumni mentor program, where a more senior alum mentors a recent graduate. Although the matches typically revolve around career affinity, participants in this program have indicated that the worth of a mentor outside of your organization can be extremely valuable, particularly when you may be facing challenges in your current position. Sometimes a perspective from someone who is familiar with your industry, but who has distance from the politics and turmoil of your own organization, can be extremely helpful in determining how best to address a challenge.

Managing Your Board

How you manage your personal board is as important as the members of the board. Keep in regular touch with your board members. A member of your board will not be in a position to advise you if he or she is not clear on your current role or doesn't understand your goals and capabilities. Table 2.1 provides guidance on how you can best interact with your board.

Table 2.1 Managing your board

To be most effective your board members must have a sense of the following:	
What you want to get out of the relationship?	Are you looking to build a skill? Is it important that you see someone model activities that you would like to learn?
What are your career goals?	Your board members can likely offer different kinds of guidance based on your varying career goals. Your board should understand your short- and long-term career goals.
What you can contribute back into the relationship?	People don't typically step up to be mentors or sponsors unless they really enjoy doing the work. However, it's important to consider what you might be able to give back. While your continued success may be all the reciprocity they seek, that shouldn't stop you from being grateful for their time and perhaps offering to assist on a special project or favorite charitable project.

Note: It is critical that the members of your board understand you, your career, and what you hope to gain by working together.

Making It Work

Make a list of who you believe has a seat on your personal board today. What angles are missing? Who you would like to add? Try to include at least two people who don't work in your current organization. If you have any significant outside of work commitments, such a position on a volunteer board, consider adding someone related to those experiences to round out the board. Keep the list in a place that will remind you to review it once a month, so that you maintain an appropriate level of communication with the various board members.

Mentoring

It Still Matters

Although much of the focus today is on the concept of sponsorship, mentoring—a term we view as more technically focused than sponsorship—continues to be an important tool for career success. Most successful people can clearly identify mentors in their careers—whether informal or formal—who helped them move up to the next level. Kathy Kram's Phases of Mentoring, first introduced in 1983,[11] continue to provide a framework for making sense of the mentoring relationship. These phases are illustrated in figure 2.2.

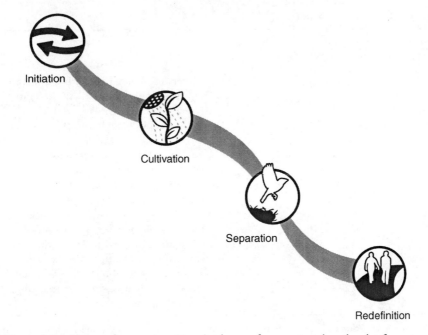

Figure 2.2 Phases of mentoring. Kram's phases of mentoring describe the four stages through which most mentoring relationships progress.

- *Initiation*: The relationship is established. Goals are exchanged and the mentor and mentee begin to share information with each other.
- *Cultivation*: The mentor begins to provide guidance to the mentee. This is the core phase of mentoring, where the mentor is actively working with the mentee to achieve the goals established for the relationship.
- *Separation*: During this phase, the mentee is likely gaining confidence and experiencing more independence in his or her career progression. The separation may occur formally or informally, but the impact is that the mentoring relationship comes to an end.
- *Redefinition*: This can be one of the most rewarding aspects of the mentor relationship for both parties. Depending on the level of the mentee, the mentor and mentee may become more like peers over time. Kram notes that often, successful mentoring relationships are redefined as friendships during this period. At this point, the person is likely to be considered a previous member of your board, available for support when needed. It's also possible that the mentor has turned into an ongoing sponsor for you.

Informal Mentoring Relationships

The most helpful mentoring relationships are often the informal ways that people become an advisor, coach, or mentor to another. These relationships are developed because those involved have a natural affinity for one another. The person doing the mentoring has chosen to enter into the mentoring role on his or her own—not because someone from human resources asked them to do it. Many senior managers like working with young people, and they're often naturally inclined to giving them advice and help.

There needs to be certain rapport between the mentor and the person being mentored. A woman may have more affinity to work with another woman than she may have with a man and vice versa. However, if there are fewer women in senior positions in the organization then there are more opportunities for people to be mentored by men, which is fine. We discuss the implications of cross-gender mentoring later in this chapter.

Formal Mentoring Relationships

An organization that has established an internal mentoring program is sending a very clear signal that the organization wants to help employees succeed. These organizations recognize that while an employee's job assignment is critical, having a mentor can truly help make the assignment contribute to the productivity of the organization, as well as enhance the employee's opportunity for advancement.

Typically, the human resources department coordinates the formal process. High-potential employees are identified and selected to be in the program. The human resources department also recruits leaders who they believe would be strong mentors. An organization's formal mentoring program is likely to involve some group activities or sessions, but typically, for the most part, the relationship is left up to the mentor and mentee to develop as they see fit. Mentors can offer significant advice to mentees. If the new employee makes a strong impression, the mentor is likely to introduce the employee to other senior members of management. A mentor can also suggest an assignment or project where the employee has the opportunity to be noticed and raise her profile in the organization.

Choosing a Mentor

What are the qualifications for a mentor? How does one find a mentor? Should the mentor be a person with very strong technical abilities and knowledge about the type of work that the woman should be doing? Should the mentor have a similar background to the mentee? The research from a study published in the *European Journal of Engineering Education* offers some informative feedback about the link between mentor characteristics and the success of mentoring relationship. The authors found that a technical background was not the prime qualification for a mentor to be successful.[12] In fact, 58 percent of the respondents responded with "no" when asked if a technical background was enough to be a successful mentor.

Professional status, however, is an important qualification to be a successful mentor according to 66 percent of respondents. Social skills are also absolutely necessary for the mentor to be effective, according to 85 percent of those surveyed. Mentors should be able to communicate with the person being mentored and be able to give the mentee the opportunity to meet people and extend their networks. A strong mentor should also have listening skills. Training experience was also considered a plus because it means the mentor is likely to understand how to help the mentee grow.

Mentors can also be sourced from outside the organization. There are a number of existing organizations designed to help people in entrepreneurial endeavors. Such examples include Service Corps of Retired Executives (SCORE) as well as many professional associations specific to an industry. You can also ask someone in your organization to be your mentor. For example, you could ask your boss's boss, a senior person in another part of your organization, or a person who is well known in the organization.

In approaching someone to mentor you, you don't necessarily need to start with a formal request. Instead, start by asking the person if you can go to lunch together to get their input on some career decisions you are considering. You can end the lunch by asking if the person would be willing to touch base again in a few weeks. If the person is receptive and the lunch goes well, it is likely to turn naturally into an ongoing mentor-mentee relationship.

Gender and Mentoring

If you are a woman, should you have a woman or a man for your mentor? First, it's important to understand that in this context we are referring only to mentors; when it comes to identifying a buddy in the organization, choosing someone of the same gender will depend on the kind of support you need. If you are new to the organization and returning to work after staying home for three years with your children, you may find that a peer mentor (buddy) who is a woman with children may be very helpful, as you are likely to be asking questions about similar logistical and cultural issues. Second, unless you work in an organization where a significant number of the senior executives are women, as you progress in your career, you may have little choice other than to have a male mentor.

There is some anecdotal data that women are not always the best mentors for other women. A 2003 article in *U.S. News & World Report* entitled "The Mentor Gap" pointed out that "older women eagerly provide advice, but young women don't like what they hear."[13] In the article, a young woman recounts her mentoring experience, in which she was assigned to a woman twice her age. The mentor told her mentee about how bad it was when she was coming up through the ranks and that she had to sacrifice time with her family for work. The younger woman had no intention of making the same kind of trade-off decisions; as a result, there was very little connection between the two. At the same time, some of the senior women felt the younger women weren't willing to "pay their dues" to make it to the top. Some of the women we have talked to have explained that they found male mentors more sympathetic to work-life challenges and more supportive of young women who wanted to try to change the expectations for their generation's path to success.

However, these reports of friction around gender in mentoring relationships still tend to be anecdotal. A study in *Psychological Reports* studied cross-gender mentoring.[14] The report indicated that in general, managerial women held no belief that cross-sex relationships were more difficult and there was no strong preference for same-sex mentoring. However, women who had actually been mentored by men reported a belief that same-sex mentorships were more desirable due to less tension, fewer complications, ease, and preference. The same women also reported more concerns about whether the cross-sex mentor relationship may appear to others as being personal rather than professional.

In general, we don't think it makes sense to close yourself to the potential benefits of a mentor who may be of a different gender. Many successful women have had male mentors. For example, Ursula Burns, a CEO of Xerox, has cited at least two male mentors who were particularly helpful to her career growth.[15] A presentation prepared by the American Psychological Association on cross-gender mentoring offers some simple tips to avoid issues.[16]

- Keep the relationship professional.
- Avoid perception of a personal relationship by meeting in public venues and being transparent about the nature of the relationship.

Making It Work

Preparing for the Start of a Mentoring Relationship
In order to prepare yourself for a successful mentoring experience, be aware of your own strengths and development areas and be clear about the goals of the mentoring relationship. An easy way to begin a mentoring relationship is for the mentee to take some type of leadership style or working preferences inventory, such as the Myers-Briggs Type Indicator or the Clifton StrengthsFinder, offered by Gallup. There are online versions of these tools and similar ones than can be completed in a few minutes and serve as a great starting discussion with your mentor.

Receiving Feedback from a Mentor
A healthy mentoring relationship should include room for feedback from the mentor to the mentee about the mentee's performance. The feedback

may be provided very directly (for example, if the mentor is actively working with the mentee, she may have the ability to see the mentee on the job) or more indirectly in the form of advice. Regardless of how feedback is given, the mentee should consider it carefully, as taking action on honest feedback can be one of the most constructive aspects of a mentoring relationship.

Tips for Receiving Feedback

- Be open to what you are hearing. Let the words sink in. Don't rush to explain why you did something the way you did.
- Write down what was said.
- Truly listen to what your mentor is saying. It is hard to give feedback well, and it could be that the mentor may not be giving feedback exactly right. Listen anyway.
- Ask questions and get clarification so that you fully understand the feedback.
- Be willing to learn and improve.
- Do something with the feedback. Commit to making changes.

360-Degree Feedback

As the name implies, 360-degree feedback includes feedback from peers, subordinates, customers, and superiors. The purpose is to identify developmental opportunities for employees. You may work for an organization that offers a 360-degree feedback program; if so, you should participate and engage your mentor in reviewing the feedback and developing an action plan for it. If your organization doesn't offer a formal program, consider asking your mentor to conduct a few informal interviews with individuals with whom you interact. This is a terrific way to engage your mentor and will likely jumpstart the mentoring relationship in terms of the insight it will give your mentor to your career.

Networking

It's a Noun and a Verb

If the term "networking" conjures up a vision of you holding a drink, standing in the middle of a busy room of people staring into unfamiliar faces looking for someone you know, then you need to change the way you think. The traditional "networking reception" common to most conferences still takes place, but by no means is networking limited to these events that are at times reminiscent of a middle school dance.

It may make more sense for you to focus on the term "network" as a noun. A network is an interconnected group of people including both friends and work colleagues; in fact, your network is made up of parts of many other networks. Think of the many connections you have made though "a friend of a friend of a friend." When you consider your network systematically, as we'll do in this section, you are likely to find that you actually have parts of your network in place that you may not have realized. A network is broader and includes many more people than your board of advisors, which is smaller and comprises only people with whom you have a stronger professional and personal connection.

The value of a strong network cannot be understated. The most commonly cited value of a network is typically around employment opportunities. In fact, most companies fill positions based on referrals; fewer than 10 percent of jobs are obtained by responding to traditional job posts. But networking is not just important for finding jobs. Networking can help connect you with potential business partners, consultants, and employees. Networking also helps you to build your personal brand, discussed in the next chapter.

Build Your Network

Think of your network from three angles: personal, professional, community, as illustrated in figure 2.3.

Your personal network includes your friends, friends of friends, your parent's friends, your friends' parents—anyone you have met outside of a

Figure 2.3   Network components. In building your network, seek to balance its composition across personal, professional, and community aspects.

professional world. Your professional network includes current and former coworkers, people you have met at association events or conferences, clients, and business partners. Finally, your community network includes people you have met through other activities such as volunteering, playing on sports teams, religious activities, parents of your children's friends, your college alumni associations, and other similar organizations. Sometimes you'll find that people transition from one network to another. For example, one of Lindsay's graduate school buddies became a client of hers, straddling the personal and professional aspects of her network. Don't spend time trying to decide where a person falls—it's more important to take stock of your network from all of these angles.

In building your network, there are some key steps to take early in your career:

- *Don't undervalue your personal network.* For individuals just out of school, while your peer network may not offer you much yet in the form of opportunities, your friends' parents can be a terrific networking resource. Your parents or relatives don't have to be an executive in the company. Any employee in a company, no matter at what level, can typically make referrals. If you have good credentials, the person who received your resume will be happy that someone of your caliber was referred and then hired and will thank the person that gave them your resume. Many organizations pay bonuses to employees who refer employees to the organization. Lindsay's sister got a connection to her first job at a prestigious financial services company through her college roommate's parents' neighbor!
- *Consciously build your professional network.* You frequently cross paths with individuals who are in a different industry or field; make an effort to understand what they do. It is now standard to add a person to your LinkedIn network after just a brief introduction. You will be surprised at how brief connections made years ago can later play a key role in your professional life.
- *Keep in touch with people from your past.* Maintain connections with people from your prior company, from college, from clubs or organizations, and from your college's alumni association. Past bosses, professors, coaches, and others may be helpful contacts down the road. Your contacts can be people who are above or below you in the organization. With all the tools available for networking, it's easy to keep in touch with people that you once worked with or knew.
- *Be a connector.* The value of your network isn't just about what it can do for you—it's also about how you can help others, which helps you build personal and professional equity with those around you. Connecting

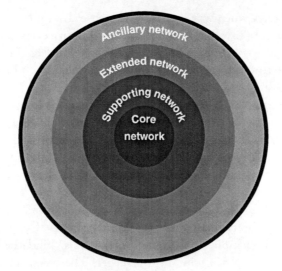

Figure 2.4 Network rings. Each ring of the network designates a common profile for a group of individuals in your network. Your strategy for maintaining a connection with each group varies with each ring.

individuals in your network is valuable for them and for you. One of the first things Jim did when he met Lindsay was connect her with a student whom he thought would be a strong candidate for employment at Lindsay's organization. He was right. The former student became a key teammate of Lindsay's and both Lindsay and the former student are grateful to Jim for the connection.

- *Reciprocate.* Networking is reciprocal. If someone contacts you about referring them or one of their children, do it. Those that do things for others will be remembered in the future when they might ask for similar favors. For example, if someone wants to talk to you about a job at your company, make every effort to do so. If someone refers a resume to you, make sure you get back to him or her. You don't have to hire them but at least respond. If someone wants you to make a presentation at his or her organization, try to find the time to do it.
- *Engage in your local community.* Early in your career you may find yourself living in a new city where you don't expect to stay longer than a few years; or maybe you moved back home with your parents to work and only plan to stay until you find a position in your field. These short-term stays offer a reason to become *more* engaged in your community—not less. If you are new to an area, becoming involved in the local community helps you meet people outside of your work environment, which is valuable for many reasons, not the least of which is offering perspective

on those days when work seems too intense! If you have moved "back home," getting involved in your local community offers a fresh and different perspective from what you had when you left. The connections you make through community and civic activities can be both personally rewarding and professionally beneficial.

- *Communicate the old-fashioned way.* Send thank you notes often. Write emails or notes to people to recognize an accomplishment. Send notes to co-workers if they did something that was helpful to you, and copy their boss if it is via email. If you notice that a colleague in or outside of your organization has been promoted, send them a congratulatory note.
- *Join industry or function associations.* If you're in human resources, join the Society for Human Resource Management. If you're in finance, join the Association for Finance Professionals. Find the organization that brings people in your field together. These associations could be national, state, or local. There are also other organizations that are more social like the AAUW (American Association of University Women) or service organizations like the Rotary or the Chamber of Commerce or the Jaycees, which are not only a valuable opportunity to do good work but also to meet other people. There are women's executive organizations in virtually every town or city in the world that offer networking across industries.

Maintain Your Network

Maintaining your network probably sounds challenging, maybe even impractical, given the advice to grow and add people to it. The key to maintaining your network is being deliberate about it. The network rings diagram (see figure 2.4) and supporting table (see table 2.2) provides a tool for prioritizing your networking activities.

It may feel a little odd to actually place people's names in the rings of this networking circle, but taking 15 minutes to do so will go a long way in helping you maintain a strong network. You should also revisit this list every few months to adjust and reconnect with individuals with whom you may not have touched based in a while.

Making It Work

Here's the thing about networking—everyone does it. It's no longer just for the high achievers in big business and government. The nature of our world has shifted. Networks—social, professional, and virtual—increasingly hold more power than organizations. If you are one of those people who still

Table 2.2 Maintaining connections with your network

Network ring	Description	Maintenance strategy	Objective
Core	Individuals with whom you regularly keep in touch through lunch, email, phone, and meetings. Includes individuals on your board, mentors, current clients, and active professional relationships.	Actively engage: keep them informed as to your status and when they have changes in their career or personal life, you should seek them out to provide your support or congratulations.	An on-demand response to your call or email with a request.
Supporting	Individuals who you are likely to tap in the near future as potential clients or employers. Examples include previous sponsors/ mentors, former coworkers in the same business, or clients with a qualified potential need.	Keep in touch—maintain ongoing reciprocity: schedule occasional interaction with these individuals—lunch every few months, a commitment to catch up at an upcoming event, or a planned phone call on your commute to work just to keep in touch.	Ability for you to approach them with a request without much set up.
Extended	Individuals in your extended network are the "friends of friends"; coworkers who have moved into a career outside your field, former classmates.	Seek situational communication but no need to actively plan ongoing communications. When you see the person at an event, make a point to connect; update them on major transitions in your professional life.	Ability to contact them when you have a specific request, but will likely require that you bring them up to speed on your status.
Ancillary	Individuals you met once at a conference, business cards you collected at a presentation.	Include them in your LinkedIn connections—no other ongoing contact is required.	Ability to tap them when needed but likely to require a reintroduction.

Note: Your approach for maintaining connections with your network should be aligned with the objective of the relationship.

finds networking too much like that middle school dance—complete with stilted small talk, and a focus on studying your drink instead of studying the nametags in a room—then you need to shift your thinking. Everyone feels uncomfortable at some point at the networking dance. The good news is

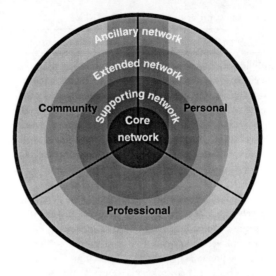

Figure 2.5 Integrated network. Your network should be composed of individuals across your personal, professional, and community networks. Based on how closely you are connected with each individual, they are placed in one of the rings. The inner rings include individuals with whom you should stay in regular contact, while the outer rings designate individuals with whom you can maintain a more infrequent connection.

that networking is not the same as dating. Don't miss out on an opportunity because of the fear of an unlikely professional rejection.

Recap

Building your own professional board, cultivating that board, and shifting its composition as you move through your career is one of the single best things you can do for your career development. The most important people on that board are those who serve as true sponsors for you, and are making a focused effort on their part to help pull you up to the next level of your career.

Mentoring, as we learn more about what makes these relationships successful, continues to be a valuable activity for people at all levels of their career as it offers an opportunity for very personal ongoing learning, sharing, and feedback. Networking complements your board, sponsors, and mentors by surrounding you with a catalog of individuals "on demand" to provide information and connections as you navigate your career. As illustrated in figure 2.5, it is important you have individuals to fill out all aspects of your network.

Finally, it's important to note that while we wrote this chapter from the perspective of you being the mentee as opposed to the mentor, it is never too early for you to look back—or over—at someone to whom you could offer support and guidance in their career.

Recommended Reading

Break Your Own Rules: How to Change the Patterns of Thinking That Block Women's Paths to Power by Jill Flynn, Kathryn Heath, and Mary Davis Holt

Power Mentoring: How Successful Mentors and Protégés Get the Most Out of Their Relationships by Ellen A. Ensher and Susan Elaine Murphy

The Networking Survival Guide: Practical Advice to Help You Gain Confidence, Approach People, and Get the Success You Want by Diane Darling

CHAPTER 3

Build Your...Brand

Josie sits across the desk facing the interviewer. The interviewer asks Josie to tell her about a time when Josie had to convince someone who was skeptical. Josie begins to answer, "Well, I haven't really been in a lot of situations like that yet but..."

Jada is at a networking reception for recent graduates of her alma mater with senior alums in the area. She spots an alum she met at an event when she was a student and walks over. "Hello Jada," the alum says, "How are you? What are you up to now?" Jada responds with, "Well I just got back from a trip to India where I was able to see the improvements in a small rural community where my management class established a micro-loan program. Now, I am focused on finding a position in the private sector where I will be able to use the skills I developed in a commercial setting."

Molly reaches to pay for lunch in her office's building café and realizes she is in line next to the manager who had originally hired her into the organization. "Hi Shenice," Molly says. They end up sitting down to eat together. Shenice says, "I heard you are doing a great job running the project management office for our global communications deployment. When that wraps up, I'd like to see if we can get you into the project management office for the trading software integration effort." Molly responds by saying, "Well, maybe. I don't know that I really want to keep doing project management work though."

The first and third instances are such glaring examples of poor brand management that you may have found them a little painful to read. Josie too quickly downplays her academic experiences, and Molly opens conversation by focusing on what she doesn't want to do. Jada, however, seizes an opportunity to work her brand statement directly into the start of a professional conversation. Building and communicating a personal brand are extremely important activities as you begin your career and transition from school to work or as you transition jobs early in your career. It's also important to manage your brand proactively through periods when you are not working or are reducing career intensity. In the previous chapter, we took the concept of a corporate board and morphed it into a personal one to guide you through your career. In this chapter, we replicate the process with another hot corporate topic—branding.

The Issue

Branding, like so many of the concepts in this book, is by no means a technique reserved for women. However, women face unique challenges—and on the flip side, unique opportunities—when it comes to the development of a personal brand. If you work in a male-dominated industry, your brand has the potential to stand out just by nature of your gender—and fair or not, it is especially critical then that you get it right. For the many women who chose to take a nonlinear career path, the management of a brand through lateral shifts or periods of no or part-time work becomes extremely important to ensure long-term professional success.

Brands have staying power—30 percent of the world's most powerful brands were established more than 30 years ago.[1] And while you can certainly expect to change your brand as you move through your career—or perhaps "grow" your brand is a more accurate term—the reality is that the brand you develop at the start of your professional career is likely to stick. As a result, it's critical to take a thoughtful approach to the composition of your brand and how this brand is communicated to others.

Making It Work

Everyone has a brand. If you don't define a personal brand, someone else will do it for you—and they may not get it right! The good news is that the development of a brand, if it's authentic to you, is actually pretty easy. There are many books, workshops, and blogs detailing how to develop a personal brand; however, most of them are targeted toward more senior executives or entrepreneurs. In this chapter, we offer several techniques to develop your first brand at the onset of your career and to adjust this brand through a career change or a return to the workforce following a break. We also offer tips for interviewing, which is one of the first opportunities you have for communicating your brand early in your career.

Branding

Definition

The concept of branding came into more regular use beginning in the 1950s as a way to differentiate products from one another.[2] Prior to that period, a consumer may have had no or very few choices for a particular product. However, as the consumer-products industry began to grow, the companies that garnered larger pieces of market share were those that invested in marketing efforts to appeal to a consumer's emotional side when it came to product selection. Branding became a way for one particular soap (or tea or cigarette) to stand out against a sea of what were actually pretty similar products. Lipton tea, Xerox copy machines, and Kleenex tissues are examples of brands that were able to differentiate themselves from the competition.

In applying the same concepts to people, personal branding then becomes a vehicle for you to make yourself stand out from the crowd. The good news is that you don't need to hire a public relations firm to help you define your brand—you already come with unique attributes that will naturally comprise your personal brand. Developing this brand simply requires you to take stock of assets you already have and identify areas of your brand that need focus.

Today, it's easy to witness the power of brands. Each year, lists are published of the most powerful brands—lists that regularly include the likes of Apple, Microsoft, and Coca-Cola—all brands that have been around for many years. The irony with brand identity today is that while branding is more popular than ever—as evidenced by the proliferation of branded products unique to discount retailers like Target[3]—it's also easier than ever to damage a brand. The growth of the internet and particularly social media mean that even our most recognized brands are only a few tweets away from a slide down the brand-value chain. Examples abound of brands damaged seemingly overnight by a high-profile incident. While it was prior to the rise of social media, Arthur Andersen's brand is a prime example. In the 1990s, the Andersen brand was so powerful that when Andersen Consulting broke apart from Arthur Andersen, part of the split that took the longest to sort out was determining who got to keep the valuable Andersen name. Andersen Consulting lost the battle over the brand and, forced to rename, chose Accenture, which turned out to be serendipitous for them, since just a year later, the Enron scandal hit, irreparably damaging the Andersen brand. A name so valuable that it had been part of a multiyear court battle, was turned into a liability in just a few short weeks.[4]

Today, with the amount of personal information online, personal brand management is more critical than ever. In a 2010 survey of US recruiters and human resources professionals, "seventy-five percent reported that their companies have formal policies in place that require hiring personnel to research applicants online" and "seventy percent of employers reject applicants over online information."[5] Younger professionals, who have grown up sharing personal information online, are likely more at risk than older workers for having their brand defined or damaged by information found online. We explore this topic in more detail and offer some tips for managing your brand online.

Building a Brand

A brand is not built from scratch. Instead, to craft your own brand, start by taking inventory of what you have and then identify gaps and steps you can take to address the gaps Consider the basic components of your brand. The most basic elements of your brand are illustrated in figure 3.1.

- *Appearance and presence*: How you talk, dress, and carry yourself are parts of your brand. The first impression you make on someone is primarily an expression of this component of your brand. Presence is also an element addressed in our chapter on leadership.
- *Professional experience*: What you know, the depth of your expertise, and your past employment comprise your professional experience.
- *Personal interests*: What you read, what you talk about, and what you do outside of work infuse your personal brand with individuality. If there was ever really a time when personal interests were kept out of one's professional brand, it has certainly passed. Although there are aspects of

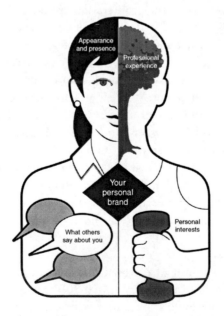

Figure 3.1   Your personal brand includes your appearance and presence, professional experience, personal interests, and what others say about you.

your life that you keep close to the vest, personal interests still comingle with your professional life. Whether those personal interests emerge through small talk about your weekend with a coworker at the start of a Monday morning meeting or more directly through your leadership role in an office charitable project, they matter.

- *What others say about you*: In the end, it doesn't really matter how you see your brand; what matters is how others see it. Information about you online falls into this component. When people enter your name into Google, what information appears?

A strong personal brand, write brand experts David McNally and Karl D. Speak, addresses three expectations by being distinctive, relevant, and consistent. They explain that "when your actions are distinctive, relevant, and consistent, your intended audience begins to see and understand your brand."[6] As you assess the components of your brand, consider how they work together to address these three expectations.

Identify Your Brand Assets
Hopefully, by now, we have convinced you that you do have brand assets. The great thing about branding is that while it needs to be grounded in accuracy and facts, branding is more about expressing emotional value than functional value. In other words, how you communicate about your experience matters just as much as the composition of that experience. Below we offer a few tips for culling out your brand assets in specific situations.

If You Are a Student with Limited Professional Employment

- *Develop a story around your coursework*: Do you have a unique mix of course experiences that help you stand out from others? One young woman we spoke with had designed her own major. Telling a story around deciding to design her own major, lining up the institutional support for it, and then executing it was very powerful. By harnessing that experience, the student established a brand centered on personal drive, creativity, and execution.
- *Focus on what your personal interests say about you*: What have you done during your time outside the classroom, and what does that say about you? If it was sports, that's notable; not many college students actually play intercollegiate sports—especially all four years. If you did, you probably have a brand around commitment to goals, the ability to balance multiple priorities, teamwork, and leadership. If your time outside the classroom centered on service to others, that also offers material rich for brand development. Did you see a need in your local or college community and then determine a way to address that

need? Have your efforts gone beyond just your campus in some way? Incorporating these experiences into your brand would demonstrate an entrepreneurial focus and an emphasis on stewardship that can help you stand out.

If You Aren't Yet Working in Your Desired Field

It may be that you have a brand based on professional experience, but that it's the not the brand you need in order to obtain a position in your desired field. Or, you may find yourself needing to update your brand following a return to work after a period of nonemployment due to family or other commitments.

- *Focus on the similarities between your current and your desired work*: One person we spoke with effectively used her experience as the office manager for a small medical practice to demonstrate a brand around a real-world understanding of the implementation of health care reform, which enabled her to transition into her desired field in health care consulting.
- *Develop your brand through other professional activities*: Identify ways to connect to your desired field through professional associations, conferences, training, and civic activities. For example, if you are seeking a position in financial services, volunteer at a local YWCA to teach low-income women about personal financial management. If you are seeking an experience in politics, volunteer to assist on a campaign. Not only does such an experience "count" in an interview setting, but it also enables you to develop a brand focused on your desired field. This suggestion also applies to women who may be taking time out of the workforce to care for young children; as you weigh volunteer activities during this time period, consider selecting ones that dovetail with your professional experience.
- *At least "Talk the Talk" if you can't yet "Walk the Walk"*: There is no reason why you can't be knowledgeable about your desired field, even if you aren't yet working in it. Identify the key publications you should read, including professional association websites and journals. Follow leaders in your field on twitter and regularly read the top blogs in your industry. Having a brand around deep knowledge of a particular market or issue is valuable in today's specialized market.
- *Be ready to evolve your brand*: If you are returning to the workforce after staying at home with a child for four to five years, you have changed and the market has changed. You should consider how your brand has evolved during this period and retool your brand. One way to help do this is through a brand SWOT (strengths, weaknesses, opportunities, and threats) analysis.

Conduct a Brand SWOT Analysis

Self-awareness is critical for the development of your personal brand. However, awareness of how you are viewed relative to your peers is equally critical. Two of the leading books on brand development, *You Are a Brand!: How Smart People Brand Themselves for Business Success* by Catherine Kaputa[7] and *Authentic Personal Branding: A New Blueprint for Building and Aligning a Powerful Leadership Brand* by Hubert Rampersad,[8] recommend that as part of the process of developing a personal brand, you conduct a SWOT analysis, illustrated in figure 3.2.

A SWOT analysis is a classic business tool for evaluating an organization's internal factors (strengths and weaknesses) and external factors (opportunities and threats) in the context of a particular business goal. To help understand how you can use this tool to evaluate your own brand, we have conducted a sample for Danielle, a 29-year-old woman who is currently trying to make the transition from team member to team leader within an agency in the federal government (see table 3.1).

Danielle's SWOT analysis reveals several things. As she talks with others about her potential to be promoted into a managerial role, she needs to consistently emphasize her strengths—she needs to articulate how her background and approach to teamwork means she is uniquely qualified for the role. She should also mention her success with a project last year that is similar to the one likely to be facing the agency next year. Danielle also needs to seriously evaluate her weakness and threats—she clearly is impacted by her lack of technical experience. Given that it is impractical at this stage in

Figure 3.2 Brand SWOT analysis. A personal brand SWOT analysis enables you to consider the strengths, weaknesses, opportunities, and threats impacting your brand.

Table 3.1 Sample brand SWOT analysis

Strengths	*Weaknesses*
What makes Danielle stand out among her peers?	*What are the gaps in her brand?*
• *Unique career path*: While most of her peers have been working at the agency since they started their career, Danielle brings experience in the public health field that is complimentary to the agency's work.	• *Technical knowledge*: Managers in Danielle's agency tend to have started their careers in more technical roles as engineers. She does not have any comparable technical experience.
• *Teamwork*: Danielle's agency includes a number of retired military members who are on a second career. She has earned the respect of many of these individuals through her approach to teamwork.	• *Presence*: Although Danielle has earned the respect of many in her office, her age and overall low-key presence make it hard for some to see how she could manage a team with so many older and more experienced staff.

Opportunities	*Threats*
How can Danielle position herself to take advantage of trends in her organization or market?	*What are the external/environmental challenges to Danielle's continued success?*
• *Retirement wave*: Danielle knows that her agency is actively involved in succession planning; a recent study showed that 60 percent of the workforce is eligible to retire in the next five years. The agency is actively seeking high performers who are interested in building a long-term career with the organization.	• *Reduction of midlevel managers*: There has been an increased scrutiny on midlevel managers in federal agencies. Agency leaders may view the role Danielle seeks to fill as an opportunity to eliminate a managerial role.
• *Upcoming deadlines*: The agency is likely to be responsible for implementing a Congressionally mandated project on an aggressive deadline. Danielle successfully led a similar project last year.	• *Background*: Likely competitors for the positions to which Danielle aspires typically bring technical experience that she does not have.

Note: In this application of the brand SWOT analysis, both areas of emphasis and potential brand gaps are identified.

her career to develop this expertise, she should seek to either downplay the value of this experience for her desired role or identify ways she can address it head-on. The first option is to focus on how her work in public health is relevant to the role she aspires to and explain how that experience actually gives her a leg up. The second option is to see if she can be assigned to a project that involves more hands-on operations work that would then enable her to demonstrate this experience. Finally, a third option Danielle could consider is that if her brand weakness—technical experience—is always going to be a problem, then she might need to move to an organization where this is not such a critical issue.

Addressing Gaps in Your Brand

Many of the gaps in your brand—for example, the weakness Danielle has around her "low-key presence"—can be addressed very tactically. For example, presence is an issue that can often be improved by increased awareness that comes from reading a skills-based book, taking a speaking class, or just asking for feedback from a colleague. Lois Frankel's book *Nice Girls Don't Get the Corner Office: 101 Unconscious Mistakes Women Make That Sabotage Their Careers*[9] may come with eyebrow-raising title, but it's filled with terrific coaching tips on how to address presence issues (chapters include "How You Act," "How You Sound," and "How You Look"). Frankel uses a mix of anecdotal and empirical evidence to offer women practical tips for improving their brand.

If the gaps in your brand are more experience or technical based, seek ways to address them through stretch roles, outside training, and professional associations. In the meantime, keep the emphasis on the strengths of your brand and how they align with external opportunities.

Branding for the Entrepreneur

Personal branding is particularly critical for entrepreneurs and small businesses. In the career path navigation chapter of this book, we discuss entrepreneurism as a growing career choice, particularly for women who want to have more control over where, how, and when they work. If you are considering starting up your own business, your personal brand and that of your business are essentially the same. In such a situation, it's not enough just to develop a consistent brand—you must actively promote it with your current and potential customer base. Entrepreneurs often engage in such promotion through blogs, websites, speaking engagements, and other forums. If you are considering establishing your own business, explore how the development of your personal brand relates to your potential area of focus and factor that into your brand management activities today.

Brand Inconsistency and Social Media

One of the best trends for women in personal branding is the increased emphasis on an *authentic* personal brand and developing a personal brand that is aligned with you as a whole person. Even just 20 years ago, it wasn't uncommon for a woman in a leadership position to feel like she had to act at work in a way that was inconsistent with her personal persona. E. Lee Hennessee, a successful female trader on Wall Street, made a name for herself by bucking this standard—for example, she made a point of bringing lunch to people's desks instead of meeting for late night drinks, and responding to offensive language by handing someone a dictionary.[10]

If your brand is authentic and feels natural, it probably means it is centered on your strengths, which will give you and others confidence in your brand. Misalignment between who you are and who you are trying to be is exhausting—and chances are you won't really be successful in such a situation. McNally and Speak address the issue of authenticity in the newest edition of *Be Your Own Brand*:

> When your values align with the values of your peers, your family, your customers, and your organizations, life becomes a much more harmonious experience. And that harmony can only be achieved by holding on to who you are. It's achieved by being committed to and holding on to your essential values. Call it integrity, authenticity, being true to yourself, or any number of other things. No matter how it is named, the results are greater peace of mind, a more rewarding life, and an enhanced sense of your own self-worth.[11]

Social Media and Branding

If people were once able to support "dual brands" by keeping personal aspects of their life separate from their professional brand, with the widespread use of social media, it's unlikely they are able to do so anymore. Although Facebook founder Mark Zuckerberg's various statements about privacy no longer being a social norm[12] have been met with much resistance from the blogosphere, Zuckerberg's statement was arguably one of fact more than philosophy. Facebook's policy of one account per user, which prevents individuals from setting up separate personal and professional accounts, is core to Facebook's success of keeping the site authentic—for the most part, people are who they say they are on Facebook. Google's then CEO Eric Schmidt expressed similar sentiments in 2010 when he wrote, "If you have something that you don't want anyone to know, maybe you shouldn't be doing it in the first place."[13]

If you want to try to keep your personal and professional lives separate online, you do have some options; of course, websites offering tricks on how to buck user agreements and set up multiple accounts can be found all over the internet. However, we suggest three basic rules of the virtual road:

- *Use different social media sites for different purposes.* Many people tend to employ one tool, such as Facebook, for their personal life, and a second tool, such as LinkedIn or Twitter for their professional life. While you aren't guaranteed of privacy in either situation, at least for the most part your followers are presented with consistent branding on the site.

- *Take advantage of privacy tools available to you.* All sites have various security options for sharing information. Set them up so that professional colleagues see less information about you on a regular basis. Pay attention to changes in site privacy settings, which change frequently.
- *Don't put anything out on the internet that is inconsistent with your brand.* Even with different sites and the use of privacy tools, one way or another most of what you do online is easily discoverable by others. That said, it's best to strive for consistency of brand across various aspects of your life. For example, a young manager explained that while she tries to keep her Facebook settings such that coworkers don't see her posts, when she does post, she still pictures her coworkers or boss reading the updates. As such, that "filter" in her mind has helped prevent the occasional lash-out post related to work. Worst-case scenario, she figures, a coworker may accidently see a post she added about her toddler son's antics. While her mommy stories are not contributing much to her brand, she figures, they aren't really hurting either.

Making It Work

Now that you have developed your brand, shored up any areas that needed more focus, and determined your strategy for managing your online brand, there are few more steps you should take to effectively manage your brand.

- *Use a professional looking photo for all business-related photos.* Organizations increasingly incorporate photos into employee directories. If you work in a small organization, they may put your photo on their website; and an effective social media account will always have a professional photo associated with it. Your picture doesn't have to look like you sat for a portrait, but it needs to look better than a head shot cut out of your extended family holiday picture. The photo should match the style of dress you follow at the office—so if you typically dress business casual at the office, your photo should at least show you in a nice blouse or sweater set.
- *Practice communicating your brand in one minute or less.* Every week you will interact with people who ask you what you do. Be ready with a clear, descriptive answer. Rarely should you only respond with an "I work at XYZ" or even worse give a response with a job title that means absolutely nothing to someone outside your organization, such as "I am an operations analyst level two." Saying you work for a particular organization does very little for your brand if you don't articulate what you do in

terms of value or results. Be specific and include numbers. Rampersad writes that what he calls a "personal brand statement" should be "unique to you, relevant to the market place, reflect who you really are (real you)," and be used at work as well as with family and friends – that is, all the relationships in your life."[14]

Examples of Personal Brand Summaries

- "I am an analyst in the financial operations division of a health care company where I focus on making sure we maximize our payment recoveries from insurers."
- "As the community relations director for a small nonprofit organization, I work with over 50 other community organizations including schools and churches, to pool our resources with the goal of reducing hunger in central Maine."
- "I just completed my bachelor's degree at XYZ University, where I focused my studies on globalization and international business through coursework in three departments on campus and two semesters in Japan."

Chances are that if you are reading this book, you have the talent and experience to deliver on a strong personal brand. Developing an authentic brand based on a realistic assessment of your current assets will help you effectively communicate the value you offer to other people and organizations. In the next section, we focus on an important opportunity you have to communicate your brand—a job interview.

Interviewing

It's Still Key

For someone who is early in her career journey, the job interview represents what might be the single-most important opportunity to communicate one's brand to a potential employer. Given that the interview is still the gateway to a position in most organizations, we thought it important to be covered in a book targeted at early-career women. Although much has changed in recent years around job searching, resume preparation, and networking, a personal interview continues to be a core part of the employment process.

Additionally, if women receive any interviewing skills training, it is likely in college. As time goes on, you are less likely to have any kind of formal interviewing experience. Jim, who interviewed thousands of people, was always surprised how hard he had to work in an interview to find out a person's talents and how they struggled to answer the simplest questions. Midcareer interviews are every bit as important as early-career interviews. What we present can help at any point in your career.

Engaging in a Successful Interview

Interviews typically take place over the phone, over a video conference application (such as Skype), or in person. For larger organizations, human resources staff is likely to conduct initial interviews over the phone with a progression to an in-person interview conducted by a more senior member of the organization.

As illustrated in figure 3.3, the interviewing process can be broken into three stages: prepare, conduct, follow up.[15]

Prepare

Prior to your first interview, conduct research about the organization. Focus on the organization's website over secondary sites. At this phase in the process, the goal is for you to get through to the next interview or to get the offer. Research focused on learning whether your salary offer is appropriate or whether the organization is a good cultural fit for you should be addressed later, once you have an offer in hand. Your

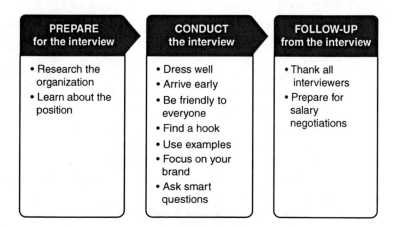

Figure 3.3   Job interview process. Breaking the job interview process into three basic stages helps you plan for each component.

preparation for the interview should enable you to answer the following questions:

- What is the overall structure of the organization? How are business units divided?
- What are the organization's current goals and strategy?
- What are the major trends in the organization's industry right now?
- How does the position for which you are interviewing fit into the larger organization?

Even if you aren't able to answer these questions completely based on your own research, the process of seeking the answers will better prepare you for the interview. You can use the information gathered in your research to help inform your responses to the interviewer's questions, as well as help to develop your questions for the interviewer. In addition to the organization's website, other sources for preparation include trade magazines and analyst reports. Additionally, your extended network can be of critical value here. Check your LinkedIn contacts to see if anyone you know currently works at the organization or in the industry. Reach out to them prior to the interview to learn what you can from a firsthand perspective.

Conduct
Phone interviews continue to be common, especially for initial screening. Typically, the interviewer is looking to confirm that your technical knowledge aligns with your resume and gauge overall characteristics such as the ability to communicate. If your interview is being conducted via phone, the following tips will improve your performance:

- Listen for the interviewer's name and title, and then use it as given.
- Keep your resume in clear view; the interviewer will certainly have it in front of her.
- Have your brand statement printed out in front of you. Use it in your introduction and then relate your responses back to your brand.
- Have a pencil and paper ready to take notes, sketch out answers, and write down questions.
- Make sure you are in a calm, quiet environment.
- Try to engage in the interview from a landline phone.
- Note how long you take for each answer; try to stick to about two minutes per question.
- Smile as you answer. Smiling offers an energy and lift to your voice.

Following a successful phone interview, you'll likely be offered an opportunity for an in-person interview. The in-person interview provides you with an opportunity to effectively communicate your personal brand. The conversation you make, how you interact with everyone in the office—it all counts and is factored in to the perception of your brand by the interviewer.

The interview is likely to start with small talk and a general opportunity for you to introduce yourself. From the beginning to the end of the interview, be specific about names, examples, and data. You want the interviewer to understand your role and your past experiences. Identify a possible "hook" to make your interaction with the interviewer more memorable. Perhaps your review of their LinkedIn profile turned up a common experience or interest.

Many interviews today include behavioral questions—that is, questions that ask you to share a specific experience and explain the thought process behind your behavior. For example, Lindsay was once asked to give an example of a time she made a major mistake and how she handled it. Always pause to consider what example you will use, explain it, and then focus on the core of the answer. For example, in response to the question about a big mistake you might say, "I once delivered a client proposal two hours after it was due and they would not accept it. I had to go back to my boss and explain what had happened. It turned out that the request for proposals clearly indicated a 12 noon deadline but I had just relied on an email exchange with a colleague that mentioned the date but not the time, so I assumed it was 5 p.m. There wasn't anything I could do about the proposal with the missed deadline, but from now on, when I am the one responsible for a project of that magnitude, I always make sure I have requirement information directly from the source. I pride myself on meeting commitments, and I don't want to be in that situation ever again." In your response to a behavioral question like this one, it's important to report what you did and offer an honest, insightful assessment of how it went and what you might change in the future. The ability to link it back to your brand statement is also a plus.

Finally, most interviews close with an opportunity for the candidate to pose any questions to the interviewer. You should still consider your questions as a data point for the interviewer. If you haven't been offered the job yet, then everything that takes place in the meeting is still part of the interview. Use the opportunity to ask questions that subtly reinforce your brand statement. For example, a question like "I noticed that your organization seems to be doing considerable work in the area of sustainable design. I was really interested in this because it was a core part of my internship. Do you consider this focus a long-term one for the organization?" gets the point across that you did your homework, that the organization's business aligns with your experience, and that you are interested in the future of the organization (which will potentially be part of your future). Interviews are not the time to ask sensitive questions about pay or cultural dynamics.

Follow up

Follow up as quickly after the meeting as possible—ideally with a brief email that doesn't require a response or if the hiring decision doesn't seem imminent you could send a note card.

A Note about Informational Interviewing

Informational interviewing typically involves the request of a job seeker to sit down with a more senior individual at the organization. Job seekers often request an informational interview of a networking contact if the contact works in the field/organization to which the job seeker aspires, even if there are no jobs currently available. Informational interviews offer the job seeker the ability to learn from the person being interviewed, and hopefully, the chance to expand the job seeker's network and job opportunities. More senior individuals in an organization often agree to an informational interview for individuals connected to them through a colleague or an organization, such as an alumni association.

Making It Work

There are many websites with good tips on interviewing. Your college career services center is also an extremely rich source of assistance on interviewing. Given the amount of information available on this topic, we focused our advice in the context of ensuring your personal brand shines through in the interview. Be consistent in how you explain your career aspirations and the reasons you feel the way you do.

Other than conducting research into the organization and preparing your responses to questions about the value you bring to the organization, the single-greatest way to prepare is to practice. If your school offers mock interviews, sign up. If they don't, pair up with a friend to take turns practicing. The more you practice communicating your personal-brand statement, the more natural it will feel.

Recap

Everyone has a personal brand. If you don't take proactive steps to assess, develop, and grow your brand, others will determine that brand for you. The in-person interview presents the single-most important opportunity for most to communicate their brand to a prospective employer; as such preparing for, participating in, and following up afterward are critical activities for successful interviewing.

Recommended Reading

Authentic Personal Branding: A New Blueprint for Building and Aligning a Powerful Leadership Brand by Hubert K. Rampersad

Be Your Own Brand: A Breakthrough Formula for Standing out from the Crowd by David McNally and Karl D. Speak

You Are a Brand! How Smart People Brand Themselves for Business Success by Catherine Kaputa

CHAPTER 4

Build Your . . . Communication Skills

During a planning session on corporate strategy, Melissa asks, "Do you think we should consider expanding into China?" when she really meant, "I think we should do business in China."

When asked by her boss if he can see an early version of a report Sara is drafting, Sara responds by saying, "OK, here it is, sorry I didn't get the graphics included yet but I can send them to you when I get them," when she should have said, "Here is the in-process version of the report you requested. I'm on track to have the graphics included by the Friday deadline."

After meeting with her assistant to explain that he is going to fail his performance review, Anne receives a call from the company human resources manager who indicates to Anne that the assistant has refused to sign the review document because it is inconsistent with the positive feedback he received in her conversation with Anne.

Cara is at a get acquainted reception with other new hires. When asked by a senior manager what interests she had in college, Cara responds, "I was on the golf team and hope to continue playing," when it would have been more accurate to say, "I was captain of the golf team for three years and have a three handicap—I'm hoping that I'm able to keep that up as I dig into my career here."

Each of these smart, articulate women made a common—but damaging—communication mistake. Could you tell? These examples illustrate that communication skills are a critical yet underdeveloped aspect of both personal and professional life. Communication is one of our earliest developed skills—one we put to use when we are just hours old (certainly a skill that Lindsay's son used early on in his life—especially when she had just settled in to work on this book). However, at times, it also feels like one of our least developed skills. Participate in an employee focus group on pretty much any topic, and inevitably, someone will raise the issue of poor communication. In a 2010 article in *Psychology Today* called "The Five Most Common Ways Bosses Screw Up," the number one reason was undercommunicating.[1] Ask any married couple about communication issues and you'll likely get an exasperated eye roll with both spouses ready to tick off a list of communication failures in their relationship. Surprising, in an era of smartphones, tablets, and bluetooth devices? Not really; the phrase "it's not what you say, it's how you say it" still rings true in today's connected world.

The Issue

If everyone needs to do a better job at communicating, what makes it an issue for women in the workplace? Extensive research and studies by a number of experts has definitively demonstrated that women communicate differently than men do, and too often, to their detriment. Women have a tendency to speak up less, apologize more, downplay their achievements, and use less-powerful body language. Not surprisingly, the basis for these gender differences in communication styles goes back to childhood.

Anna Fels, a psychiatrist and author of *Necessary Dreams, Ambition in Women's Changing Lives*, describes how women view ambition and achievement. Her work demonstrates that in early childhood women learn to avoid visibility and recognition. For women, ambition implies negative traits— "egotism, selfishness, . . . the use of others for one's own end."[2] Women often deny success and their achievements. Men—and boys—are just the opposite; Fels writes that men view ambition as a necessary and desirable part of their lives. Directly linked to this issue of ambition, Fels catalogs the myriad of studies demonstrating that as a result, women solicit and receive less recognition than men receive. This indifference about ambition may help you get a date (though arguably not with the type of guy you want for a life partner) but in the workplace it turns out that it won't get you much in terms of a promotion or a raise; and it certainly doesn't serve women well when it results in women communicating in ways that downplay their achievements.

According to Flynn Heath Holt Leadership, a leadership development firm with a track record of working with women leaders, part of the problem is that women are too modest—they believe accomplishments should speak for themselves.[3] Viewing raises and promotions as good things that *happen to* them instead of successes that *resulted from* their own hard work, means that women may miss opportunities to be to rewarded or recognized for their efforts. Similarly, in her article entitled "Why Women Lose Out," Sandi Mann points out that women are aware of politics but dislike this aspect of organizations.[4] For too many women, they see these communication issues as an obstacle—something that gets in the way of their goal to simply do the job well. The reality, though, is that if women do not engage in the political aspects of organizations, they are put at a disadvantage when competing with men.

Deborah Tannen, who is perhaps the most well-known researcher on gender differences in communication, has studied and identified a number of critical differences in the communication styles of men and women. When conversation rituals are studied in girls, Tannen points out, girls focus on building rapport with others while boys learn to focus on building status. Girls often have a best friend and tend to play with one best friend or in small groups; they downplay ways in which one is better than the other, and emphasize ways in which they are all the same; and they don't like to sound too sure of themselves, fearful that they will not be popular. Boys, however, play in larger groups where everyone is not treated equally; they display their abilities and knowledge, and emphasize, rather than downplay, their status. After years of this socialization pattern, young women often fall into the same patterns in the workplace. Women are reluctant to talk about their accomplishments; yet avoiding such discussion hinders their opportunities for recognition and advancement.[5] Unfortunately for young women, what worked on the playground doesn't do much for them in the boardroom.

Making It Work

Awareness of communication nuances and the impact they have on your career goes a long way in helping you to position yourself well at work. We have organized this chapter into three focused sections to help you recognize and improve your communication skills:

- *Linguistic Style*: Linguistic style is *how* you say something. There are some specific stylistic patterns that are more effective in the workplace than others.
- *Direct and Indirect Communication*: Many women are indirect in their communication style—the cause behind the commonly used request from men for women to please "just say what you mean!" When women learn to be more direct in their communication styles, they typically find that the results of their communication are more aligned with their intent.
- *Nonverbal Communication*: Women have different nonverbal communication patterns than men do; just as important, women's nonverbal communication is also *perceived* by others differently than men's is. It's important to recognize these patterns and how to counterbalance some that may have negative effects in order to be treated more fairly in the workplace.

In each section, we describe the particular aspects of the communication issue, illustrated through examples and case studies, and provide practical exercises and approaches to make your communication style work *for*, not against, you in the workplace.

Linguistic Style

Elements of Linguistic Style

In Deborah Tannen's groundbreaking book, *Talking from 9 to 5: Women and Men at Work*,[6] Tannen, a linguist, explains how the conversational styles of women and men differ, and the far-reaching effects these differences can have in the workplace. In Tannen's work, linguistic style refers to a person's characteristic speaking pattern. Many workplace communication issues are actually caused by differing expectations and perceptions of linguistic style. Tannen identifies a number of different elements of linguistic style, discussed below.[7]

One Up, One Down
When Tannen refers to "One Up, One Down," she is addressing elements of linguistic style that have to do with power and positioning yourself in the workplace. There are three aspects of linguistic style included in this category as discussed below.

Getting Credit Men are more likely to be attuned to the power dynamics of a conversation, while women focus more on the rapport elements of a conversation. For example, to avoid seeming boastful, a woman may use the term "we" when referring to an achievement she actually performed on her own. However, being specific and direct about your contributions, while giving appropriate credit to the team, is the best way to communicate your value. Lia, a guest speaker in one of Jim's classes, was very good at this:

> Lia is the cofounder and CEO of a high-tech company, the third one that she has started. She has raised several hundred million dollars for her start-up firms and she does not hesitate to take credit: "I am very good at raising money," Lia said when she introduced herself to Jim's class. When we talked about her management style, she credited hiring and developing good people for her success. A coworker described her greatest strength as, "her ability to get that internal team aligned. She's very much about the team. She cares about them and cares about developing them." While Lia willingly takes credit for her successful fundraising, she gives the credit for the success of the entire company to her employees. "The people are why we have been successful." She takes pride in hiring the best people and then lets them do their jobs.

Confidence and Boasting Women are socialized to downplay situations when they are certain about something while men are socialized to minimize their doubts. In other words, when questioned, a woman is quick to say, "Well, I could be wrong, I'll double-check," while a man is more likely to say, "I remember discussing it. I'm quite sure it's correct." These habits have been reinforced throughout childhood and adolescence. The problem for women is that the norms of the US business world are based primarily on a male style of interaction; as such, a perception of indecision or uncertainty damages a woman's credibility.

Displaying uncertainty can be particularly damaging for women when it's in the context of their ambitions and career trajectory. Robin's story illustrates this issue:

> I graduated from law school and went directly into a really good firm. I took maternity leave when I had children, but generally I kept up the pace expected of candidates for partnership. Like many of my peers, at times I had doubts about my ability to commit to the intensity of such a role long term, especially with two young children. I made the mistake of occasionally sharing my concerns with individuals in the organization and the year before I was supposed to be admitted, I was repeatedly asked if it was what I really wanted. Clearly, the word had gotten out that perhaps I wasn't as committed as I needed to be. Everyone has doubts about what they are doing. Just don't discuss them with everyone you meet. Save the discussion for a trusted mentor.

We aren't suggesting that you ignore legitimate doubts you may have about the path your career should take; just be sure to share those doubts with a more limited group of people who are in a position to provide you with good counsel.

Asking Questions Many men believe that asking questions might reflect negatively on them. As such, these same men may form a negative opinion of others who ask questions in situations where they would not.

Conversational Rituals
Conversational rituals refer cultural-specific nuances of language—"how" we say things. Tannen focuses on four as below.

Apology Tannen writes that apologies tend to be regarded differently by men, who are more likely to focus on the status implications of an apology. Men are more likely to avoid an apology because they view it as putting themselves into a "one-down" position. We explore the concept of apologies in more detail in the next section.

Feedback Typically, you will deliver feedback how you like to receive it. People tend to fall into two feedback camps, and often these two camps also fall along gender lines. Some managers buffer criticism by beginning with praise; others may start by announcing what needs to be changed. As a result, in the workplace, how individuals like to receive feedback and how they actually receive it may not be aligned, resulting in muddled exchanges about performance. In the opening to this chapter, Anne was giving feedback to an employee and was surprised to learn that what she thought she said wasn't what the employee thought he heard; this kind of misunderstanding may have been due in part to Anne's personal preference of using praise along with negative feedback when delivering a performance review. Neither way is more, or less, correct, but recognizing how you are communicating improves the likelihood that it will be received the way you intend.

Compliments Tannen has found that exchanging compliments is a common ritual, especially among women. But again, a mismatch in how this ritual plays out can confuse exchanges in the workplace. One of the rituals young girls learn is taking the one-down position ("I don't really like my new hairstyle") assuming that the other person will recognize the ritual nature of the self-denigration and pull them back up ("Really? I think it looks great"). However, since men are not as accustomed to this ritual, they are more likely to respond with advice ("Well, you can always try a new stylist"). When this plays out at work, a woman may feel like her male colleague is honing in on her project by telling her what to do when he thinks he was just offering suggestions for a problem.

Ritual Opposition This is a linguistic-style element that can solicit very strong responses. When using ritual opposition, a person presents an idea with certainty and then prepares to defend it. He or she views the defense of the idea as an opportunity to test it out and see if it sticks; however, to an individual who expects a more bilateral exchange of ideas, such an approach is often viewed very negatively. Men are more likely to use ritual opposition; this topic is discussed in more detail later in this chapter.

Negotiating Authority
Authority refers to power. There are different kinds—formal, which come from the position one holds, and actual, which is something that has to be negotiated day to day. Linguistic style is often directly linked to establishing your own type of authority.

Managing Up and Down In the workplace, everyone adjusts his or her linguistic style based on the status of the person with whom they are speaking. (Think about it—how often do you consider a person's title before you respond to his or her email? You use a different tone with a peer vs. a high-level executive.) However, the style you use can have a significant effect on the image you are promoting for yourself. For example, in Tannen's research and that of others, it has been found that women are more careful to "save face" for the other person if that person is a subordinate; in other words, women are more likely to "soften a blow" when delivering a hard message to a direct report. This situation is a tough one—Tannen writes that though it might make for a more positive workplace, it is also likely to draw criticism that the woman manager isn't projecting the proper authority. Either way, it makes sense given that, as we discussed earlier, even young girls are socialized to downplay, rather than flaunt, their superiority.

Indirectness Women are especially likely to be indirect when telling some- one what to do (that childhood reluctance to be called "bossy") while men are likely to be indirect when admitting fault or weakness (again, this one stemming from a childhood desire not to be the one who is pushed around). The challenge comes when there are differing expectations for this linguistic style. Lindsay learned this firsthand, when after giving a junior female colleague some very specific advice upon the colleague's request ("Should I push for a promotion again this year?"), the colleague requested a new mentor. Lindsay thought she was helping her out by giv- ing her off-the-record, honest advice. Turns out the colleague didn't see it that way; she later told a friend that Lindsay was just "too direct." Clearly, Lindsay and her mentee had different expectations for the nature and rap- port of the relationship (and yes, as you guessed, Lindsay's answer to her question had been "no"). This story illustrates the core issue with linguistic style; it's not that one way is always better or worse than the other; the issue is often a mismatch between styles that results in misperceptions about the other person.

Apology

Tannen's work identified apology as a conversational ritual used by girls to establish rapport. Until recently, there was only anecdotal data that sup- ported the perception that women apologize more than men do. However, in 2010, Karina Schumann and Michael Ross published a study offering specific evidence and explanation. The study design was fairly simple; men and women kept diaries logging "offenses" they committed or experienced and whether or not an apology was offered. The results? Women not only apologized more than men did—but they also reported more offenses. Upon further study, Schumann and Ross determined that women didn't necessar- ily experience *more* offenses—it was just that women had a lower threshold than men for the types of situations that required an apology. In other words, women perceived the same offense more severely than men did, which led women to apologize more.[8]

Apologizing is generally not in and of itself a bad idea; any successful married couple will tell you that "I'm sorry" goes a long way regardless of your gender. But in traditional organizations, apologies may lead to a woman being perceived as weak and as a result, limit her influence and opportunities. This is not to say that there are no situations that merit an apology. However, women need to understand when it is appropriate to apologize and when it is unnecessary. Schuman and Ross identify eight actions that require an apology (see table 4.1):

The above examples indicate when both women and men should apologize. However, women have the tendency to apologize for situations that are not their fault or are out of their control (see table 4.2).

Remember our example in the opening to this chapter—where Sara apologizes for not having the graphics in a draft report? Instead of apologizing for something that is not her fault (it wasn't even due yet), Sara should just offer a status of the document as way to gently remind her boss that it was not expected to be complete yet."

The other aspect of Shumann and Ross's work presents the finding that men apologize less because, well, they have a higher threshold for offense severity. Shumann and Ross found that women perceived offenses more severely—both offenses they perpetrated and offenses perpetrated on them. Linking the two aspects of their work, Schumann and Ross suggest that the reason men apologize less frequently than women is because they have a higher threshold for what constitutes offensive behavior.

Table 4.1 Actions requiring an apology

Actions requiring an apology	Example
Remorse	I am sorry that your father passed away.
Acceptance of responsibility	I am sorry I forgot to swing by your desk before lunch.
Admission of wrongdoing	I am sorry that I shared confidential information with the team. It was wrong of me to do so.
Acknowledgment of harm	I am sorry that I neglected to forward the email I received which caused you to lose the client.
Promise to behave better	I am sorry I was late to the meeting again. I will make every effort to not let it happen again.
Request for forgiveness	I am sorry I was rude to the vendor. Please excuse my comment.
Offer of repair	I am sorry that I left the projector on the plane. I will call the airline to see if I can get it returned.
Explanation	I am sorry your copy isn't in color. The color copier is out of service.

Note: There are only eight key actions that require an apology at work.

Table 4.2 Situations that do not require an apology

Situation	Instead of this...	Try this...	Why
A flight is cancelled for a planned client pitch.	I'm sorry our flight was cancelled.	It's so frustrating our flight was cancelled.	It's out of your control.
A conference room is double-booked for a meeting you are leading.	I'm sorry. I know I booked the room.	It appears the room is double-booked. Let me go see about an alternative.	It's not your fault (or, at least assume it's not!).

So, are men insensitive or are women too easily offended? For the purposes of this book—and your career—it doesn't really matter. What matters is how you choose to act and how you are perceived. Lindsay saw this dynamic in action through her professional adult softball league. After a female team member missed a play, she would usually jog back in at the inning's end with an apology to the team, "I should have had that one; it was my miss—I'm sorry," while after a male team member missed a play, he might swat his glove at his knee in frustration, but by the time the inning was over, he had seemingly let it go and moved on. This is one situation where women may find that letting things go a little more will lead to being perceived as more authoritative (generally a good thing at work) and less angst over mistakes (generally a good thing in life!).

Ritual Opposition

Tannen writes about ritual opposition in her book as one of the linguistic rituals that is common for men at work, and is often taken literally by women. Ritual opposition is used every day in organizations. It is a form of decision making where one uses all the arguments she can think of to make sure the other side is well prepared and confident in their proposal, which is believed to ensure the success of the proposal. Most often, ritual opposition is used when a proposal or plan is presented—particularly when a subordinate is presenting a proposal for action to a boss or to a group of superior individuals. The senior person is testing the person's commitment to the plan or idea by looking for inconsistencies and gaps in their logic.[9]

Commercial loan officers and investment bankers often use ritual opposition with individuals who are asking for money. These exchanges are often very intense. Investors want to know if the person requesting the funds has her facts straight and has confidence in her own proposal. In a way, the investors are giving the money to the person requesting it, not to her business; so, it is important that she demonstrate confidence, commitment, and belief in her business plan. Any indication of lack of confidence, feelings of insult, oversensitivity to criticism, or self-doubt will make an argument seem weak and could lead to doubt as to whether the idea is worthy of their investment. The reality television show *Shark Tank* has turned ritual opposition into a form of entertainment. Entrepreneurs with ideas make a pitch to a panel of investors. The investors (the "sharks") drill the candidate with tough questions, to which many sharks already know the answer. At the end of the show, the sharks indicate if they will invest in the idea or pass; more often than not, the tougher the questions and the more intense the exchange, the more likely the shark is to invest in the concept.

Women need to be prepared for ritual opposition and become comfortable responding to it and recognizing it is not a personal attack. Women who are prepared will likely be perceived as committed and confident about their proposals and ideas.

Politeness

Politeness is defined by the concern for the feelings of others. Nancy Bonvillain's writes in her book *Language, Culture, and Communication* that women use more polite speech than men do.[10] Politeness is characterized by a high frequency of showing respect for the person you are talking to and the use of softening devices such as hedges and questions. While respectfulness is a good thing, if you use too much of it, you inadvertently put yourself in an inferior position. For example, saying to a potential client, "George, I would love for us to grab lunch to continue this conversation," puts you on a much more even playing field than "Mr. Smith, would it be ok for me to get on your calendar for lunch?"

Similarly, softening devices, or hedges, take away from the assertiveness of the statement and soften the impact of the words. For example, saying, "If you get a chance, will you please write up the meeting notes and send them to me at your convenience?" is an entirely different statement than, "Please go ahead and write the meeting notes and send them to me tomorrow." The work of Pamela Hobbs, a professor at University of California, Los Angeles (UCLA), suggests that women are more likely than men to use politeness strategies in their speech.[11] When you avoid excessive use of these terms, you can still be polite but at the same time, make it clear that you expect to receive that for which you are asking.

Making It Work

When it comes to understanding how the elements of linguistic style— including the use of ritual opposition and apology—can impact your career, the most critical thing you can do is to identify and be aware of the potential impact of linguistic style in your workplace communications. Consider these exercises:

1. Review the elements of linguistic style identified by Deborah Tannen. Which one of these elements resonated with you the most? What's one thing you might do differently based on what you know now about linguistic style and the differences between men and women?
2. Clue yourself into the phrase "I'm sorry." For a day, be sensitive to how often you say it. How many times are using it when things are not your fault or not in your control?
3. Think back to situation when you felt picked on or attacked in a setting at school or work because of an idea you proposed. Reevaluate what happened in the context of virtual opposition. How does it change how you might have prepared for or managed the situation?

Direct and Indirect Communication

Elements of Direct and Indirect Communication

There is a critical aspect of indirectness that can be detrimental for young women: self-promotion. When indirectness spills over into how a woman speaks about herself and her accomplishments, the results can mean that despite much hard work, she won't get the credit or accolades she deserves.

Carol Gilligan has extensively researched adolescent girls and young women. Her work provides a deeper understanding of why many women do not seek recognition and why they feel uncomfortable taking credit—why they use "we" instead of "I." From childhood, girls are taught to care for others; they see concern for themselves as selfish. She writes that "teenage girls and adult women get caught on the horns of a dilemma: is it better to respond to others and abandon themselves or respond to themselves and abandon others."[12] Too many women see this desire to seek recognition as an either/or situation—"I'm either selfish or I care about others." Unfortunately, this reluctance to appropriately claim credit for success means that too many women are waiting for someone else to recognize their value.

Peggy Klaus is a Fortune 500 communication and leadership coach and author of *Brag! The Art of Tooting Your Own Horn without Blowing It.* Working with thousands of clients (most of them women), Peggy has identified seven "Bragging Myths" listed in table 4.3.[13]

Becoming more comfortable with directly and specifically describing your accomplishments is a skill that will help lead you to success in a wide range of situations. Agnes's story provides a great example.

When Jim first met her, Agnes was working as a student assistant in an academic department in college. She was soft-spoken, nice to those around

Table 4.3 Peggy Klaus's bragging myths

The myth	The truth
Myth #1: A job well done speaks for itself.	With constant changes in leadership and organizational structure, you can't count on the person in charge to always be aware of your contributions.
Myth #2: Bragging is something you do during performance reviews.	You are surrounded by opportunities to promote yourself and need to be ready and comfortable to take advantage of them.
Myth #3: Humility gets you noticed.	Humility may be praised at home as a virtue but in the workplace, it's critical to learn how to sell yourself with ease and sincerity.
Myth #4: I don't have to brag; people will do it for me.	Letting others brag for you can be an effective way to promote yourself—but it can't be your only way. Klaus puts it simply, "No one is going to have your interests at heart the way you do."
Myth #5: More is better.	Klaus reminds us that while bragging is important, it's also important to tailor your approach to the situation in order to make it authentic.
Myth #6: Good girls don't brag.	Klaus writes that the disinclination among professional women to self-promote can significantly impact a woman's trajectory and ability to negotiate in the workplace.
Myth #7: Brag is a four-letter word.	Bragging doesn't have to be distasteful, Klaus says. Learning to brag is not about becoming something you are not—it's actually about becoming more of who you are and bringing forward your best.

Note: Women may have a reluctance to brag that limits the ability for others to recognize their professional value.

her, and presented herself well. As Jim got to know her though, he also saw competitiveness, strength, and a little toughness emerge. She had all the attributes to be successful on campus and in her chosen career. However, Agnes seemed almost unable to talk about her numerous accomplishments. She asked Jim to review a letter she wrote to apply for a job at the prestigious government agency. Jim was stunned about what she had left out. This was her first paragraph:

> I am currently a senior majoring in the sciences. I will be graduating this May, and would be honored to pursue my research interests at the National Science Foundation. I heard about the wonderful opportunities presented by the Foundation's rotational program from professors and students who have previously had the opportunity to participate in this program. The

National Science Foundation seems to provide the perfect environment for research.

This is the letter after a little coaching:

> I am very interested in the research opportunity presented by the National Science Foundation Rotational Program. I am currently a senior biology major with a grade point average of 3.8 out of 4.0. I have made the Dean's List every semester of my college career and believe my characteristics of competitiveness, determination, and dedication would contribute to any research team. In addition to my academic achievements, I have also been a competitive runner and held positions of leadership in my nationally recognized sorority.

Agnes had the right stuff—she just needed to get more comfortable telling people that she did.

Rachel, a college senior and very good soccer player, was another one of Jim's students. She was focused, hardworking, and goal oriented. Jim had heard about the result of the soccer Conference Championship and her role in the victory leading to the championship. The next day he asked how she did; she replied, "Pretty well." Jim continued, "Did you get any goals?" "Yes," she replied, "one." "Rachel," Jim said, "that's true but that's not enough. You should say you played well, worked hard, and were lucky to score the championship-winning goal with two minutes left in the game. That tells the story and gives you the credit you earned." Rachel smiled. In this case, Rachel's humility was probably appropriate with her teammates in the room—teammates who would already be aware of her accomplishments—but if she is telling this story in just about any other setting, it's critical that she accurately describe her role in the win. Rachel learned from her athletic success and when it came time to look for a job, she was more comfortable talking about her accomplishments and her traits that would make her an asset to her employer.

Making It Work

In the examples with Agnes and Rachel, they both had the goods / the right stuff / —whatever you want to call it. When you think about it, that's the hard part, right? Winning the game, making the Dean's List, creating a winning proposal—these are things you have stayed up late to finish, pushed yourself to revise one more time, worked through with a problematic team situation. It was hard. You did do a great job. And unfortunately, no one will probably know about it unless you tell them.

Lindsay has a communication exercise she does with college students and entry-level staff. It's basically a modern version of preparing your "elevator speech." The idea behind the traditional elevator speech was that you needed to be ready to clearly sell yourself in your accomplishments if you happen to share an elevator ride with the CEO of your organization. The good news is that due to the increased use of texting, the generation just entering the workforce now is very accustomed to communicating a lot in just a few words.

To do this exercise, prepare a template like the one below. Choose every word carefully (think about a 140 character limit!). Write it down, punch it up, practice it, and then use it the next time you introduce yourself in some kind of professional setting.

Write It Down
You should write down the elevator speech and be prepared to explain to anyone you meet what it is you do and why it matters. Table 4.4 lists the basic components of an elevator speech.

Punch It Up
What works best? When you speak with details and examples about your accomplishments, you will communicate your value without appearing over the top. Table 4.5 provides some examples of how you can 'punch up' your elevator speech.

Most young people are skilled in developing strong resumes—using action words, including specific details; but that same style of communication you use to make your resume stand out needs to be used when you are speaking about yourself and your accomplishments.

Practice It
Every day you will probably come in contact with someone who asks you about yourself. Be ready with your story. Clearly, you need to adapt it to your audience (the delivery person probably doesn't want to hear it) but you will be

Table 4.4 Your elevator speech

Name	
Demographic details	• Years with current organization
	• Role
	• Previous work experience/school
Value overview	• Articulate what you do and the value it provides to people around you
	• Include metrics, numbers, and examples
	• Use words that are easy to quickly understand

Table 4.5 How to punch up your value statement

Which works better?	
This...	*Or this...*
During my internship, I developed a training guide for the new computer system.	I developed training programs that were used for a global deployment of a new inventory tool used by 15,000 employees in 6 countries.
I used SPSS in class.	I conducted analysis using a statistical software tool that enabled me to quickly conclude from a lot of data about breast cancer.
My group redesigned a business process for a local nonprofit organization as part of our class assignment.	I was a member of three-person team who revamped the intake process for women arriving at a local shelter. My role was to document the new process so that it could be used by new employees. The new process reduced intake time from 2 hours to 30 minutes, reducing the stress on both the employees and the women arriving at the shelter.

surprised at what doors will be open to you when you speak with specificity and confidence about who you are and what you have accomplished.

Nonverbal Communication

How you present yourself impacts how you are perceived. It is particularly important in organizations to be aware of how others see you. Nonverbal communication ("nonverbals") contributes to this perception. Nonverbals are especially important because we are often unaware of their presence and influence.

Michael Argyle's Seven Categories

In order to help you fully understand the implications of nonverbal communication, we will present some of Michael Argyle's views, one of the original researchers in nonverbal communication from the 1970s, as well as Amy Cuddy, a social psychologist and assistant professor at the Harvard Business School, whose recent work helps us understand some of the gender differences in nonverbal communication.

In his research, Argyle indicated seven categories to describe nonverbal communication:[14]

- Facial Expressions
- Eye Contact
- Gestures
- Posture

- Touch
- Space Relationships
- Appearance

Facial Expressions

The face is a very important area for nonverbal signals. It can be exceedingly expressive and is usually the most easily observed feature of a person. There are many muscles and individual features of the face that can convey messages beyond common speech. Specifically, the mouth, eyes, eyebrows, and skin can work together or separately to deliver a message. The mouth can manipulate itself into a smile, frown, and anywhere in between. The eyes can also be very expressive; the term "smiling eyes" refers to this effect. Narrowing the eye is perceived as an expression of anger or annoyance. Raising eyebrows also sends signals of surprise or incredulousness. Blushing or perspiring facial skin also sends messages to the observer. Much of the time, we are unaware of our expressions but our faces often give us away. Feelings of confusion, disinterest, and annoyance can be hard to hide—just ask participants of any heated presidential candidate debate, many of whom have won or lost based more on facial expressions and other nonverbal communications than from the content of their message.

Amy Cuddy's research has demonstrated that within a second, people use facial features to infer certain things about another person. She has identified warmth and competence as the two variables that account for about 80 percent of our evaluations of people. Warmth, which is perceived first, is basically whether you feel good (warm) or bad (cold) about someone. Competence, which follows, refers to our perception of whether someone possesses the capability to carry out their intentions. Cuddy explains these variables in the context of survival instincts. Assessing warmth is essentially a way to determine if another person is going to harm you ("friend or foe"); assessing competence is determining whether or not they would be capable of acting on their intentions. The combination of the two variables leads us to quickly make some inferences about a person. For example, Cuddy explains that if a person is an enemy who is competent, "we probably want to be vigilant."[15]

This work has significant application in the workplace, as it gets to the heart of why individuals are selected for jobs, stretch opportunities, raises, and promotions. People tend to see warmth and competence as inversely related. Cuddy says this means that in the workplace people may feel, "The more competent you are, the less nice you must be. And vice versa: Someone who comes across as really nice must not be too smart." The implications can be particularly problematic for women as Cuddy's work goes a long way in explaining the "motherhood penalty" and "fatherhood bonus." Studies have demonstrated that working moms are seen as significantly nicer and less competent ("I'm sure she is a great mom, but I can't see how she could do as well at work with all she has on her plate") while a working father who leaves on a Friday afternoon to see his child's holiday program at school gets our admiration for being warm *and* competent ("Isn't that great that he works so hard and still makes time for his kids"). Cuddy's work is especially important for managers to understand where they may be inappropriately relying on the wrong factors for decision making.

Eye Contact
Eyes are the key receptors of information. It is especially important when being introduced to someone for the first time or presenting your case to a client, interviewer, or superior. By maintaining eye contact, you can also convey confidence in yourself and in your ideas and abilities. This applies to many organizational situations such as negotiations and presentations.

Gestures
Usually gestures are done with your hands, for example, raising your hand in a meeting or class. Cuddy observed that in class men raise their hands straight up while women raise their hand with a bent elbow, commanding less space. Jim observed this behavior in class as well as during his years in business. Gestures can be both encouraging and discouraging. A beckoning hand wave, shoulder pat, or head nod all qualify as encouraging behavior. At the same time, a curt hand motion can cut off a person in midsentence.

Posture
The main postures in organizations are standing or sitting. The way one stands or sits indicates whether they are determined, attentive, indifferent, or dominating. Cuddy has identified some nonverbal postures that are either warm or competent. Cuddy points out that there are high-power poses and low-power poses. People make inferences of competence based on how dominant someone appears. Postures taking up minimal space are seen as low power and expansive positions are associated with high power, as illustrated in figure 4.1.

It is important that you sit and stand in a way that projects competence. Lois Frankel, in her book *Nice Girls Don't Get the Corner Office*, reinforces the important of posture. Some of the mistakes she points out include "taking up too little space," "sitting on your foot," and "sitting in meetings with your hands under the table."[16]

Touch
Touch is another nonverbal way of communicating. The most prevalent way of touching is shaking hands. Some handshakes are accompanied by

High power

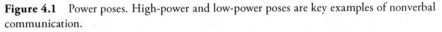

Low power

Figure 4.1 Power poses. High-power and low-power poses are key examples of nonverbal communication.

the other hand patting the person's shoulder or shaking with two hands. In other industries such as media or fashion, hugging and kissing is a common greeting or farewell between men and women. However, this is generally not accepted in most organizations. A conservative approach to touching is usually best. Lindsay still notices occasional awkward moments involving touch in the workplace—usually involving young women who offer or are offered hugs at work. When in doubt, don't hug at work! If you are in a situation where someone seems to be unsure as to whether they should hug or shake your hand, quickly extend your hand to shake—you can't go wrong.

Space Relationships
Personal space, is just that—it's personal. There is no single rule that applies to all people. Still, you need to be aware of how close you are when you speak or interact with your coworkers, clients, or superiors. Should you sit behind your desk when you are interviewing or meeting with someone? Or should you move to a less dominating setting to encourage conversation?

Appearance
In all societies and organizations, clothes are used to send information about personality and status. A woman's appearance comprises her clothes, hair, makeup, and jewelry; as such, it certainly can be difficult to reconcile style with professionalism in an organizational setting. You want to be remembered for what you say or do, not for what you wear. You should not be defined by brands or inappropriate work clothing. Anything too low, too

short, too tight, or too sheer, should be left in the closet. It is very important to determine what kind of clothes women are wearing where you work. You can determine that by observing what senior women are wearing and by asking what is appropriate attire on casual days, meetings with clients, or weekend company social gatherings. Especially when starting out, it is better to be overdressed rather than underdressed.

Making It Work

Similar to linguistic style, the key to effectively using nonverbal communication is to identify nonverbal communication and be aware of how it may influence other's perception of you. If you have an opportunity to take a presentation skills class that includes video recording and feedback from the audience—do it. You will become much more aware of your own nonverbal communication style and where you might want to change it. If you don't have access to a class, share the list of nonverbal communication elements with a friend or a coworker. Ask them to pay more attention to you for a few days and provide some feedback on how they perceive your nonverbal communication.

Appearance as a form of nonverbal communication is an extremely convoluted topic. There is a plentitude of social research demonstrating the impact of appearance on our perceptions and thoughts. As our society has become more pluralistic and casual, guidelines for appearance in the workplace have become more and more confusing. However, it is clearly a topic that young women want to know more about. Lindsay was asked to do an evening presentation on "Dressing for Success" to a group of undergraduate students, during the middle of finals. She expected two students to show up and then leave halfway through the session. Instead, there were not enough seats to accommodate all the young women who paused the night before exams to hear the presentation; about half of them stayed an hour past the advertised program end time. Lindsay was almost shocked by the specificity of the questions (Nude pantyhose or black? Closed or open-toed shoes? Capri pants or full-length?). It turned out that so much flexibility and acceptance has made making decisions about appearance more confusing for young people, especially women. While you will always have to make decisions based on your own style and the standards in your industry, when in doubt, go with the more conservative alternative—you can always bring out the knee high boots, nose ring, and sleeveless shirt later—though hopefully, even then not at the same time! See table 4.6 for some guidance on dressing for successful first impressions.

Table 4.6 Cheat sheet for professional dress

Yes	No
✓ Jacket with matching skirt or pants	✗ Party, cocktail, or sun dresses, even with a jacket or a sweater
✓ Black, navy blue, grey, or brown	
✓ Closed toe shoes with one- to one-and-a-half-inch-high heel	✗ Heels over two-three inches
	✗ Brightly colored shoes
✓ Shoes darker than your hem line	✗ Colored or white stockings
✓ Nude or black stockings	✗ Heavy jewelry
✓ One purse or bag in an interview	✗ Sheer or low-cut blouses

Note: While acceptable dress standards vary widely across industries and geographic regions, there are some general standards that can ensure you are dressed appropriately, particularly for interviews and the first days at a new organization.

Recap

In the beginning of this chapter, we gave examples of women falling into common communication pitfalls at work. Go back and look at those statements now. Can you identify what is wrong with them? Here are the takeaways:

- Consider how you both use and perceive the elements of linguistic style. Consider how *others* around you might use and perceive these elements.
- Don't apologize for things that aren't your fault or are out of your control.
- Be ready if someone engages in ritual opposition with you. Demonstrate your knowledge of the facts and don't take the exchange personally.
- Be direct when the situation calls for it—especially when talking about your accomplishments.
- Be aware of your nonverbal communication style and be willing to adjust it based on feedback.

Communication may always be one of the top workplace challenges, but is a skill that gets better with awareness and practice.

Recommended Reading

Brag! The Art of Tooting Your Own Horn without Blowing It by Peggy Klaus
Talking from 9 to 5: Women and Men at Work by Deborah Tannen

CHAPTER 5

Build Your ... Negotiation Skills

Maya hangs up the phone and quickly dials her mom. "I GOT THE JOB!" she exclaims. "Congratulations honey," her mom says, "That is great! When do you start? What is your salary offer?" Maya smiles, "Mom, I have no idea. I guess I will find out about all those things soon, but I am just so excited about this job right now that I want to go out and celebrate."

Abby is talking to Kathy, one of the well-respected senior vice presidents in her company. Kathy is talking with Abby about Abby's willingness to go stand-up a project—and potentially a small office—in Shanghai. Abby wants to do it, but getting it done in Shanghai, without the benefit of the supporting functions they have set up in the United States, will be a challenge. And then there is her husband; she is not sure that he would be able to come to Shanghai for as long as she will likely need to be there. "I think I may need to pass on this opportunity Kathy," Abby says with some hesitancy.

Think of the last time you got something you really wanted from someone else—without asking (or hinting) for it. Chances are that you got it from a parent, a significant other, or maybe a friend if you're lucky ... but when was the last time you got it from an employer? Your mom may be able to figure out what you really want, but unless you are a famous celebrity, not too many people are sitting around thinking about what you want. Turns out you usually have to actually ask for it—and asking for what you want is negotiation.

The Issue

You may be thinking that you are going into a career where you can't really negotiate your salary—maybe you are a teacher; or joining an organization through an established trainee program. Or, like Maya in the opening story, you may be so grateful and excited for the opportunity to do your "dream job" that you just don't see a need to negotiate your salary. If you have felt this way at times, you are not alone. Research has shown that women expect less and ask for less when it comes to getting what they want. The results can be significant. In their book *Get Paid What You Are Worth*, Robin Pinkley and Gregory Northcraft estimate that a woman who routinely negotiates her salary increases will *earn over one million dollars* more by the time she retires than a woman who doesn't.[1]

But we aren't just talking here about negotiating your salaries; what you may not realize is that you are faced with opportunities to negotiate all the time—how you do your work, where you do it, who you do it with, which projects you work on, what resources you are given, and so on. As you'll learn in this chapter, you can even negotiate what is negotiable. Abby, the woman who was offered the opportunity to run a project in Shanghai, is ready to turn it down because she is presuming that she won't have the professional resources to be successful in the project and that the situation won't be appealing for her spouse. In fact, it's likely all of those areas are open to negotiation as part of her decision to accept the assignment.

Making It Work

The good news is that negotiation is a skill that can be taught. We offer a flexible process you can use to negotiate virtually anything, and then we specifically focus on salary negotiations, which are particularly important early in your career.

Rethinking Negotiation

It's Not Luck—It's You

Social cognition theory categorizes people as "Internals" or "Externals" (see figure 5.1).

Internals are those who believe they will realize outcomes as a result of their own behavior, drive, and ambition. "I worked hard. I got results. I asked for the job and I got it." Externals think outcomes are controlled by other people, fate, or luck. They might say, "My boss will notice my talents and accomplishments and see that I get recognized." Studies show that women are more likely to be externals than internals, while men are just the opposite.[2] When it comes to getting what you want, you just can't count on leaving it to others. One of the managers we spoke with recounted this story about one of her team members.

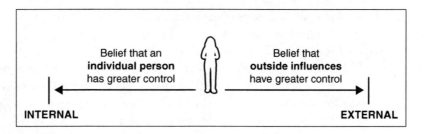

Figure 5.1 Locus of Control. People with a more internal Locus of Control (further to the left) believe that individuals have greater control over what happens to them. People with a more external Locus of Control (further to the right) believe that outside factors have more control.

I was approached by one of my team members, Jen, with a request that she be able to work from home two days a week. Jen was clearly struggling with work, getting time with her children, and a long commute. When Jen came to talk to me, she started out by, well, just asking to work from home two days a week—no summary of her high performance, no discussion on how to mitigate challenges being off-site. She just figured I was aware of the value she brought to the team and didn't see any reason to state it. I found out later that she had worked from home successfully in the last department she worked for. She just thought I knew all this. Unfortunately, I didn't (at that time at least) and I told Jen to come back with a better proposal.

Even though Jen may have had a solid case for the request, her discomfort in speaking about her positive performance history was a real detriment. She thought the decision was out of her hands because it was the manager who would approve her request; however, she missed the opportunity to influence the manager's perspective by providing relevant data about the likelihood of success with the arrangement.

The Locus of Control scale also helps to explain the internal versus external view of the world. People who score lower on the scale think their fate is determined more by internal than external factors. These people beat down the door to get their proposal considered; they tell an interviewer that they should get the job because they are the best qualified; they think it is better to apply for an open job even though they don't quite meet the stated qualifications; in short, they don't wait to be asked. Too often, women fall on the higher end of this scale thinking that luck, circumstance, fate, and other people control their success in organizations.

Research and data pointing out the reluctance of women to take control of their success and put themselves forward is the subject of many books. Mika

Brzezinski, in her book *Knowing Your Value*, writes, "Knowing your value means owning your own success. Owning your own success means acknowledging your achievements. By acknowledging your achievements you build confidence."[3] Brzezinski reports in an interview with Lesley Jane Seymour, editor of *More* magazine, that Seymour had this to say about luck, "You are going to hear a lot of women use the word luck. I hear executives say all the time 'I'm lucky to have gotten here, I'm lucky'...I can't even tell you how many successful females, CEOs of companies, will say 'I just got lucky.' But if you think it's just luck that made you successful, then if you ask for too much, the luck might just run out."[4]

If you consistently attribute your successes to luck, other people, or an accident, then when you do choose to negotiate, you will set your targets too low. In fact, Linda Babcock and Sara Laschever write that one of the reasons men outperform women in negotiations is because when women do negotiate they set targets that are too low.[5] Additionally, they write that setting high targets helps prevent women from making the common mistake of conceding too much and too quickly. Deborah Kolb and Judith Williams's work on "Shadow Negotiation" also places importance on recognizing and articulating your value and write, "People negotiate because they need something from you. Being clear about the value you bring empowers you in a negotiation."[6]

Learning to Ask

It's not as simple as flipping a switch from "Don't Ask" to "Ask." There are all kinds of other factors tied up in a woman's reluctance to ask. Theories about the reluctance of women to speak up or to put their ideas forward are integral to understanding how women approach (or don't approach) negotiation. In the chapter on communication, we discussed Anna Fels's work studying women and ambition. Because women are taught that ambition implies negative traits like egotism and selfishness, women solicit and receive less recognition than men receive. This ambition ambivalence leads directly leads to a reluctance to negotiate for promotions, salaries, or anything else at work. We also introduced Carol Gilligan's work in the last chapter; Gilligan's book, *In a Different Voice*, is largely based on in-depth studies of girls in all-girls schools. Gilligan's research shows that girls often feel it is wrong to act in their own self-interest. As adults, this can mean that women actually feel bad when they ask for a better shift, less weekend work, or a job with more responsibility, especially if these requests put them in competition with other women or men.

Some of the most groundbreaking research around women and negotiation has been done by Linda Babcock at Carnegie Mellon University. Using a mix of Babcock's own research, her experiments, and those of others, Babcock and her coauthor Sara Laschever lay out the reasons behind women's failure to negotiate in their books *Women Don't Ask* and *Ask for It*. They write that the pressure women feel regarding the needs of others first manifests itself in a variety of ways; one is that while women may feel confident asking for things on behalf of their children, their parents, or their spouse, when it comes to asking for things for themselves, even very successful women feel uncomfortable. And it's not just that women *feel* uncomfortable when they negotiate; sometimes women are even viewed negatively when they negotiate because their behavior violates gender stereotypes.[7]

Deborah Kolb, Judith Williams, and Carol Frohlinger have written extensively on how women can use negotiation to bolster their careers using the concept of shadow negotiation. Their work is particularly important in understanding how to frame your negotiations. Their research shows that in many cases, with high-achieving women, they are often making "the ask." But what becomes more critical is figuring out *what to ask for*. Their work demonstrates that negotiating the terms of an opportunity, assignment, or challenge is just as critical to a women's long-term success at negotiating promotions and salaries.[8]

Learning to Just Ask

Negotiation doesn't have to be complicated. Results can be seen simply by asking. Babcock and Laschever dub this concept the "Asking Advantage"— the idea that sometimes simply asking can lead to significantly better results than not.[9] This is particularly important when it comes to negotiating starting salary in an organization when future raises are likely to be incremental increases over your starting salary. Numerous studies have demonstrated that people who negotiate starting salary, even when they were happy with the initial offer, make more money for the same work than people who don't negotiate. It seems simple then, right? Not necessarily though—there are legitimate challenges for women when negotiating.

The first challenge is understanding and articulating your value as it relates to the issue being negotiated, which we discussed in the preceding section. Another challenge is overcoming the reluctance to do something that may seem too self-centered, given that our society expects women to be focused on the needs of others. Babcock and Laschever write that "wanting things for one self and doing whatever may be necessary to get those things—such as asking for them—often clashes with the social expectation that a woman will devote her attention to the needs of others and pay less attention to her own."[10]

A third challenge women may face when "asking" is that their behavior may be perceived negatively because it is inconsistent with gender stereotypes. In other words, it may be OK for a man to make an ask ("He's just making a case for what he has earned") but not for a woman ("On top of all we have already done for her, she is asking for a raise?). Alice Eagly's work on leadership, discussed in her book *Through the Labyrinth*, coauthored with Linda Carli, demonstrates that there is a double standard in place regarding our expectations of men and women's leadership abilities. Eagly and Carli write that "prejudice against women leaders flows from the usual mismatch between people's mental associations about women and leaders... this inconsistency results from people associating communal qualities [affectionate, helpful, friendly, kind, sympathetic and interpersonally sensitive] predominately with women and agentic qualities [aggressive, ambitious, dominant, self-confident, self-reliant] predominantly with leaders... [This prejudice] results in a attitudinal penalty, or lower evaluation, of the person who is stereotypically mismatched to a role."[11]

Women also need to consider the scope of what is even on the table for negotiation. Women don't just need to learn to "ask"—they need to learn what is on the table to "ask for." Deborah Kolb and Judith Williams introduced this concept in their book *Shadow Negotiation*. Shadow negotiation "is where hidden agendas and masked assumptions play out";[12] in some ways, it is the act of negotiating how you are negotiating. They write that "all the time when they are bargaining over issues, they are conducting a parallel negotiation in which they work out the terms of their relationship and their demands."[13] The concept of shadow negotiation is critical for women to consider. Stereotypes or expectations linked to gender are often going to be part of the shadow negotiation. If a new mother is trying to make a case that she be assigned a high-profile assignment in another country, she has to recognize that it's very likely a shadow negotiation is going on—perhaps in the form of assumptions that a new mother would not want to be away from her child, or that child-care arrangements might preclude such an assignment. A person in this situation will need to consider how to address these "shadow" issues—whether directly or indirectly—but the critical part is recognizing and acknowledging that indeed these types of assumptions are very likely to be in play during a negotiation.

Making It Work

First, recognize that you are probably worth a lot more than you think! To get a more realistic picture of you and your value, ask three friends or coworkers to list your three strongest traits; ask them for examples of situations where you have demonstrated these traits. Then you should do it too, by writing down your proudest accomplishments in the past three years. When you are approaching a specific negotiation situation, you may need to repeat this exercise, tailored to the situation.

If asking others to tick off your strengths feels too uncomfortable for you, then consider taking a strength-based assessment such as Gallup's StrengthsFinder (www.strengthfinder.com) to help you articulate your value.

You also need to "ask more" and often, "ask for more." That said, we've clearly presented a case that women face some unique challenges when they do ask. There is no one way to address these challenges, but being aware that certain challenges may be impacting your negotiation effectiveness is important as you determine your approach to negotiating in a particular situation.

Integrated Approach to Negotiation

Overview

It's important to understand that while you may not call it negotiation, you actually negotiate all the time about almost everything. You negotiate with your friends, children, parents, boss, coworkers, local businesses, people that you want to provide services to, and people that want to provide services to you. You negotiate with other drivers at a four-way stop sign. Who goes first? With your friends, you negotiate where to go for dinner. You negotiate bedtime with your children starting when they are five years old and if they are visiting you at home, their curfew, until they are 25. You negotiate with your parents about who gets the car, and later in life, whether they should give up their driver's license or move into assisted living. You negotiate with your boss over pay and responsibilities, your office space, flexible work schedules, and lunch times. You negotiate with your coworkers as to who should do what on a project. You negotiate with local businesses about how much they will charge to cut your lawn, fix your car, and finance your refrigerator. Like it or not, you are a negotiator. In addition, your negotiation skills are an indicator of who you are. Are you confrontational? Are you a peacemaker? Are you firm or timid? Are you flexible or close minded?

The world is changing. Nowadays, negotiation is more important than ever. It used to be that organizations looked like pyramids, with decisions and policies made at the top. Procedures and policies were directed and were instituted at all levels of the organization. Now, organizations have flatter structures and decision making has purposely been moved lower in the organization. Policies have turned into guidelines, which must be negotiated. Organizations want employees to take initiative. Often that means proposing and then negotiating new practices and procedures that will make the organization a better place. Most negotiations used to have a winner and a loser. They were almost always adversarial; unions versus management, subordinate versus boss, buyers versus sellers. When Jim was hiring mid- to senior-level employees 20 years ago, there was a much older human resources manager who would always ask Jim how much he offered a new employee. The manager would say, "You could have gotten him for less!" Finally, Jim said, "I didn't want to get him for less. I wanted him to think he was paid more than fairly; after all, he's coming to work for us and will be a key player for our team." The manager never understood this and fortunately for Jim, he retired. Negotiation does not have to be adversarial.

Twenty-five years ago, Jim attended a negotiation course to learn how to negotiate with unions. Back then, there weren't nearly as many negotiation courses in existence as there are today. Most negotiation seminars were specific to dealing with unions or big real estate and purchasing deals. To meet the new need for negotiating, training companies that present negotiation courses and training have proliferated. Almost all business or management curriculums in colleges and universities have full-semester negotiation courses. In this section, we provide a high-level process for negotiation, recognizing that there are many books solely on the topic of negotiation (we provide a list at the end of this chapter) that are available to you if you want to learn more about this topic, which is clearly "here to stay" as part of a successful career.

Often, you really don't even have to negotiate. You just need to ask for it and present a well-thought-out and reasonable argument, as Jim has found in teaching. College professors know a grade is very important to students so they work very hard to make sure a student's grade accurately represents the work they do. If you know teachers at any level—middle school, high school, or college—you know that they are very busy at the end of the semester. There is a compressed time for exams and lots of student grades that need to be submitted. In Jim's first year of undergrad teaching, students would often send him emails after they received a grade that was lower than their expectations. They would often write, "I would have liked a better grade." He would think to himself, "Well, I'd like to play centerfield for the Phillies." It's not a good idea to present your first position as, "I'd like something." The most successful request he received was from Leslie. Her email request said that she attended every class, was prepared when he asked for her opinion, got good grades on the homework assignments, paper, and final, and said she learned a great deal in the class. Jim's grade for her grade was a B+. Because she added much more to her request than simply asking for a better grade, he looked at her request in greater detail. Jim realized he had made a mistake. She had earned an A. He immediately sent her an email apologizing and completed the paper work to get her grade changed to an A. Leslie is an example that if you believe you are right, you should speak up. Make a case with facts to the decision maker and you will likely prevail.

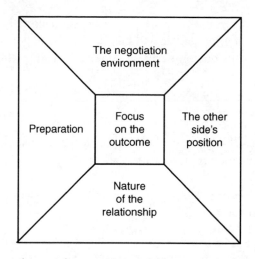

Figure 5.2 Integrated approach to negotiation. Addressing each of these negotiation components can help you achieve your desired results in just about any type of negotiation.

To help you navigate your next negotiation, we offer a five-step process, illustrated in figure 5.2, for negotiating just about anything in your professional or personal life.

Preparation

First, most of the negotiations with which you will be involved will not be adversarial. To lessen the adversarial relationship, make your position one of cooperation. You want to create a friendly relationship with the other party. Your goal should be agreement, not victory (the commonly used phrase in negotiation to describe this is "win-win").

To prepare for a negotiation, do some reflection about the negotiation and about your position.

The Negotiation
- What is the ideal outcome?
  - If the negotiation is related to your career, consider what you really want from your career. Challenging, stimulating work? Autonomy? Flexibility? Being allowed to be creative? Opportunities to learn new things? The ability to have a balanced life?
- Consider fairness in what you want
  - If the negotiation is related to home, is it that you are doing too much of the household work?
  - If it is at work, are you being paid what you are worth?
- Identify how many decision makers there are on the other side

- What's your relationship with the party in negotiation? Make sure you know if other people will be affected if you get what you want.
- Determine if the outcome will be public or private. How will it look to others?
- Find out if there are precedents related to what you are seeking.

Your Position
- Be confident. One way to build confidence is to make a list of your contributions and achievements. What are your unique and relevant strengths?
- Identify points of flexibility. For example, are you willing to work weekends or overtime?
- Consider why your position makes sense. Why should the other side do what you ask?

Identifying these issues and putting them on a piece of paper will help you recognize your strengths and help you to articulate them to the other party. You should be interested in getting what you want from others; but, you should also want to improve your relationship with the person you are negotiating with—and certainly not damage the relationship (ever hear the phrase "We can disagree, but let's not be disagreeable?"). Your negotiation should produce a balanced agreement. Shared interests are often not in the open (remember the shadow negotiation), but you should look for them and build on them.

Nature of the Relationship

Evaluate the context of your relationship with the person you are negotiating with. Is it someone you have known for a long time and have a history of seeking to come to an agreement? Is it someone you have worked with for several years and have a good relationship with? Is it someone that you've not gotten along with and who is now in a position to say yes or no to you?

Consider who has the power in the negotiation. For example, if you are negotiating a higher starting salary, and the company is having financial trouble and the unemployment rate in your area is high, that would seem to lower your negotiating power. In such a case, the person making the employment offer would have more power than you would. Understanding if one party has more power helps one to realistically determine an approach and may make the other participant more receptive to alternatives.

Focus on the Outcome

Have a goal for the negotiation and a plan with detailed steps to obtain that goal. Rather than have a singular expectation, it is better to have a range of acceptable outcomes. This is called the Zone of Possible Agreement, or

ZOPA. For example, through internet research and talking to others, you have determined that the salary range or ZOPA for the position you are offered is $75,000 minimum, $100,000 midpoint, and $125,000 maximum. You have decided that you will not work for that company for less than $100,000. They first offered you $80,000 and then moved to $90,000, which was as high as they said they could go. What do you do? If you are firm, you will consider what your options are—pursue other job offers, continue negotiations, or accept.

Another concept is BATNA, Best Alternative to a Negotiated Agreement. You are in a much better position to make a decision if you have determined what your BATNA is before you go into any negotiation. How many issues are you negotiating? If there are five, is attaining three of them enough? Or do you need all five? Should you separate the five issues and talk about them one at a time? Deciding whether to separate issues is not a right or wrong decision, it simply determines how you go about achieving your goals. You may have a specific goal in mind, but have you invented any alternatives? Look for creative solutions and identify them. Consider the following example:

> Lauren and Bill are two married 35-year-olds, both with demanding careers. They both are very active and involved in caring for their children. In the evenings after the children are in bed, Lauren is usually packing lunches, emptying the dishwasher, going through the mail, and trying to tackle whatever household task is most overdue. Bill seems to spend his time in the evening catching up on work on his laptop or watching TV. Lauren feels tired and wishes she had just a little more time to herself; she is jealous that Bill seems to get more downtime than she does.

What should Lauren do? First, she should not turn this into an adversarial position. "You watch too much TV," isn't going to get her very far. What would work better is if she develops some options where they can both get some downtime. That might be finding out how much it would cost to hire a person to help clean the house, the availability of additional child care, or ideas as to how they might divide the housework and child care. She might find out that if she asked, Bill would be happy to bathe and put the kids to bed while she got a jump start on some household tasks, so that once the kids were asleep they could both watch a little TV together. The options here for a better solution are endless. The key is to think of this as a negotiation and how both of them can improve their situation.

Identify multiple options for agreement. You should be looking for mutual gains, which means you should fully understand the other person's point of view. Your results should be based on some form of objective standards. It is key to focus on interests—not positions. A position would be, "I want a

$5,000 salary increase." An interest would be, "I would like to increase my compensation." A second example of a position would be, "I will not pay a penny over $200,000 for your house." An interest would be, "The price seems to be a little bit high for our first house; would you be willing to make it easier for us to buy the house by including some other things like furniture or appliances?" If your first negotiation point is one of looking for a solution, you will put the other party in a cooperative state of mind and they might come back with an offer that exceeds your expectations; or their proposal might be something you have not thought of that could be very helpful to you.

The Negotiation Environment

What is the negotiation environment? Will the outcome be private or public? Who else is involved? If you were to negotiate a new contract, and everyone else knew the details, would they want the same? Can the person you are negotiating with make a decision or does it need to go to a higher level? Is your company having financial problems? If the company is having financial problems, and you are simply asking for more money, the answer might be no. But if you are asking for more money because your job will be expanded and those new responsibilities will increase the productivity of the company, the chance of the answer being yes is more likely. If you are moving from New York city, with a very high cost of living, to Indianapolis, with a much lower cost of living, you need to consider that the level of pay may be lower in a low-cost living area. It's important to consider the supply and demand level for your skills. You must use research to adequately understand the negotiation environment and prepare for the negotiation.

The Other Side's Position

What is the other side's position? Are there strict policies and rules precluding the outcome you want? Are there very few decisions your boss can make? You need information about even simple things in life like asking for a hotel upgrade. Are you asking for an upgrade on a Sunday night when hotels are usually relatively empty? In such a case, you might be upgraded to a suite. However, on a Wednesday night when there is an enormous convention in town and the hotel is probably sold out, you will likely get the room assigned to you. When you walk into a car dealer and tell them you want to pay cash, thinking they will like that, you need to know that car dealers sometimes get a commission when they refer a financially qualified person to a bank. Offering cash payment may not enhance your position. If you are buying a house, you need to know everything about the owners. How much is left on their mortgage? Does the owner have an out-of-town-job needs to sell? Have the people who lived in the house, lived there for 30 years, have no mortgage and want to sell to a young couple with children who will enjoy the house as much as they did?

Making It Work

It is very important to be confident in your abilities and presentation. You can become confident if you have written down the details in your proposal. You also need to know or anticipate what the other person's point of view and arguments might be. Any argument you have should be based on objective criteria and factual information.

Ask someone who is knowledgeable about the issues to play the role of devil's advocate. You should practice talking about your proposal out loud. Because this is important, you should spend a very significant amount of time preparing. Talk to someone who has been down the same path you are preparing to go down. Another great way to prepare is to put yourself in the other person's shoes and then do all the thinking and data analysis for them. In other words, present a completed plan listing all the reasons why your request makes sense for them. Dani's situation illustrates the value of preparation.

Dani was a recruiting assistant for a company with a large recruiting department and she wanted to be promoted to being a full recruiter. The recruiter jobs were always entry-level Human Resources jobs and were filled with college graduates, usually high-potential candidates. There was an expectation that the recruiters would move on to other jobs within two to three years, so the turnover rate was high. Dani had been a recruiting assistant for six years and was by far the best performer of all the assistants; but she did not have a college degree. She and the senior vice president had worked together over the past six years and had a very good relationship. She went to the vice president because she knew he would be the decision maker for her proposal and the recruiting director would have to go through him to get it approved. Dani said that she had been thinking about being a recruiter for some time and she felt she would do a very good job in that role. She pointed out the following:

- She fully understood the recruiter's job.
- She had become an excellent evaluator of job candidates, and paid attention to who was selected, who was not, and why.
- She would stay in the job for a longer period of time than another new hire; she commented that the learning curve of the new hires was three

to four months and in this time, she observed, some mistakes were often made.

- She could get up to speed on the job very quickly. She knew that all new recruits were sent to a one-week class to learn recruiting skills and said that between that training and several books she had already read on recruiting, she would have a solid background for the job.
- She had an in-depth understanding of jobs in the organization and a good relationship with the hiring supervisors.

The senior vice president immediately went to the director of recruiting to get her opinion on offering the recruiting job to Dani. The director said, "Yes, she is a super employee. I wish I had thought of hiring her into the position in the first place." Dani got the job, a 20 percent pay increase, and did exceedingly well.

If Dani had not brought a well-thought-out plan to management, they would not have thought of offering her the job. Her proposal considered the pain points of the person with whom she was negotiating (the high turnover in the job) and anticipated concerns about her lack of formal education by proactively explaining how she was prepared for the job. Dani's story demonstrates that you may just get what you want by presenting a well-thought-out proposal.

Tips on Negotiation

- Make your position one of cooperation.
- Don't make demands—even if it's something to which the other party can agree.
- When it's appropriate, make concessions on issues that are not critical to you.
- Be soft on the people and the problem. Don't take hard positions.
- Assume you can trust the person you are negotiating with.
- Make offers, not threats.
- Look for an outcome that will be acceptable, don't focus all the time on the offer you will accept.
- Seek agreement; don't insist on your position.
- Yield sometimes and don't threaten or apply pressure on the other party.
- Make it easy for the person you are negotiating with to make a decision that is easy for her.

Table 5.1 Impact of negotiating a starting salary

Starting pay	$50,000.00	$55,000.00
Increase	5% per year	5% per year
Year 1	$52,500.00	$57,750.00
Year 2	$55,125.00	$60,637.50
Year 3	$57,881.25	$63,669.38
Year 4	$60,775.31	$66,852.84
Year 5	$63,814.08	$70,195.49
Year 6	$67,004.78	$73,705.26
Year 7	$70,355.02	$77,390.52
Year 8	$73,872.77	$81,260.05
Year 9	$77,566.41	$85,323.05
Year 10	$81,444.73	$89,589.20
Total earnings	$628,894.60	$691,784.10

Note: Over time, even a small difference in a starting salary can have a long-term effect.

Salary Negotiation

Salary negotiations can have a tremendous impact on how much an individual is paid over his or her career. We have added specific information to this chapter on how you can successfully negotiate compensation. The following example in table 5.1 points out how much money is at risk if you don't negotiate and end up accepting an offer for less money than you might have negotiated.

This is a modest analysis that does not consider the differences in benefits and additional compensation that are linked to base salary. For example, if a bonus is based on a percentage of pay, the individual who negotiated a higher starting salary will always make more.

Most people, women included, feel uncomfortable about asking for more money when they are offered a starting salary. But Jim's experience with human resource managers is that they are willing to negotiate increasing salary and benefits. Knowing that they are willing to increase the offer should make it easier for you to ask. In addition, many recruiters are expecting you to ask for more. Many recruiters make their first offer at 10–20 percent less than what their maximum offer could be. They may actually view whether or not you choose to negotiate as a test that indicates whether you have a high opinion of yourself or not. Sometimes their opinion of a candidate is actually diminished when the candidate does not ask.

In terms of when to discuss compensation in the hiring process, midway through the process typically makes the most sense. As you move through the process, you should get all offers in writing. While you don't necessarily want to bring up compensation during your first interview, it can be to your advantage to be the first to make a proposal, since the other side will have to respond to what you proposed. Your negotiating position is at its highest before you accept an offer. If you resign your current position or take yourself out of the job search and accept the offer, your negotiation position is greatly diminished. In the following section, we use the integrated approach to negotiation and apply that to salary negotiation.

Preparation

As we introduced through our negotiating model, preparation is the most critical aspect of the negotiating process. Every candidate must be familiar with compensation ranges and rates if they expect to maximize their salary offer. Begin by conducting the following research online:

- Average pay offered by other companies for the position you are offered. If you were offered a marketing job in the telecommunications industry, you need to know what companies in that industry pay for the position.
- Average pay for marketing managers in all companies.
- Average pay for marketing manager positions in your geographic area.

If you find the pay range for the job you are offered to be $45,000 minimum, $55,000 midpoint, and $65,000 maximum, and you are offered $45,000, then you know there is a lot of room for the company to increase the offer. But if you are offered $60,000, there is likely less room for the company to move up. In addition to getting increased income, there are other benefits to being paid at the top of the range. Generally, companies have high expectations of success for individuals at the top of the pay range, which may open additional opportunities for stretch assignments and early promotion.

Be prepared to answer the following questions listed in table 5.2 during the hiring process.

Nature of the Relationship

You can more easily highlight your capabilities and talents if you know about the other individuals in the department or company. Will you be the only one who knows how to deal in a certain market or has certain skills that others don't have? Listen to what is said in the interview process and pay attention to what qualities the company seeks so you can highlight how you have those qualities. For example, if in talking to others you find that they have all

Table 5.2   Answering common compensation questions

Questions about compensation	Tips on how to answer them
What salary are you looking for?	You should know before the interview what the ranges are for the area, the industry, and your specific experience and knowledge. You should tell them honestly and if you know the range, there's not much risk that you will underestimate yourself.
What is your current compensation?	In a negotiation process, the company wants to know what your current pay is so they will be in the driver's seat when the first offer is made. If you're low in the range, they know they can hire you without going to the top of their range and you've already given them the information they need. If you know your current salary is low because you've done the research, you may answer it by telling them your current compensation but adding, "One of the reasons I'm interested in another position is because I believe, based on my talents, accomplishments, and work ethic, that I am underpaid where I am right now."

been there a long time, you might say that you can bring a new perspective to the group.

Earlier, we talked about the BATNA, your best alternative to a negotiated agreement. If you're already working at a great company or just getting out of school and have five offers, you're in a better position to negotiate than you are if you've been out of work for a year or are looking for your first job and have found nothing. You should also know what the company's BATNA is. How long has the job been open? Is there more than one opening? Is it a very difficult position to fill? Is their market expanding? Are they moving into new businesses? Do they have a lot of openings in lots of different areas?

The negotiating process should not be adversarial. It is not a win-lose situation. It's best if you can determine together how the company can meet their needs and you can meet your needs. You should establish that you want to work for the company. They should know that you are flexible. Often, employers stop negotiating because the candidate indicated to them that they were really not interested. This lack of interest may have been due to a candidate's casual attitude or request for concessions that they should have known that the company could not accommodate. For example, if you're working at a retail environment, you need to know you're going to have to work some weekends. If you can't, then the negotiations aren't going to go very well.

In any negotiation where there is a range of issues, it is important to prioritize them. What's an issue that would cause you to walk away? What are the issues that can be resolved easily? It's often easier to get a "yes" on issues easily resolved before you move onto a hard one. You must state your positions clearly. You want a 10 percent signing bonus, not just a signing bonus. You want a salary 5 percent more than the one they offered, not just more. An important negotiating strategy is to be very clear with the employer and let the employer know exactly what it will take for you to agree. If your requirements are clear, the employer will know how to quickly come to an agreement.

Focus on the Outcome

Don't focus only on negotiating your salary. Your base pay is only one element of your compensation. For example, if you are near the top of the pay range, you could ask for a signing bonus, say 10–15 percent of your pay. This is not part of your base compensation, so it does not get highlighted as being above the range and it is less expensive for the company than increasing your salary.

If you are being relocated, you should know what the company's relocation benefits are. Even if you are not, it may be helpful to know. For example, if they were to pay for the cost of moving someone else 500 miles and you are local, a negotiating point is you are saving a lot of money because you're right around the corner versus someone who is 500 miles away. If you are not being relocated, you should remind the hiring organization that they are saving a significant amount of money if you accept the job. Find out what the relocation costs might be and use that as a starting point for your negotiation. If you are relocating and single, your relocation costs would be cheaper than relocating a family with children and a larger house.

It can be a negotiation point if you found the job on your own versus coming through a search firm, which typically charges 30 percent of the first year's pay. In our $50,000 example, the fee for search firm charge is likely $15,000. In this case, you could ask for a signing bonus based on the money the company is saving by hiring you versus somebody else. If you're relocating, you may ask for three to six months of temporary living paid for by the company. You may want to ask them to waive a waiting period for the medical plan or tuition aid reimbursement. Sometimes, organizations may have more flexibility in some of the ancillary benefit options than in compensation.

Options for Negotiation Other Than Salary

- Stock options or equity interest
- Time off
- Child care
- Personal time to attend to children's issues
- Flexible work schedule
- Telecommuting
- Supplemental insurance coverage
- Adoption assistance if you have plans to adopt
- Student loan reimbursement for your college or graduate school
- Training programs/continuing education
- Wellness/fitness center benefits
- Trailing-spouse job-search assistance

The Negotiation Environment

Your preparation and research will help you better understand the negotiation environment. Consider whether you are in direct competition with others or if the organization is accepting a number of people for your role. If the organization has already invested significantly in the recruiting process (multiple interviews with you for example), then you are in a better position to ask for more, as they will want to realize the benefits of their investment – the benefit being a new hire for the role. Use all of your interactions with the organization to better understand the hiring environment and what you are being asked to do. It's likely to become more clear through the interviewing process how quickly they need you to come on board and what the expectations will be for your new role. Use this information in the negotiation process. Perhaps you can ask for a higher salary and agree to start more quickly, allowing time for transition with the current person in the role; or if you are going to be expected to meet significant sales targets in your first few months, you can raise that point in the negotiation process. All data points are important when gathering information about the negotiation environment.

The Other Side's Position

Try to make it easier for them to give you more. Negotiating more pay is typically not adversarial and you should make sure that you aren't perceived as adversarial. You're going to become an integral part of the organization, and the hiring organization wants you to be happy; but they also have certain restraints. If you can help the company figure out a way to make you more likely to join them or compensate you in nontraditional ways, they're often willing to do that.

It's perfectly alright if the salary offer is not what you expect it to be. If you discuss with managers in the hiring company what your issues are, and if they want you, they can often come up with ways that meet the needs of the company and your needs. However, the best negotiating position by far is to point out the talents, skills, and abilities that will make you a key asset to the company. Ultimately, your talent and potential are the reason you should be compensated more highly.

Making It Work

Some executives use a career coach to advise them through the salary negotiations. While career coaches can be very helpful working with you through the negotiation process, you don't necessarily have to pay someone to be your career coach. You could ask a relative or a friend with experience to serve as an outside coach to you as you negotiate your pay package.

Recap

We have outlined some of the challenges women face in negotiating—but more importantly, we hope we have convinced you that with some preparation and practice you can both be comfortable and successful in asking for what you want. Simply asking will often improve the results. Additionally, it's critical to recognize that just about any aspect of a situation can be negotiated—you can negotiate revised annual goals, the resources you have to accomplish a project, or how you and your spouse will split household duties. Finally, understanding and being able to articulate your value in the context of the other party's needs will position you to do well in the negotiation.

Recommended Reading

The Shadow Negotiation: How Women Can Master the Hidden Agendas That Determine Bargaining Success by Deborah M. Kolb and Judith Williams

Her Place at the Table: A Woman's Guide to Negotiating Five Key Challenges to Leadership Success by Deborah M. Kolb, Judith Williams, and Carol Frohlinger

Women Don't Ask: Negotiation and the Gender Divide by Linda Babcock and Sara Laschever

Ask for It: How Women Can Use the Power of Negotiation to Get What They Really Want by Linda Babcock and Sara Laschever

Knowing Your Value: Women, Money, and Getting What You Are Worth by Mika Brzezinski

Getting to Yes: Negotiating Agreement without Giving In by Roger Fisher, William Ury, and Bruce Patton

Negotiation Genius: How to Overcome Obstacles and Achieve Brilliant Results at the Bargaining Table and Beyond by Deepak Malhotra and Max H. Bazerman

The Mind and Heart of the Negotiator by Leigh Thompson

PART II

What Women Need to Consider throughout a Successful Career

CHAPTER 6

Consider . . . Ambition

Kim receives an email with the subject line "Congratulations." Upon opening it, she learns that her company has selected her to participate in a two-year leadership development program that includes quarterly international sessions and intensive mentorship and coaching. She needs to accept or decline the invitation by the following Monday. That weekend she discusses the offer extensively with her family and close friends. Two years? That seems like such a commitment. She'll be 35 by the time it's over. What if she decides to have a child during that time? Or shift careers? She thinks it may be best to decline.

Ana gets a call from one of the directors in her office. The director tells Ana that the company was just awarded a research grant from a prestigious foundation. He wants Ana to be the lead researcher for the project. Ana is nervous; she has never held the lead researcher role; and she has generally worked under Karen, another lead researcher. Ana doesn't think she is ready to do it on her own and tells the director this, asking if Karen could be the lead. The director admits to Ana, "I'm confused. Karen is the one who recommended you for the position. She said that you basically ran the last two projects you were on."

Ambition is a complicated word for women. "She is pretty ambitious" may sound like code for "she's not collaborative" or "she is just focused on getting ahead." What does ambition really mean? The truth is that ambition is a healthy by-product of confidence, security, and belief in oneself. Being ambitious indicates thinking about the future and making decisions today that will position you for the future—in both work and personal life. Ambition "is the desire for personal achievement."[1]

The Issue

Much discussion still continues on the topic of whether women are less ambitious than men. Some of that discussion stems from the inability to explain why more women don't occupy leadership roles in our society. Many organizations have had women's leadership programs in place since the early 1990s: Discrimination may still exist but certainly not in the structural ways it did 30 years ago: If women wanted to be in leadership roles, some have reasoned, wouldn't they be there by now?

The numbers fueling this debate are telling:

- According to Catalyst, a leading nonprofit membership organization expanding opportunities for women and business, women earned only 36.8 percent of MBAs in 2011.[2]
- Fewer than 20 percent of members of Congress are women.
- In an oft-cited study of women with Harvard MBAs, researchers learned that 15 years later, 28 percent of the women were not working.[3]
- Only 4 percent of Fortune 500 CEOs are women, although women comprise 46.6 percent of the US workforce.[4]

Knowing the opportunities that are now open to women, how does one reconcile these numbers? The reality is that ambition requires more than just setting goals and taking advantage of opportunities. As we discuss in this chapter, ambition relates to one's self-image as well as the recognition one receives throughout life.

Making It Work

Articulating ambitions and recognizing how feelings about ambition impact work and personal life is critical for success—in whatever it is you choose to do. In this chapter, we discuss

- how ambition changes in girls and women as they mature;
- the psychology behind ambition; and
- how ambition plays out for women in organizations.

Being ambitious is a good thing; in this chapter, we'll discuss how to become comfortable with ambitions and use them to sustain and grow a healthy career.

Ambition in Girls and Women

Ask any young girl what she wants to be when she grows up and one will typically hear an answer ranging from the noble (a teacher!) to the interesting (a dog walker!) to the aspirational (president!). So what happens to that little girl who at age 5 wants to be an astronaut but at age 30 is pleased to accept a part-time job in a research lab so that she can be home each day to get her children off the school bus? Is she less ambitious? Well, the short answer is that it's complicated.

Ambition in Young Girls and Adolescents

In her groundbreaking book, *In a Different Voice: Psychology Theory and Women's Development*, first published in 1982, Carol Gilligan points out the underlying male bias in most theories of developmental psychology. Theorist after theorist—from Freud to Piaget to Kohlberg—puts forth a model for development that eventually explains why women seem to *lack* something—courage, ambition, or in Freud's theory a piece of anatomy. Gilligan reexamines these theories in the context of her research and others like it; what she finds is that it is not so much the research that is flawed—but its interpretation that is. For example, a number of psychologists have followed in Piaget's footsteps by pointing out the differences in childhood play between girls and boys—that boys tend to play competitive games with increasingly complex rules, while girls gravitate toward more cooperative play such as jump rope. Many of these researchers use these observations to posit that boys, with more opportunities to practice, become better and more comfortable with conflict, competition, and winning; while girls, without the opportunity to learn through play, miss out on these building blocks of long-term career success. However, Gilligan's work offers us a different interpretation of these play tendencies. In fact, Gilligan observes that in these girl's games, one child's success does not necessarily imply another's failure. The reason girls are more likely to end a game when a quarrel breaks out is not so much because they are "avoiding conflict" but because for girls, continuing the relationship is more important than continuing the game. By redefining success in a more gender-neutral way, Gilligan offers a model for girl's development that is more complex than the deficit-based models that dominated psychological development theory. Both girls and boys, though through different experiences, learn behaviors that position them well for long-term success.

However, Gilligan's ongoing work studying girls as they grow into adolescence and adulthood[5] demonstrates that somewhere along the way between about age 11 and age 16, many girls emerge from adolescence with less confidence and self-esteem. Gilligan's explanations for this effect and how to address it influenced much of the "girl power" movement of the 1990s and what has expanded into the anti "mean-girl" movement prevalent today. Regardless of the explanations for why this effect exists, the bottom line is that girls' ambition—just like boys'—is something that needs to be developed and nurtured as they traverse through adolescence, which is a challenging period of development for both genders. Consider this question in your own life—how did your own aspirations change between age 10 and age 16—and why do you think that was?

Anna Fels, a psychiatrist and author on the topic of women and ambition, offers a premise that the absence of recognition prevents the development of expertise that is required for pursuing any ambition.[6] As they grow, girls are less likely to seek recognition, deflect it when they get it, and fail to put themselves forward for new opportunities. Young women often find out about other's accomplishments through friends rather than learning them directly from the achiever. This pattern prevents the recognition that is essential in the development of ambition.

The work of Jerome Kagan, a theorist and leading researcher at Harvard University and Howard Moss of the Fels Research Institute in Yellow Springs, Ohio, supports Fels' theory. In their book, *Birth to Maturity*,[7] Kagan and Moss use the results of longitudinal research to reveal links between early experiences and adult characteristics. The results of their work demonstrate that achievement is encouraged when a person places oneself in a situation where competent performance is essential and achievement occurs when one obtains positive reinforcement for demonstrated competence. In other words, individuals who achieve success in adulthood typically had opportunities to do so early in their lives. Considering Kagan and Moss's work in the context of ambition in young girls, it becomes clear that both girls and boys should be put in situations that enable them to demonstrate competence and receive recognition for it.

Ambition and Gender

Today, there continues to be differences between men and women when it comes to ambition, though perhaps not quite what you think. A 2012 Pew survey of 2,500 women and men demonstrated some significant shifts in priorities related to work and family.[8] The survey revealed that women placed a higher importance than men did on both "being successful in a high-paying career" *and* "being a good parent." In fact, 66 percent of women between ages 18 and 34 cited a high-paying career among their top life priorities, compared to just 59 percent of young men. These findings are a reversal from 1997, when 56 percent of women rated a high-paying career high on their list of priorities compared to 58 percent of men. Clearly, women continue to demonstrate ambition in their orientation toward both career and family.

Yet, there are still many career fields where the gender gap is significant—for example, politics. Fewer than 20 percent of Congressional members are female. However, women who run for office do just as well as their male counterparts and are just as likely to win as men are. The problem, according to a recent study and survey by Jennifer Lawless of American University and Richard Fox of Loyola Marymount University,[9] is that so few women choose to run. Women competed in less than a third of congressional races in 2012. In short, Lawless and Fox write, the main challenge is that women lack political ambition. The factors contributing to that lack of political ambition, though, are telling. Some of the reasons echo Fels's work—in that women aren't encouraged to run as often as men are, women think they are less qualified than men are, and they are less confident than men that they will win. Another factor identified includes, according to the authors, the reality that the women are still responsible for the majority of child-care and household tasks.

Leslie Bennetts draws some similar conclusions in her 2007 book, *The Feminine Mistake*, where she pushes back on the view that lack of ambition is partly what drives some women to stop working and care for their children full time. She recounts a study by Hunter College sociologist Pamela Stone. What Stone found was not that these women lacked ambition and left their jobs; in fact, many reported planning to return to work when their children were older; it was more that the women were pushed out of jobs that didn't provide the flexibility the women needed to care for their families.[10] This point is a critical one; the reality is that marriages where both partners have highly competitive, demanding careers present significant challenges for raising a family. In fact, it's not uncommon for women in particularly powerful positions to have a spouse who slows his career down in order to care for their children. Its likely that these decisions have much more to do with the logistics and demands of young children than they do with the ambitions of either parent. Parents with ambitious careers often have what one might call an ambitious orientation to parenting, with high expectations for their children's development. Meeting the desired expectations of both parents toward their careers and family, even if possible, can be emotionally and physically exhausting. Bennetts acknowledges this challenge in her book, but offers some perspective. One of the ideas Bennetts offers in her book is the concept of "The Fifteen Year Paradigm," where Bennetts points out that in the context of one's entire career, the logistical challenges of childrearing account for less than a third of an individuals' working life. Bennetts writes that from her perspective, the career rewards of staying the course in the workforce not only brought economic benefit to her family, but also enabled her to have a rewarding career that sustained her before, during, and after the period of "intense mothering" required from birth through high school.

A well-known female COO, Sheryl Sandberg of Facebook, spoke about women and ambition in a 2010 TED talk (also captured in a commencement speech at Barnard), offering what has since become remarks including her challenge to the students that they not "leave before they leave."[11] Sandberg was referring to the tendency she has seen in some women to pull back just as they are reaching a high point in their career, because of concerns about children they don't have yet, or a different pace of life they might want in the future. Her point was that if women start gently pulling away from their ambitions, it becomes a self-fulfilling prophecy, eventually leading women to work that isn't aligned with their passions, and hence even harder to sustain at the same time they have a family. Sandberg implored the class to help close the "ambition gap" by "leaning in" and taking leadership roles. Kim's story in the beginning of this chapter is a prime example of a woman facing this kind of challenge—should she turn down a developmental program because she fears she may not want to sustain the same level of career engagement over the next two years? Instead of passing on the opportunity because she isn't sure it will work for her down the road (in effect carrying out what Sandberg calls "leaving before you leave") Kim may very well find that this program is exactly the type of opportunity she needs to give her more career options as she moves into another phase of her life.

Making It Work

1. Consider how your ambitions have changed since you were a child. What has changed and to what might you attribute the changes?
2. Consider how you feel about the decisions of the women around you. How did you feel when they have pulled back or pushed forward in their careers? How does that compare to how you feel about men in similar situations?
3. Write down your ambitions in your career and your personal life. Do you feel like they are mutually exclusive of each other? How might you do both concurrently?

In her book *Men and Women of the Corporation*, Rosabeth Kanter, a professor at the Harvard Business School, has a chapter called Opportunity. In her study of an unnamed, multinational company, which she describes as "among the biggest and most powerful of the multinationals that dominate American industry," a key reward was the ability to be promoted. The company installed a career planning process to monitor the promotion and advancement of top performers. Similar plans have been implemented by almost all large US companies and many midsized companies. To make the most of these opportunities, women (and men) need to get noticed early. Employees who are on the fast track often get plum assignments, are asked to take on additional tasks, and will be noticed by senior executives.

If your organization has a developmental program for high performing employees, find out how people are selected for it and seek an opportunity to become part of the program. Whether you are able to become part of the program or not, study those people who have been selected. Watch their behavior, understand their accomplishments, and note how they handle recognition. Doing so will help you develop and become comfortable with your own aspirations and successes. In the next section, we discuss how important this type of recognition is for one's success in an organization.

The Psychology behind Ambition

Reluctance to Take Credit

Anna Fels' work also explores ways in which women are brought up to avoid recognition and visibility in favor of traditional and feminine values and why women choose to nurture and defer rather than compete with men. As a result of this tendency, Fels writes, women often limit the recognition they accept for an achievement, which in turn makes it more difficult for them to be successful in an organization. This pattern can sidetrack the careers of even the most high-potential women—remember Ana in the beginning of the chapter? Reluctant to take credit and acknowledge her role in past research projects, she is hesitant to take on the position of lead researcher—an opportunity that might not come again if she says no. Jim often sees this reluctance in his classroom. Recently, as part of a discussion in class on this topic, Jim asked a woman in his class to say her GPA, (he knew it was a 3.9). At first she refused to say it. After asking her again, she became very flustered, blushed, and finally said she had a 3.9. One of the men in Jim's class remarked that if he were to earn a 3.9 GPA, the whole world would know.

Social cognition theory offers a lens from which to view this dynamic. Julian Rutter (1954) explained that individuals differ in the degree to which they see cause and effect links between their behaviors and outcomes. Some people believe in internal factors, such as their own behavior, and recognize outcomes as a reflection of their own actions. Others are inclined to believe in external factors and think that outcomes are controlled by other people, fate, or luck. Women often believe that external factors control results and therefore attribute their successes to forces beyond their own skill. Anna Fels argues the reason for this reluctance to attribute success to a woman's own actions is deeply rooted in society's view of femininity. Femininity is defined by qualities such as yielding, compassion, sensitivity to the needs of others, and gentleness. All of these adjectives position femininity in the context of a relationship where a woman is providing something for another person.[12] Our society offers positive social reinforcement when they perform feminine behaviors and very negative social reinforcement when they do not. Girls receive more reinforcement for being thoughtful and considerate of others than they do for being ambitious and competitive. From an early age, the importance of feminine behavior is a clear rule women obtain from their surroundings; unfortunately, that means that girls may miss out on critical opportunities to be nurtured and developed into ambitious women.

In their 2011 book, *Break Your Own Rules*, authors Jill Flynn, Kathryn Heath, and Mary Davis Holt write that while the "old rule" is "Be Modest," the "new rule" is "Project Personal Power." They explain that the new rules include "take credit for your hard work" and "don't confide your insecurities." In fact, the key to success is not just about projecting personal power— it is also important that women personally value their own contributions. If a woman does not see the direct relationship between her own skills and a successful outcome, too often she will not do enough to ensure that her colleagues or superiors recognize any connection. When she attributes successes to external sources such as luck or other people, she might not feel justified enough to toot her own horn. Women are at a disadvantage because they "refuse to claim a central purposeful place in their own stories, eagerly shifting credit elsewhere and shunning recognition"[13]. When women shift recognition elsewhere, they are decreasing the likelihood for promotion or attainment of a new job. Too many women wait for external events to give them a chance or breakthrough; in doing so, they may miss opportunities waiting for their advancement to happen to them instead of taking the initiative to make it happen. As a result, they may find themselves in a passive position compared to male colleagues who are more likely to speak openly about their accomplishments and seek credit. Tina's experience with the internal promotion of a sales win illustrates these points:

> In our company, whenever a team makes a sale over $5M they send out a companywide email. Typically, the lead sales manager writes the announcement describing the win even though it goes out from a central email account. It is unusual for two of those big wins to come from the same office in the same day, but that happened in my office. I wrote up the description of the win I had led and a male colleague wrote up the description of his. When both came out, in succession, the differences I saw were huge. In my write-up I mentioned everyone's contribution but my own; in his write-up, he listed his name prominently. At an office event later that week, our office manager mentioned my colleague by name in referencing the win; when they acknowledged my win, they asked for a round of applause for "the team." I was afraid people would think I was taking too much credit for my team's win; as a result, I didn't get any.

Tina recognized the role she played in the sales win, but in her effort to avoid being perceived unflatteringly as a self-promoter, she missed an opportunity for important recognition. A better approach would have to been to write the announcement in a way that recognized both the team and Tina's role in the win.

Recognizing Her Own Contributions

Even more damaging perhaps than a reluctance to take credit, is a reluctance to even recognize the value of one's role in the first place. This belief—that external factors influence what happens to people more than internal factors—can create other problems in the workplace. Individuals have very different behavioral tendencies when they credit internal reasons for what happens to them. "Internals" place higher value on their skills and experience, possess higher self-esteem, and display better social skills; "Externals," however, believing things happen to them, may see little value in exerting any effort to improve their situation[14] (see figure 5.1 for a related discussion). If women are more likely to look externally to explain outcomes, it could at least partially explain the differences in success between men and women in organizations.

In the opening of this chapter we introduced Ana, who was surprised that success on past research projects had been attributed to her; so surprised in fact, that when asked about it, she attributed the success to her previous boss. In this case, Ana wasn't just playing into a societal expectation that she be demure about her accomplishments—in fact, she actually thought that the success of her past projects was more a result of her manager's work than her own. It's easy to see how this kind of failure to see the value in the role one plays in organizational success could be damaging long term. In Ana's case, when she didn't see the value of her own work, it led others to doubt her abilities.

There are numerous examples of well-known women who failed to take recognition for their own success. Katherine Graham, publisher and owner of *The Washington Post*, in her autobiography, *Personal History*, diminished her role in Watergate. "I have been credited for backing the Watergate investigation. In truth, there was not much of a choice to do so."[15] Graham did not want to be recognized in the movie, *All the President's Men*. This incredibly accomplished woman, who made the decision to risk her paper's reputation on the work of two young reporters, seemingly avoided any credit at all for such an important event in the nation's history. At the same time, she acknowledged in her book that despite the fact that she didn't take credit—she expected to receive some type of recognition, writing, "My feelings were hurt by being omitted all together." Graham's story adds punctuation to the point that one must take credit for one's own work versus just hoping people will notice.

Avoiding Organizational Politics

Waiting for those external events to happen—such as receiving public credit for a significant accomplishment—may also decrease the emphasis a woman places on organizational politics, or what is sometimes called social capital— the relationships between people and the feelings of mutual obligation and support that these relationships create.[16] Believing outcomes to be the result of external sources, one reason that women are less likely to engage in the building of social capital is because they see such positioning as something that does not directly relate to the quality of the work, and hence not worth the investment time that it takes away from child care or family obligations. Conversely, if people see that advancement in their career is the result of internal sources (their own abilities), they recognize that the potential to move up is in their control and act accordingly in order to get a step ahead.[17]

A study cited in Alice Eagly and Linda Carli's book *Through the Labyrinth*, suggests that building social capital is even more necessary to managers' advancement than skillful performance of traditional managerial tasks. As a result, if women resist certain aspects of "the game," as one woman we talked to called it, they may loose.

Self-Perceptions of Confidence

Albert Bandura, the major contributor to the Social-Cognitive Learning Theory, thinks a belief in one's own competence is a major factor that influences how one approaches goals, tasks, and challenges. Related work by Charles Carver and Michael F. Scheier demonstrates that confidence in one's perceived ability to carry out a desired action develops from external experiences and self-perception.[18] It is not enough to *know* what needs to be done in a task, but one must have confidence in one's ability to *perform* that task. Differences in one's degree of confidence in performing a task determines whether or not the individual engages in that behavior. Confident individuals believe they can perform a task, and are more likely to perform it successfully. Those with less confidence in their abilities are less likely to succeed at a task. Confidence is a major factor in determining motivation and aspiration. We develop confidence through previous success and achievement, observation of others performing successfully, and verbal encouragement.

Confidence is largely developed through recognition and receiving feedback on tasks. A study by Albert Bandura and Robert Wood further revealed that confidence was affected by feedback from prior accomplishments and influenced subsequent organizational performance and achievement of goals.[19] Confidence is a major factor that either contributes to or hinders our success in organizational settings. If one does not receive positive recognition, he or she will be less confident. In a 2011 study conducted by the Institute for Leadership and Management, it was found that half of the female managers in the study admitted to feelings of self-doubt about their performance and career but only 31 percent of men reported the same.[20] Considered in the context of Bandura and Wood's work, these feelings of self-doubt could lead to poorer performance on tasks and the setting of lower personal goals, which over time could result in missed opportunities and promotions in the workplace. It's a vicious cycle of self-doubt—she's not sure she can do it, maybe she actually does it well, but even if she does, she doesn't promote her accomplishments, and she is passed over for opportunities for advance and growth. This cycle is illustrated through Caroline's story:

> I was asked by my leadership to serve as "Auditor-in-Charge" for an important study. I had led similar reviews before, but none in this subject area, and I didn't know a lot about it. I said yes hesitantly with a lot of qualifications about my knowledge. I got the report completed on time and I don't think there were any issues with the work; in fact, it was cited in some media reports. But then a follow-up study was requested and they asked someone else to lead it. I'm not sure why.

Caroline may have created a successful report; we don't know—but from what she describes, even if she did do a great job, it sounds like she did little to promote that success or accept her role in it. As a result, for whatever reason, she was passed over when the next opportunity came around.

Even the most talented women sometimes struggle with issues of confidence. Virginia Rometty, selected as IBM's chief executive in 2012, is an example of how a clearly talented business executive was reluctant to put herself forward and appeared to lack ambition. "Early in my career, I can remember being offered a big job," she told a *Fortune* magazine conference on women and careers in May 2012.[21] "I right away said, 'You know what? I'm not ready for this job. I need more time, I need more experience and then I could really do it well.' And so I said to the person offering the job, 'I need to go home and think about it.'...And my husband, he's just sitting there. And as I'm telling him about this, and I told him I would get back to them tomorrow, he just looked at me and said, 'Do you think a man would have ever answered that question that way?' And I sort of sat there—and it taught me a lesson. And he said, 'I know you, you go do it, you're going to—six months you're going to be bored.'"

Making It Work

All of these studies provide women with both practical tools and options to shift their thinking in order to best position themselves for success. One particularly helpful piece of work in understanding how to embrace ambition and best position oneself for success is the Rimm Report, or *See Jane Win*,[22] which was authored by Dr. Sylvia Rimm, a clinical professor at Case Western Reserve University School of Medicine. She was assisted by Dr. Sara Rimm-Kaufman, a research psychologist at the University of Virginia, and Dr. Ilonna Rimm, a pediatric researcher in Boston. Their research included a survey of approximately 1,000 women who achieved success in their careers. The survey identified what successful women had in common and pointed out what young women could learn from the survey to help them be successful.

First, they found, women should set high educational goals for themselves. That includes college and attending graduate school. They should also take courses or workshops throughout their career. For example, one woman with a successful Wall Street career, who was interviewed as part of the research for this book, cited the importance of taking early advantage of a particular financial services accreditation course. Over Jim's 25 years working as a human resources manager and executive in organizations, about the only account that was always under budget was the company tuition-aid fund. Make sure that you take advantage of your company's tuition refund program or consider options at community colleges. When Lindsay found herself increasingly engaged in information technology projects, she audited a graduate-level information technology course at her alma mater for a small donation.

Successful women often describe themselves as nurturing, sensitive, caring, and compassionate—traits mostly ascribed to women. Rimm reports that although these words have not been typically attached to leadership or management characteristics, they do not interfere with success. In fact, according to the Rimm report, the model of the aggressive, noncaring, harsh, victory-at-all-costs leadership model attributed to men is no longer as prevalent as it once was, and has been replaced by a more caring, employee-focused leadership style that is more productive. Traits that perhaps once were considered detrimental to leaders are now considered desirable. We explore this trend more deeply in the chapter on leadership.

The Rimm survey also found that developing math, science, and computer skills are essential for women's achievement. College women should take a course where women are typically underrepresented. Organizations truly want diversity; and career fields where women are traditionally underrepresented are likely to offer significant opportunities to young women. We would also suggest that taking even just one class in human resource management, marketing, accounting, finance, organizational behavior, and economics will give you an edge in finding a job and doing well when you get it.

Recap

Ambition connects directly to the future—it allows you to set goals and achieve them. Critical to developing your ambition is recognizing the role you played in your successes, and then making sure others recognize that role.

Recommended Reading

Necessary Dreams: Ambition in Women's Changing Lives by Anna Fels
See Jane Win: The Rimm Report on How 1,000 Girls Became Successful Women
   by Sylvia Rimm, Sara Rimm-Kaufman, and Ilonna Rimm
Lean In: Women, Work, and the Will to Lead by Sheryl Sandberg

CHAPTER 7

Consider ... Leadership

Amy sat across from her boss and listened to her performance evaluation. After reviewing the glowing report, her boss set it down and took off her glasses. "Look," her boss said, "There are things that go in the review and things that don't. Because I think you are a strong performer and I know you can continue to do well here, I'm going to tell you something and I need you to hear what I am saying." Her boss paused and then continued, "Well, the thing is, people feel you are abrasive at times. And some of your staff say that you are too hard on them when you aren't happy with their performance." Amy was surprised; she knew she held the team to a higher standard than the manager before her; but she didn't think she was any tougher on the team than he had been.

Justine looked around the table. The team was celebrating the submission of a huge grant application to a major potential funder. They had had only four days to pull the application together, and it took a lot of heavy lifting. When they first found out about the opportunity, Justine spent an entire afternoon meeting one-on-one with each member of the agency from whom she needed a contribution, determining how each could best assist in preparing the grant. She raised her glass to the group and offered a toast, "I have a good feeling about this one," she said. "We came together to get this done, and we are going to come together again to expand our agency's work when we get this funding!" Everyone at the table clapped; it felt good to know they had done such a great job on the application.

Leadership and gender can be a confusing topic. Are women or men better natural leaders? Should women be more "like" men—that is, more decisive and directive? Or should women be themselves, motivating employees through personal attention and collaboration? What does it even mean to be "like" a man or "like" a woman? Mix in topics like ambition, as discussed in chapter 6, and it gets even more confusing: maybe women don't occupy formal leadership roles because they *choose* not to. In the examples above, would Amy get the same feedback if she were a man? And is Justine's collaborative approach to managing her team a direct result of her being a woman?

The Issue

In fact, few would disagree that the characteristics of leadership have traditionally been male: decisive, bold, visionary, and strong.[1] Perhaps, you picture George Washington at the front of a boat crossing the Delaware River; Lincoln standing his ground to hold together the United States; or Julius Caesar, the statesman, making an impassioned speech on the Senate floor. When images like this come to mind, it's probably hard to replace these famous men and consider women in these roles instead. Even today, data shows that women are missing from leadership positions, and many successful women struggle with their own identity as a leader. Additionally, while as a society we have grown more accepting of women leaders, public women leaders often find a disproportionate focus on their appearance and personal style compared to their male colleagues; they are also often criticized simultaneously for being too soft and for exhibiting qualities that are too masculine.[2]

However, as more study has been given to leadership and gender, some have made a case that women are better candidates for modern leadership, because women are more likely to demonstrate compassion, openness, and the people focus valued in today's leaders. In this chapter, we explore the traditional views of leadership, how they have changed, and what it means for you today.

Making It Work

Throughout this book, we've cited data that shows how women continue to be significantly underrepresented at the highest levels of business and government; and we've talked about a number of steps women can take to increase their opportunities for success. Improving your negotiation or communication skills, planning ahead for potential career path shifts, and lining up sponsors are all concrete steps you can take to be successful at work. But when it comes to leadership, there is no three-step process to ensure success. In fact, earlier theories of leadership actually indicated that leadership couldn't be taught—that it was a characteristic innate to certain people. What we offer in this chapter is something in between the recipe-for-success and the you've-either-got-it-or-you-don't approaches. Understanding different types of management styles, becoming more self-aware, and developing your own leadership style are all vital areas in the context of leadership.

Leadership and Gender: A Historical View

Shifting Views of Leadership

As mentioned in the introduction to this chapter, historical perspectives on leadership have been very male oriented. The first theory of leadership was called "The Great Man Theory," which clearly left little room for women. This view of leadership, popular in the late nineteenth and early twentieth century, posited that certain men simply possessed the necessary attributes of leadership. The qualities they possessed were thought to be natural and intrinsic.[3] The Great Man Theory supported further development of the concept of "trait theory," the idea that certain traits made people leaders. The early traits identified through studies were based significantly on military and political leaders and were decidedly masculine, including traits such as aggressiveness and dominance. Today, the trait theory persists, though the traits identified as desirable for successful leaders have been expanded and updated based on more inclusive modern research. In fact, today, there has been somewhat of a comeback of the Great Man Theory, in a form of what we might call the "Great Woman Theory," with some now making the argument that women have an intrinsically better way of leading in today's world because they are cooperative, communal, and supportive of others.[4]

Many find the trait theory, even with its resurgence (an example is the continued widespread use of the Myers-Briggs Type Indicator, which is based in part on trait theory), is limiting in its understanding of how some leaders are successful while others are not. The idea that leadership could be taught gained support through the concept of behavior theory, which indicates that the approaches taken by leaders can lead to their success. A related concept, referred to as situational leadership, maintains that the behavior should be varied based on the unique aspects of the environment or people. We will draw on all of these theories in this chapter as each of them contributes in a different way to current views of leadership.

Leadership Theories and Gender

Gender Bias

The traditional theories of leadership continued to influence perceptions about gender and leadership well into the middle of the twentieth century and beyond. These traditional theories of leadership contributed to the "sex-typing" of work. Research by Virginia Schein demonstrated an effect she dubbed "think management—think male." Her research, initially published in 1973, found that the attributes people identified as making a successful manager were those more commonly ascribed to men than women. She writes that "women were perceived by both male and female managers as less likely than men to possess the characteristics, attitudes, and temperaments required of successful managers. Characteristics such as leadership ability, desires responsibility, and objectivity were seen as requisite management characteristics and more likely to be held by men than by women. To 'think management' was to 'think male.'"[5] Schein used this research to demonstrate that women were indeed facing a bias in seeking managerial roles. She and others revisited this work in the 1980s and 1990s and found that the attitudes of males were still similar to those in the early 1970s; but the attitudes of women had changed. Women saw women and men as equally likely to align with the characteristics of a successful manager.[6]

Schein's work helps explain why a "deficit" model sometimes emerges when discussing women and leadership. A deficit model would view the issue of "think management—think male" as needing to be addressed by women "fixing" themselves and acting "more male"—that is more assertive and direct. Deficit models are problematic for many reasons, not the least of which is that such a perspective fails to recognize that different leadership styles can be successful in different situations.

Gender Differences in Leadership
The increased focus on gender and leadership has in some cases led people to suggest that women make better leaders than men. For example, in the book *Mother Leads Best: 50 Women Who Are Changing the Way Organizations Define Leadership* by Moe Grzelakowski, the author makes a case for the benefits of "maternal leadership," identifying characteristics and behavior such as patience, spontaneity, and crisis management as ones that women develop during the stages of motherhood.[7] Certainly, the ability to learn from life experiences and translate those in a way that they help refine one's leadership style is critical for all leaders—whether those experiences include motherhood, fatherhood, being immersed in another culture, living through a serious illness, or any other life-changing experience. We don't think women are better leaders than men are; but we do think that most women have key strengths that should be incorporated into their leadership style.

In their groundbreaking book *Through the Labyrinth: The Truth about How Women Become Leaders*, Alice Eagly and Linda Carli tackle most of the tough issues around women and leadership. In particular, they consider whether women lead differently than men. Their presentation of the topic demonstrates little research that has turned up actual evidence of differences in women and men's style; instead, they find more claims about differences in articles written for management audiences and the general public.[8] These perspectives generally suggest that women's style of leadership—one that is more interactive, collaborative, and inclusive—is more appropriate and successful for modern organizations that rely more on team-based environments.

Eagly and Carli partially reconcile these perspectives in the context of situational leadership, presenting the idea that leadership roles may be more likely to lead to differences in style than gender. For example, a role that typically requires an authoritative style—they use an orchestra conductor as an example—is going to require similar characteristics regardless of gender. They write, "Women generally split the difference in these masculine and feminine demands by finding a middle way that is neither unacceptably masculine nor unacceptably feminine...women also modulate their style to meet the demands of their particular leadership roles."[9] We think their perspective is one that offers women a path forward to develop personal leadership styles throughout their careers and adapt these styles to the needs of unique situations.

Making It Work

Women still face bias when it comes to perceptions about their ability to be an effective leader. Yet at the same time, there is a perspective, however anecdotal, that women possess characteristics such as friendliness and collaboration that make them better modern leaders. This is one of those situations where you need to sort through the perspectives and cull from them what works on a personal basis. It is important to adjust your leadership style to needs of your team members and the situations in your organization. In the opening case study, Justine used a very personalized and communal approach to assign work; she felt that it was needed in light of a difficult deadline where she had to find a way to get people to voluntarily put in extra hours. At the same time, be aware that when you need to employ a more directive or autocratic approach to your work that, as a woman, you run the risk of being perceived negatively—even if the approach isn't radically different from one utilized by a male colleague. As Eagly and Carli wrote, "splitting the difference" seems to be the way most women successfully navigate this leadership paradox of needing to be simultaneously viewed as both agentic and communal. In the next section, we discuss a common framework for modern leadership that works for both genders in a variety of situations.

Leadership Styles

Introduction

As mentioned previously, leadership styles have been categorized, analyzed, and studied by consultants and scholars. Three styles that are particularly helpful for offering a lens on leadership are transactional, transformational, and laissez-faire styles. Laissez-faire, essentially an abandonment of any leadership style, is dysfunctional in most situations; for that very reason we won't explore it further. However, the concept of transactional and transformational styles can be very helpful when considered in the context of situation and gender.

Transactional and Transformational Leadership Styles

Eagly and Carli, in *Through the Labyrinth*, write that "women are associated with communal qualities indicating a concern for treating others compassionately. They include being especially affectionate, helpful, friendly, kind, and sympathetic, as well as interpersonally sensitive, gentle, and soft-spoken. In contrast, men are associated with agentic qualities, which convey assertion and control. They include being especially aggressive, ambitious, dominant, self-confident, and forceful, as well as self-reliant and individualistic. The agentic traits are also associated in most people's minds with effective leadership—perhaps because a long history of male domination of leadership roles has made it difficult to separate the leader associations from the male associations."[10] The traits listed for men are consistent with the *transactional* leadership style. Transactional leaders operate with clear rules of authority, follow a chain of command, and believe employees should do what the boss tells them to do. They are strong, direct, aggressive, dominant, blunt, hardworking, and results oriented.

The second style, *transformational* leadership, was first coined by James McGregor Burns, a longtime political science professor at Williams College and the author of *Leadership*, published in 1978.[11] Transformational leadership occurs when the leader engages others in the department, company, or organization to raise motivation to a higher level. Transformational leaders believe that people can be lifted to higher levels of performance by leadership. Leadership is a positive process, which leads to positive organizational outcomes. Leaders who use a transformational leadership style, one often viewed as having more female characteristics, have better organizational outcomes than transactional leaders. In this respect, the recognition of the value of transformational leadership is good for women—and their organizations. It's important to note, however, that many men routinely use a transformational leadership style with great success.

Transformational Leadership and Employee Involvement

In the 1970s, concurrent to the growing emphasis placed on the transformational leadership style, a new and different management concept evolved. It went by several names: employee involvement, employee empowerment, total quality management, and team concept. An employee involvement philosophy is based on the elements of transformational leadership and has proven effective in improving the outcomes of the organization. This philosophy elicits the commitment and hard work of the employees in the organization in order for the organization to be high functioning and stay in business. The same adjectives used to describe transformational leadership are those that are used to describe leaders who successfully engage employees in running the organization. Everyone—at any level of an organization—can benefit from the use and practice of techniques to help one become a very effective transformational leader.

Employee involvement utilizes the knowledge and capabilities of all employees in the organization to solve the problems of the business. Employee involvement occurs when knowledge, skills, operating information, decisions, rewards, and control usually reserved for managers is appropriately shared with all levels of the organization.

The philosophy of employee involvement relies heavily on involving employees in day-to-day processes and enabling them to use their knowledge and skills to make decisions that enhance the organization's performance and their individual satisfaction. Concurrent to improvement in organizational results, the satisfaction, financial well-being, and job security of employees increases. Any assumptions made by managers about employees are positive ones. The more productive organization believes that people are responsible, intelligent, and want to work; and that all jobs are necessary and therefore, important. The person performing the job is viewed as the expert on that job. Consider the following situation when a hotel clerk is empowered to make room-rate pricing decisions.

> A potential guest shows up at 8:00 p.m. when the hotel is only three-quarters full. The guest asks the price of the room and the clerk says $120, the standard rate. The guest indicates that the rate is too high and begins to walk away. The desk clerk, who is authorized to give flexibility in the rate, offers the room for $100 a night, and the customer books the room. The desk clerk, because she was empowered to make a decision, added $100 in revenue to the hotel.

Employees who have the authority to make a decision built into their job description find more satisfaction in their job and are encouraged to take action that supports the organization's objectives. In this example, the desk clerk is best positioned to determine what the rate should be to secure the customer. Involving the desk clerk indicates that the hotel trusts employees to make important decisions. In fact, the Ritz Carlton Hotel chain has a policy that anyone in the hotel—bellhops, desk clerks, and housekeepers, can spend up to $200 to make a single guest happy.[12] They report they have very few cases of the misapplication of this policy.

Your role as a leader is to establish a framework where employees can develop the ability to make important decisions about the management of their work activities. It is your job as a transformational manager to elicit commitment from your employees rather than control them. Jim frequently observed that when employees are engaged in the decisions about the management of their work, the result is greater organizational effectiveness and reduced employee turnover. The traditional way that decisions were made in organizations was that the managers did the thinking and controlled the employees. The people who were doing the work carried out instruction or complied with very strict rules and procedures. In contrast, an organization led by a transformational leader would be one where managers focused on the strategies, and the people at the bottom of the pyramid did the thinking, controlling, and performing. This concept is illustrated in figure 7.1.

Particularly helpful for understanding these differences is a 1985 article in the *Harvard Business Review*, "From Control to Commitment in the Workplace," by Richard E. Walton. This important article spelled out a new management philosophy that had the potential to improve the productivity

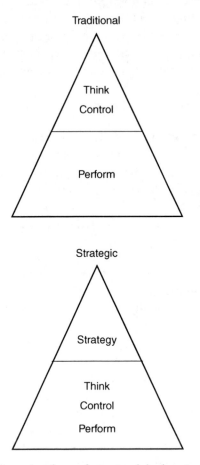

Figure 7.1 Management style of transformational leader. An organization led by a transformational leader is one in which lower-level employees are empowered to make decisions about how to best achieve the organization's goals.

and success of the organization. Walton put forth the idea that employees are more creative and more productive when they are not tightly controlled by management, placed in narrow jobs, and treated like an unwelcome necessity. Instead, employees are successful when they are given broad responsibilities, encouraged to contribute, and enabled to take satisfaction in their work that pays tangible dividends for the individuals and for the company.[13]

Walton's view was a radically different workforce strategy at the time, but it

---

Ways to Elicit Commitment from Employees

- Support a high performing team member's arrangement for a flexible work schedule.
- Give more responsibilities to individuals seeking to grow. A job can often be made more interesting by adding complexity to the position.
- Employ the concept of "Completed Staff Work." Completed Staff Work is a way of operating in which the study of a problem and recommendation of a solution is the job of the subordinate; the manager only needs to give approval or disapproval of the completed recommendation. This concept not only improves productivity but also allows the person doing the work to get the recognition of completing a whole task.
- Take responsibility for setting high standards for new employees entering the organization or being promoted. Selection of staff is one of the most important tasks a manager can perform. Employees with these traits help the organization thrive and contribute significantly. It's the leader's job to make sure that employees who are selected for the organization are individuals who will thrive in and contribute to the organization.

---

offered a way for managers to increase organizational outcomes and simultaneously improve employee satisfaction. Walton's model has become a very popular management philosophy throughout the world. Jim was fortunate to be in Professor Walton's class and can recall, almost as if it was yesterday, when Walton said, "There is no tradeoff between employee satisfaction and productivity. In a way, you can have your cake and eat it too."[14]

Making It Work

It's important to understand how you can draw from various leadership styles in developing your own and adapting it to the situation and your team members. In particular, some of the transactional techniques can be appropriately used to compliment a transformational style. For example, decisiveness is an attribute of the transactional leadership style. All leaders need to be decisive, but good leaders can still be transformational in their approach to decision making. Consider this example:

> A software company faces a decision of whether or not to invest signifi-cant cash in the purchase of a smaller competitor. The decision needs to be made quickly as there is a limited opportunity to make the purchase. There are many hours of discussion while the leadership team weighs the options and tries to determine the best decision. Finally, the night before they need to make the call, the ten members of the group go around the room and indicate whether to buy the competitor or pass. Seven of the employees want to pass and two want to make the pur-chase. The CEO says she wants to make the purchase and after jokingly saying "majority rules," she lays out a compelling case for why the pur-chase should be made. Given their engagement in the previous analysis, her perspective makes sense to the rest of the employees, including even those that had previously voted against the purchase. Everyone is satis-fied that they had an opportunity to give input to the decision and now that it is made, they do everything they can to make sure the purchase is successful.

Most team members desire an opportunity to give input—but in the end, it's the role of the leader to make decisions. Indecisiveness can be worse than making wrong decisions. Decisiveness is a critical leadership trait regardless of the particular leadership style being used in the organiza-tion. In the same light, consider how you might merge attributes of both the transactional and transformational styles to strengthen your role as a leader.

Leadership Elements

Strategy

Some elements of leadership are so important that they should be consid-ered separately. These elements are strategy, culture, leadership presence, and power. These topics prove critical for any man or woman to consider when laying the groundwork for a successful career.

Strategic thinking is an essential part of being a leader. In fact, by defi-nition, leaders must be strategic. We have used the terms "manager" and "leader" somewhat interchangeably in this chapter, which makes sense given that this book is targeted at women who are in early or midcareer stages.

However, one of the important distinctions between the two roles is strategy. Managers and even the CEO of many organizations may be very effective, get good results, and operate a well-run company. However, in the words of Michael Porter, "Operational effectiveness is not strategy."[15] Strategy is the process of competing to be unique rather than competing to be the best. It involves deciding what not to do as much as deciding what to do. Deciding what not to do seems to be even more difficult for managers than starting a new initiative because it involves giving up on something that may have been a key part of the organization for decades. Analysis of the recent demise of Kodak pointed out that the company invented digital photography and holds digital patents but was reluctant to move aggressively into the digital business because it would have a negative impact on the highly profitable film business. Because they were reluctant to give up something previously successful for them for decades, they lost almost everything.

Porter and other thinkers helped companies and organizations focus on implementing strategy in nonmilitary organizations. If one reviews management books prior to the 1960s, it is very rare to see the term "strategy." Strategy became a term on every manager's lips in large measure because Michael Porter wrote *Competitive Strategy* in 1980. In a *Harvard Business Review* article, Porter says that operational effectiveness is necessary but is not sufficient for long-term success.[16] Operational effectiveness means performing similar activities better than competitors do. To be successful, a company must establish a difference that it can preserve in order to stay ahead of others. Many very well-known companies focused on performing the same processes that their competitors performed but in an extraordinarily effective way. We recount a few of the ones that have been well known and successful.

Toyota flourished over a 30-year period because they created a strategic manufacturing process that centered around reducing waste in the process (waste of any type of resources—time, goods, energy, etc.). The process was different from those used by other automobile manufactures to make cars. This new manufacturing concept, clearly a strategic change, allowed Toyota to be a leader in manufacturing processes for years. It took a long time for other auto manufacturers to replicate what Toyota invented, but over time they were able to do so. Once other companies replicated Toyota's process and caught up, Toyota lost its preeminent manufacturing position. The Toyota story illustrates that strategic thinking needs to occur continuously. Organizations should always be looking for a new strategy or the next new idea, which will keep the company moving forward. If you're not progressing, you're falling behind.

Southwest Airlines is another company that is widely studied and has been the basis of many business school cases. Southwest is an example of a business that created a unique strategy that led to an extraordinarily success-ful business. Their strategy is based on point-to-point air travel instead of a hub-and-spoke system. Prior to the creation of Southwest, hub-and-spoke was the predominant airline strategy. Southwest also added a transforma-tional leadership concept, employee involvement, to their business strat-egy. These practices included sharing responsibilities for multiple jobs and implementing employee practices that led to extraordinary dedication by Southwest employees. They used only one type of airplane—Boeing 737. This led to significant training and maintenance savings. It was impossible for other airlines to quickly replicate Southwest practices and processes, in part because they had already committed to a hub strategy, which was much more costly than Southwest. Those of you who have flown Southwest know that there are no seat assignments, no connections with other airlines, limited use of travel agents, 15–20 minute gate turnarounds, extremely low ticket prices, and a highly motivated, humorous cabin attendant workforce with pilots wearing leather jackets. Other airlines are now attempting to rep-licate Southwest strategies. Even given their great success, it will be vital for Southwest to keep looking forward and develop new strategies. Even the best strategies don't last forever.

Dyson, which started as an everyday vacuum cleaning company, is an example of how a well-thought strategy can upend traditional competitors. Dyson was a newcomer to the vacuum cleaner business. Their strategy was not to make a better vacuum cleaner and compete with companies 100 years old, but rather to use a new air-moving strategy. They have gained a large share of the worldwide vacuum cleaning market with their strategy of mov-ing air faster. Their focus on air movement also allowed them to enter the restroom paperless hand-drying business. Dyson is replacing a company that had a huge market share with the same hand-drying product for 50 years. They defined a unique air-moving concept through which Dyson has been able to maintain their competitive advantage.

These three examples indicate what can happen when a newcomer enters a market with a new business model, with competitors who either underesti-mate their impact or fail to respond quickly enough in the market. A high-tech business has a greater risk than a traditional business that a newcomer will overtake its business not in a 15-year period, but in a 15-month period. Examples of large, powerful companies who have witnessed this challenge are Yahoo, AOL, and Research in Motion, the company behind the Blackberry.

Starting in the 1980s, many organizations implemented a formal strategic planning process. Figure 7.2 offers a generic strategic formulation model that can be used as a starting point for a strategic planning effort. Each of the related components should be considered as part of the strategic planning process.

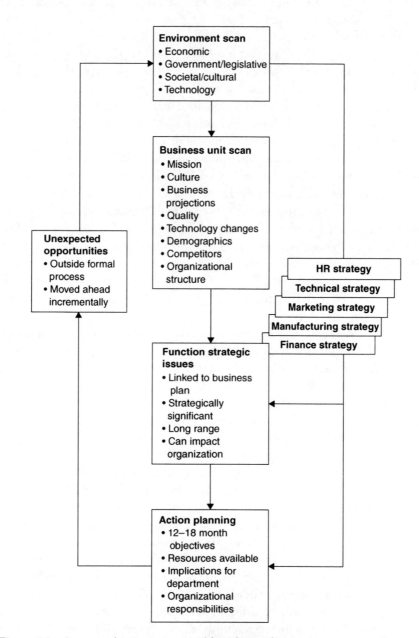

Figure 7.2 Strategic planning process. Although specific processes may vary, this model includes the basic elements of any strategic planning process.

When conducting the environmental scan, the impact of external shifts and trends must be understood. For example, are there any new laws or regulations (planned or in progress) that may significantly impact the organization's business? For example, the health care reform legislation passed in 2010 continues to have a far-reaching impact on many industries. Another key issue to consider through an environmental scan is technology. Today, technology continues to be more and more "disruptive"—meaning that new technology can enable an organization to entirely change the nature of a market; on the flip side, such disruption can quickly put an organization out of business by rendering its model moot. For example, as discussed earlier in the context of Kodak, the widespread use of digital cameras disrupted the film business. Successful organizations both identify such environmental trends and develop ways to minimize them or use them to their advantage.

The business unit factors, in the center of the diagram, identify the many internal factors that need to be evaluated through the planning process. For example, does the business unit face significant employee turnover due to retirement or is there a new competitor entering the business? Supporting business units, captured in the far left of the diagram, must also be evaluated, including human resources, technical departments, marketing, manufacturing, and finance.

Strategic issues for each function need to be identified. The issues must be linked to the business, strategically significant, long range, and if the issue is successfully addressed, have a significant impact on the organization. Finally, the organization must identify action plans over the next 12 to 18 months and consider how to implement the plan. Are resources available? What are the implications of working on these plans in the department and who in the organization should be responsible for implementation?

Additionally, it's common that unexpected and unplanned opportunities may arise (the far left of the diagram). For example, a competitor may be for sale or a new investment option may become available. Considering all of these factors and using this model as a strategic planning tool will help guide an organization in the development and execution of a successful strategy.

There is no evidence that women are more or less strategic thinkers than men. But being a leader means being strategic. It's not uncommon for bright women to be promoted into increasing positions of responsibility because they are excellent managers—they can get things done, solve problems, find solutions, and meet deadlines. Making the jump to a leadership level in an organization requires an increased emphasis on strategy. When you first start in an organization, even if you are at an entry-level position, learn and understand the organization's strategy. Be able to articulate how your service supports that strategy. As you move up in the organization, you must set aside an increasing amount of time to pull your mind out of the daily rush of activity and take a strategic view of your organization's environment and long-term success.

Culture

Understanding, creating, and sustaining organizational culture is one of the most important requirements of a successful leader. Edgar Schein, whose work is discussed in more detail in the chapter on working globally, offers a helpful perspective on organizational cultures. Schein writes that culture is a deep phenomenon; it is complex and difficult to understand. Culture is a set of beliefs and assumptions that are shared by members of an organization. Generally, these assumptions and beliefs have been developed because they have enabled the organization to solve problems and successfully adapt to their external environment. The culture is then sustained through internal integration—another common term for this is "socialization"—in that new members are taught the correct way to perceive, think, and feel in relation to those problems.[17]

Culture and leadership are intertwined, and Schein implies that the leader is responsible for creating or changing the culture to ensure that the culture remains a productive one. He says that leadership plays a key role during the times the team faces a new problem and must develop new responses to the situation. He points out that one of the crucial functions of leadership is to provide guidance at precisely those times when habitual ways of doing things no longer work or when dramatic changes in the environment require new responses.[18] A leader must not only ensure the invention of new and better solutions, but must also provide some security to help the group through the anxiety of giving up old stable responses, while the new ones are being tested.

Leadership is critical in situations where an organization or group is confronted with unanticipated problems and must develop solutions that will eliminate the problem. A leader should be equipped to provide guidance and support when something occurs either internally or in the environment that makes it necessary for the group to devise new responses to the problem. This would be a stressful time for the members of the group, and the leader must be the one to provide a sense of well-being for the members to inspire them and help them to deal with the anxiety of giving up the old culture.

Leadership Presence

Leaders are expected to have a certain sense about them. Comments like "I just can't see her in that position yet" or "She needs a little more seasoning" are getting at what is called "presence." One may think that being hired into a management or leadership role and being in charge of a number of people automatically provides leadership presence. It absolutely does not. Yet, presence is a critical part of obtaining and being successful in leadership positions. In the earlier chapter on developing a personal brand, we discussed a variety of suggestions on how to establish a positive presence.

Leadership presence has a number of components, a few of which we capture here:

- Ability to connect with others
- Integrity and trust
- Authenticity
- Confidence
- Energy
- Sincerity
- Positivity

What would you add to the list? Consider someone you look up to as a leader. What do you admire about that person? What do you observe about how he or she talks, thinks, and interacts with others?

Shakespeare's words from *As You Like It* are better than ours. "All the world's a stage, and all the men and women merely players. They have their exits and their entrances; and one man in his time plays many parts." Presence may seem elusive, but in fact, there are some simple things you can resolve to do in order to strengthen yours:

- Make a point of *building relationships* with junior staff in your organization by spending time with them, helping them with their assignments, and setting high goals. Empowering others, which we've discussed as employee involvement, enhances your leadership presence. You should understand a subordinate's career and personal goals and do everything you can to help that person achieve them.
- When you are talking with someone, *listen to them*. Keep your entire focus on the person talking to you. Turn away from your computer and put down your phone. Learn everyone's name even if it's a large organization.
- Think before you speak. It's important to *present ideas succinctly using declarative sentences.* As long as you are being respectful, don't apologize for offering a firm or different perspective.
- Establish a physical presence that *projects confidence.* If you need to, fake it. If you were up late with a crying baby or feel overwhelmed about the volume of work on your plate, address it, but don't walk around with the weight of the world on your shoulders or commiserate with coworkers. Your mom was right—stand up straight, speak so you can be heard, have a twinkle in your eye, be positive and optimistic, and people will sense your energy.

- *Dress the part.* This is one area where hands down, men have it easier. Men can look great with a couple of suits and ties and two nice pairs of shoes. Women have many more choices (and hence, more opportunities to get it wrong!). Your clothes should fit well, be tailored, and be spotless. Dress codes typically describe the minimum standard of dress—not the style of dress to which you should aspire. You should dress for the job you want to have, not necessarily the one you have. Accessories should be in good taste and be prominent enough to compliment your clothing. You can learn how to dress appropriately at your organization by observing others. At the same time, you should also consider your audience when you decide what you're going to wear. What you wear to company headquarters might not be what you would wear to a manufacturing plant.
- *Ask others for their perspective.* People are more supportive of an effort when they have been engaged in the process. Ask others how they would address a problem and be willing to discuss your thoughts on their ideas.
- *Be authentic.* You must be yourself, know yourself, and be comfortable with yourself. These three things build trust in the people you are dealing with or work for. When a person is able to align her identity (professional, gender, and culture) with her work, the result is full engagement and satisfaction at work and home.[19]

When President Reagan was asked, "How can an actor be President?" he responded, "How can you be President and not be an actor?" That comment has been repeated for years as an indicator of his understanding of the role presence plays in leadership. John Keegan, a well-known author who writes about leadership in the military, titled one of his books *The Mask of Command.* The title indicates that leaders need to develop leadership presence. It's important to be authentic, and it's important to be real, but different circumstances and audiences may require a shift in your persona.

Power

Leadership has been written about extensively. Power's relation to leadership has been written about to a lesser degree, likely because of a reluctance to use a term that is often associated with an autocratic leadership style. Power can have an unfavorable connotation because it can be seen as dominating and controlling others. Yet power, when one uses it, is clearly an element of leadership.

Abraham Zaleznik, a psychiatrist and professor at Harvard, and Manfred F. R. Kets De Vries, also of Harvard, wrote an influential book entitled

Power and the Corporate Mind. The book was written years before Anna Fels's *Necessary Dreams*, but there are many connections. Many people have a reluctance to want to control others, to dominate others, and even to be in charge. "Yet, it is power, the ability to control and influence others, that provides the basis for the direction of the organization and for the attainment of social goals." Zaleznick and De Vries's definition of leadership sums up their perspective: "Leadership is the exercise of power."[20]

We have noticed reluctance in the women we spoke with around the use of the term "power." There are likely many reasons for this, but part of the reluctance is likely linked to women's desire not to be perceived as bossy. This is a bit of a challenge for women—the term "bossy" is rarely applied to men, but commonly applied to women who are seen as offensively self-assured and claim an unwarranted use of power. We encourage you to challenge any concerns you might have about being identified as bossy. If you incorporate the strategies we describe here, you will likely be viewed as confident and powerful in a positive way. It's also important to challenge a commonly held assumption that men use direct power that is status derived and women use indirect power that is personally derived (the "woman behind the man"). In fact, research has shown that what matters is who has the power, more so than what kind of power it is.[21]

Men and Women of the Corporation by Rosabeth Moss Kanter, written in 1977, was an early landmark book on women in organizations with a focus on corporate power. Kanter writes that job-related activities can build power if those activities are extraordinary, visible, and relevant.[22] In the context of Kanter's points, we offer the following ways to help build your own power in an organization:

- Exceptional performance offers a road to power. However, most activities are not exceptional. Volunteer for difficult problems.
- A visible job can lead to power. Jobs that include responsibilities across several units, being a member of a task force, and opportunity to deliver presentations to senior staff, can offer you significant visibility in an organization.
- Work on relevant tasks. We all have choices as to what we do in our jobs. Time spent on important tasks or solving problems is more valuable than time spent doing routine work.
- Form alliances in the organization. Become part of informal social networks outside of your immediate work group. Go on a service trip with your organization; volunteer to lead the annual picnic; or join an office sports team. If the activity is well done and you were involved, that's a way to increase power. Invite your coworkers and their spouses to your home or a restaurant for dinner. If you find it difficult to juggle hosting

duties with work, come up with a way to engage socially that incorporates your family and your lifestyle. You can build alliances with sponsors, mentors, peers, and subordinates.

- Subordinates can be helpful in establishing influence. Encourage the people on your team to accept new assignments in other units that help build their own career. If you become known as a developer of people, you will find that before long, there will be a large number of employees who used to work for you who have significant positions in other parts of the organization—including positions above yours. People remember who helped them learn, gave them important assignments, and was instrumental in promoting them for jobs in the organization.

If you are seen as a powerful, influential individual in the organization, people will want to work for you and senior people will want to see that you are promoted. Observed power and influence leads to success. Additionally, if your work and effort is recognized by somebody higher in the organization, you will be remembered and you will have a sponsor at a high level who will often bypass the hierarchy to work with you. Or perhaps a person in another part of the organization will feel free to pick up the phone and give you a call because they saw your work on a cross-divisional project.

Making It Work

We have touched on a wide variety of topics in this chapter. In figure 7.3, we summarize the key takeaways in developing a leadership style that works for you.

Some managers think that the approach described here is a soft management philosophy. It is not. The best leaders are "hard on the work but easy on the people."

Leadership is inherently a positive process. The employee involvement philosophy works best when leaders are focused on building relationships, building consensus, being collaborative, being supportive, sharing their powers with others, caring for the people in their group, and at the same time being confident, forceful when necessary, decisive, and impatient for results.

Although we have discussed the concept of presence in the context of acting, if it really feels like you are acting most of the time, then it probably isn't working. Authenticity is a critical aspect of leadership, even more so in an age with less privacy, when it becomes quite easy to see when someone isn't being authentic in their professional life.

Across the board, managers need to improve. An article in the *Wall Street Journal* cited a report from Towers Watson, a risk-management consulting company, which asked employees what they think of their bosses. The bosses

Figure 7.3 Your personal leadership style. Your personal leadership style is based on how you interact with others and how you project yourself.

received low marks. Many workers said their managers weren't trustworthy, didn't provide enough guidance, and failed to inspire good work. Fewer than half of the workers surveyed said they had confidence in their senior managers, and only 44 percent believed managers were sincerely interested in their employees' well-being. The Towers Watson report points out that there are enormous opportunities for managers to learn how to be a better boss, which will lead to more satisfied workers and improved organizational success.[23]

Recap

Some of the content of this chapter may seem more relevant to you later in your career. To some extent, that may be true. However, you don't need to be the head of the organization to be a leader. And, even if you aren't in a position of leadership, you can still benefit from developing and exuding your own personal leadership style. Leadership style drives better quality, higher service ratings, improved productivity or profits, and improved organizational success.

There are still biases toward women as leaders, and women may face some paradoxical challenges when it comes to leadership. Balancing the need to be decisive, direct, and in control with the expectation that women are also friendly, engaging, and kind can be a challenge. Understanding various styles of leadership and recognizing the need to adjust them in different situations can help you navigate challenges due to gender or other roadblocks. Leadership elements such as strategy, culture, power, and presence are tools that can help you be a successful leader throughout your career.

Recommended Reading

Through the Labyrinth: The Truth about How Women Become Leaders by Alice Eagly and Linda L. Carli

Women and Leadership: The State of Play and Strategies for Change by Barbara Kellerman and Deborah L. Rhode

Handbook of Leadership Theory and Practice: An HBS Centennial Colloquium on Advancing Leadership edited by Nitin Nohria and Rakesh Khurana

CHAPTER 8

Consider...Work-Life Fit

Susan hands over the revised financial analysis to her boss, wishing she could go over it one more time, but she is late. She jumps in the car, rushes over to the kindergarten graduation, and slides into her seat 20 minutes after it started, as her daughter finds her in the crowd, smiles at her, and starts singing a song. After she and her daughter enjoy cookies at the reception, Susan heads back to the office and her daughter attends her afterschool child care program and is picked up by her father later that day. When Susan sees her daughter the next morning, they talk about how the program went.

It's 6 p.m. and Mara is in front her computer when she sees a calendar invitation display for a 7 p.m. conference call to prepare for a sales pitch taking place in two days. On her calendar she also sees the time she blocked with a trainer—the same time as the call—to help her condition for the upcoming triathlon. She picks up her mobile phone, calls the organizer of the conference call, and explains she can't make 7 p.m. work tonight but can do it early the next day; they reschedule for 8 a.m. the next day and Mara makes it to her training session on time.

Jana opens a new file on her computer and begins editing the photo, hoping it doesn't require as many changes as she thinks it does. She had promised these photos to her client by the next day and she still had to get through half of them. She finishes the photo and gets through five more when she hears a cry on the baby monitor. "The boss says it's quitting time!" she thinks as she smiles and saves the file. She goes upstairs to greet her bright-eyed toddler and they head to the park. Later that night, after the baby and her husband are asleep, Jana finishes up the files, and drops them off to her client the next day.

Each one of these women has something in common—they figured out a way to make their work and their life *fit*—for today, at least! When it comes to women and work, there is hardly a topic more popular than "work-life fit" and in fact, the issue, for the most part, is truly no longer a woman's issue, as you will read in this chapter. As we prepared the topics to address in this book, we felt it would be incomplete without a discussion of work-life fit. However, it is a topic on which so much has been written, presented, dissected, and discussed that at times we questioned what we might possibly add to the subject. But that information overload is exactly why we decided to include it. Most people who struggle with work-life fit don't have the time to read five books, check blogs, and hire a professional life coach. So whether you are trying to figure out how you can "have it all," or if you have seen how others do it and question whether their approach is one that would work for you, this chapter offers various perspectives when considering how you are going to fit the demands of your work life with the "rest" of your life.

The Issue

Work-life fit is often labeled as an issue for working moms, and though work-life fit is just as important to working dads and childfree adults, it is still very much an issue for the 71 percent of women with children under 18 years who work outside the home.[1] Why? Let's let the numbers tell the story:

- *More workers are seeking a better fit between their careers and their personal life.* According to a survey by the Families and Work Institute, in 2008, 49 percent of employed men with families reported experiencing minor or major work-family conflict, a significant increase from the 34 percent reported in 1977.[2]
- *The issue continues to be a challenge particularly for working moms.* When asked in general how they feel about their time, 40 percent of working moms said they always feel rushed, compared to 24 percent of the general public, 25 percent of stay-at-home moms, and 25 percent of working dads.[3] (It is worth noting that in the same study, there was no difference in stress or happiness between working moms and stay-at-home moms). Additionally, 62 percent of working mothers said they would prefer to work part time, presumably to give them more time for childrearing and household duties.
- *Workers increasingly feel as if they need to choose between career and home.* In the Families and Work Institute's 2008 survey, 41 percent of respondents agreed that employees have to choose between advancing in their jobs or devoting attention to their family or personal lives, compared to 33 percent in 1997.[4]

Clearly, work-life fit continues to be an elusive target for most and a topic that is important to many workers.

Making It Work

In this chapter, we'll look at work-life balance from both a strategic lens and a tactical one. From a strategic angle, work-life balance coaches encourage you to focus on what it is *you* want: What's important to you? What makes you happy? What do you want to spend your time on this earth doing? The tactical angle is just that—more focused on the nuts and bolts of the "how" to balance it all: Which industry is the most family friendly? What are the pros/cons of a flexible work arrangement? Should I hire household help?

To help you consider your options and guide your career decisions, we discuss both strategic and tactical considerations. However, before we address those topics, we start with some perspective on the work-life balance journey, because when it comes to work-life fit it's *all* about perspective. We discuss

- history of work-life balance;
- factors impacting work-life balance; and
- strategic and tactical considerations.

In this chapter, we focus on the issues concerning women who are working. A number of women, however, choose to temporarily stop work for some period of time following childbirth, either for an extended maternity leave or to care for their children full time until the children are school age. This decision, how to approach it, and the implications of it are discussed in the next chapter entitled "Consider...Career-Path Navigation."

A Historical Perspective on Work-Life Balance

On the surface, many articles about work-life balance open by indicating that work-life balance emerged as an issue when families transitioned from the "traditional" 1950s family with a father working outside the home and the mother being a homemaker, to the model that exists today with the preponderance of dual-earner couples. This perspective, while accurate, is actually quite narrow. Taking a more historical look at the evolution of work and family in American society provides valuable perspective for today's working women. Women have always contributed to their families' economic sustainability, but the nature of their contributions has changed.

Eileen Boris and Carolyn Herbst Lewis, of the University of California, offer a historical basis for work and family in the context of three models (see table 8.1).[5]

Table 8.1 US work and family historical trends

Models offered by Boris and Herbst	Description	Time period
Model 1: The household economy	All members of an individual household labored together to produce goods for household maintenance; sites of work and home were virtually indistinguishable. For example, family farm.	Colonial through the early nineteenth century
Model 2: The male breadwinner / female caregiver	As a new industrial market economy developed, men increasingly "left home" to earn a wage and become the economic provider for the family. Because women's work (still at home) did not earn a wage, it began to be viewed as nonproductive. For example, husband is a clerk employed at a factory while the wife cares for the house and children.	Mid-nineteenth century through mid-twentieth century
Model 3: The dual breadwinner / female caregiver	A new consumer economy, higher standard of living, and rising prices led mothers into the workforce. For example, husband has a full-time job outside the home and the wife has a full- or part-time job also outside the home.	Mid-twentieth century through present

Note: All parents balance work and family demands. How families have done that has shifted as our society has changed.

The household economy model dominated the American economy for over 200 years, with everyone's work centered around the household. As such, domestic duties and child care were simply integrated into the household rhythm. Additionally, more children often meant more support of the household economy. In many families, in the late nineteenth century, women took on extra work to add to their families' income—through boarders, sewing, or washing. This was particularly common in immigrant families in urban environments. Additionally, many African American women, particularly in the South, worked in-home for affluent white families, often living in and only returning to their own families on Sundays. Surely, had you had a conversation with any of these women, they would have indicated that they worked very hard to help support their families.

A number of factors came together to shift more families, particularly white ones, away from the household economy model. Boris and Lewis point out that innovations in transportation and banking led to a model where the husband was more likely to be working away from home, resulting in the need for the mother to manage domestic duties closer to home. While some point to more cultural shifts as the driver to the dominant model in the United States today—the dual breadwinner / female caregiver model—Boris and Lewis cite work by economists that identifies the drivers as a new consumer economy, higher standard of living, and rising prices. While social debates regarding working mothers persist, it is our perspective that such a debate is of limited use, given that that 71 percent of women with children are working outside the home.[6]

So when placed in a broader historical perspective, one sees that women have been contributing to family income through paid work for many years, all the while balancing child care and domestic duties. This historical perspective is important for women today for a number of reasons:

- You are neither the first to struggle with work-life fit; and nor were your mothers. With the exception of affluent families, most mothers have always had to balance domestic requirements with the need to earn income or otherwise support their family.
- Much of the discussion around "having it all" and "opting out" result from disproportionately focusing on the challenges of more privileged families; in fact, there are few families where mothers are actually able to make a choice about whether to work outside the home or not.

It is clear that women have been integrating work and life for at least the last 250 years (and surely long before that). To help you think through your situation today, in the next section we shift to a discussion about factors that influence the present realities.

Different Perspectives on Work-Life Fit

One Person's Fit Is Another Person's Fiasco

In the opening to this chapter, we shared illustrations about how three women were making their work and their life coexist. Chances are, as you

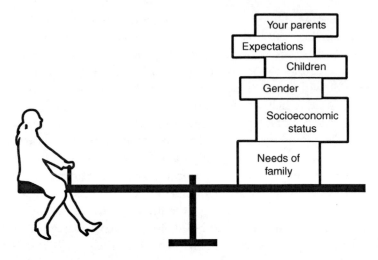

Figure 8.1 Factors influencing your perspective on work-life balance. Work-life balance is very personal. A number of factors impact how you approach it in your own life.

read at least one (maybe all) of the stories, you found yourself saying, "That is not for me." Filling every moment your baby is sleeping by sprinting to the computer only to find you have absolutely no life other than caring for the baby and squeezing in work during very nap? Thinking that a 40-minute drive-by to rush in and out of kindergarten graduation is actually *enough*? You get the picture. There is no one way that works for everyone. Lindsay worked with a professional coach following her return to work primarily on work-life fit issues. She remembers asking her coach (and dutifully expecting an answer) about how many hours a week most people actually work as part of Lindsay's effort to search for balance based on simple math; she thought if she could just determine the "right" number of hours to work a week, that would give her the path to work-life fit. And, of course, the answer was simple: "it depends."

And indeed, it does; as illustrated in figure 8.1, your perspective on work-life fit depends on your expectations, your gender, whether or not you have children, your socioeconomic status, your own parents, and the individual needs of your family. In this section, we explore each one of these topics in more detail.

Gender

It's true—today, men too want work-life fit:

- In 2008, fathers reported spending 3 hours per workday (on average) with their children, up significantly from 1.8 hours per workday in 1977.[7]

- In the same study, fathers reported spending an average of 2.3 hours per workday on household chores, up significantly from 1.2 hours in 1977.
- There is an increasing recognition about the value of fathers far beyond being an economic provider. Engagement of fathers is linked to better educational outcomes, emotional security, and confidence.[8] This recognition is likely one of the drivers behind men increasingly placing a higher value on fatherhood than on their careers. According to a study conducted by Julia McQuillan, professor of sociology at the University of Nebraska—Lincoln, 77 percent of US men rated being a good father as very important, while just 49 percent said the same about having a successful career.[9]

In fact, 3.4 percent of stay-at-home parents are dads, which while relatively small, is a percentage that has doubled in the last decade.[10] And over half of all dads indicate they would be willing to be a stay-at-home parent if their finances allowed for it.[11] There is a widespread perspective that having more men push for work-life fit is good for everyone because it broadens the issue. Instead of being viewed as a woman's issue, requiring a special solution just for women, thinking around work-life, and specifically work-family integration has been broadened to include mothers and fathers. Most adults have children (about 85%).[12] Most adults with children work (70% of mothers and 93.5% of fathers).[13] Even with good child care, children require a lot of time, energy, and attention that cannot always be relegated to after 5 p.m. and before 8 a.m. Therefore, most adults need flexibility in their work schedule to appropriately parent their child.

There is, however, always an undercurrent to the gender discussion when it comes to work-life fit. Lindsay has been waiting for a researcher to figure it, but until then it's just one of those *things* that no one can explain but everyone gets. Women struggle more with the issue than men do—emotionally and logistically. Lindsay has never heard of a father crying into a pillow because he missed his infant's bedtime; but this is such a common occurrence for women, that it was actually captured in Allison Pearson's popular fiction book *I Don't Know How She Does It* when Kate Reddy (played by Sarah Jessica Parker in the film production) cries into her child's laundry hamper when she rushes home only to find the baby asleep. Lindsay has canceled important civic commitments and weekend getaways with her girlfriends to be with her children after being away at work all week, while in the same situation, her husband (who loves his kids tremendously) bounds out of the house on Friday with a kiss and a "see you all Sunday" as he heads off for a weekend with the guys. And even though dads do more around the house than ever before, they are more likely than moms to prioritize their own leisure time.[14] Again, ask most working parents who responded to the last wedding invitation or returned the soccer registration . . . and the answer is likely to be mom. A famous story frequently told by former Congresswoman Pat Schroeder still rings true today. Just after being elected to Congress for the first time in 1972, Representative Schroeder's husband reported in an interview in *Redbook* that in the future he would take the children to the pediatrician. When she read the interview, Schroeder immediately telephoned her husband and said, "For $500, what is the name of the children's pediatrician?" He responded, sheepishly, that what he had meant was that he would be willing to take the children, if she asked him to.

It's not a good thing that men feel more work-family conflict than in the past—but the growing recognition that mothers and fathers need to be able to care for their families while being successful at work is good for all working parents. Today, although men still report a stigma associated with using them, most companies have made programs originally designed for working mothers open to all employees.

Being a Parent versus being Childfree

The numbers on this topic are very interesting:

- Of women aged 40–44, 19 percent do not have children[15]
- The rates are higher for educated women. In 2008, 24 percent of women aged 40–44 with a bachelor's degree had not had a child.
- Nearly half of women with annual incomes over $100,000 do not have children[16]

Researchers cite multiple reasons for the trend. It is likely due to a number of factors, including the fact that delaying pregnancy has meant for some women that they have been unable to get pregnant. But it is also due to shifts in society's thinking about parenthood—there is less stigma associated with not having children. Some women—and arguably a growing number—choose not to have children, in part at least due to their desire to maintain their career trajectory. Based on the case studies we completed for this book, we found that few of these women set out specifically to be childfree—instead, personal circumstances together with a successful developing career meant that some women describe simply "finding themselves" at a point where they are nearing the end of their childbearing years, not yet having had a child. Instead of initiating an intense effort to "find" a partner or move forward with single parenthood through adoption or fertility treatments, they recognize the value of the trade-offs they are making (by purpose or happenstance) and embrace them. As one woman we talked to put it,

I always thought I would work hard until I was 30, get married, and have 2 or 3 kids by the time I was 35. And then when I actually turned 30, and wasn't married yet, I assumed that if I wasn't a mother by 35 I would pursue adoption. And then I turned 35, and then 36, and now I am 38; I still think about having children—and I still may—but I recognize that compared to my friends with children, I enjoy a great deal of personal balance in my life. I work very hard, and travel extensively all over the world; but I also have time to help my parents around the house, vacation with my friends, pursue my artistic hobbies, and visit my nieces and nephews.

By no means are we advocating that the solution to work-life fit is for women to avoid having children. However, for some women, and particularly ones in careers with extensive travel, long hours, or unpredictable schedules, the decision to be childfree is one possible solution for work-life fit. In effect, it's not that these women have said they are choosing not to have it all; instead they have redefined what "all" is.

Socioeconomic Status

There is a growing recognition and attention placed on socioeconomic status and what it means for work-life balance. There is ample evidence that the focus on work-life balance is inappropriately dominated by the perspectives of high-earning women with expectations based outside of economic realities for most people. In 2012, Ann-Marie Slaughter's cover story in *The Atlantic* called "Why Women Still Can't Have It All" set off days of intense media discussion on a number of related topics. Once the initial discussion over the inflammatory nature of the title had taken place, a more thoughtful discussion began to emerge indicating that Slaughter's article, which focused on the high-profile job and experiences she felt she needed to give up in order to appropriately care for her children, didn't address some of the toughest issues for many working moms.

Certainly, women who earn more money are able to hire more help; more help at home typically means more time spent with their families than performing household chores. However, the vast majority of families with two working parents are not debating whether to hire a housekeeper to come twice a month versus every week. Instead, they are focused on finding quality, affordable child and health care.[17] Additionally, flexible work arrangements, which many cite as enabling them to have career-life fit, are typically not available to the 60 percent of Americans in hourly jobs.[18] In fact, in some of the literature about low-wage work-life fit, the subject is actually labeled work-life *conflict* due to the constant challenges families face on a daily basis to patch together child care and adjust to emergent issues, such as a sick child.

Given the target audience for this book, it's more likely than not that our readers have a socioeconomic status that enables them access to high-quality child care and workplace flexibilities. However, even in middle-/ upper-middle-class families, income still factors significantly into the decisions parents make about their families. As you work through your career, you will make decisions that impact your current salary, your earning potential, your hours, and the demands on your time. It's important to recognize these trade-offs as you make decisions about your career. For example, choosing a career with long or unpredictable hours can lead to significant child care costs unless you have family support to help care for your children. If you are a single mother, and you accept a job that means you have to leave the house very early in the mornings, you will either need to arrange for nonpaid care for your children (often a family member) or expect to pay a premium for early morning care. As such, you need to consider the career trade-offs of location, hours, and pay. On the flip side, if you and your spouse are able to coordinate nontraditional working hours around each other's schedule, you may find that you don't have to pay for child care. Lindsay's husband Adam was a police officer early in his career, and we meet a number of dual–police officer couples who were able to alternate their shifts and avoid child care costs.

Your Own Background

Your recollection of your own childhood, how much your parents worked, and how they fared in achieving work-life fit (before it was even called that) also has an impact on how you approach it for your family. Research has indicated that with Generation Y (Gen Y; born after 1980) there has been decrease in career ambition in favor of more family time, less travel, and less personal pressure. Gen Y watched their parents spend more time at the office and today, they are eschewing the perspective that a career is the most important aspect of a person's life, but increasing the priority they place on family life.

If you remember, fondly, that your parents were home each night for dinner together with the family then you may find that you place a high emphasis on establishing a similar schedule in your family. Or if you recall, that your father, as a surgeon, was often at the hospital in the evenings, then you might find your expectations are impacted by that experience. For some, it means such a schedule may be "normal" to you; for another, who recalls missing her father during all those nights away, she may be intent on doing things better and finding better career-life fit in her own life.

The Needs of Your Family

Of course, any working woman with family responsibilities (whether children or aging parents) will tell you that this is the part for which you really just can't plan. Faced with an aging parent or a child with special needs, working parents may have to redefine their work-life fit. In many of these situations, it means working less and accepting the career impacts, as part of a trade-off to provide necessary attention to a parent or child.

> One woman we interviewed, Amy, was progressing quickly in her career with a trade association agency in Washington, DC, working on exciting and important issues. She married a man with a similar career path and five years later they found themselves with two beautiful children, both of who required extensive in-home supports, therapies, and treatments for chronic medical and developmental conditions. Amy reduced her workload to part-time; her husband tried, with some measured success, to build more flexibility into his job. For them, slowing their career pace and taking advantage of these programs was not a case of traditional work-life-fit because "I want to spend more time with my kids while they are young"—it was simply a case of having no other options in order to be able to properly care for their children.

Even parents of children with less intensive needs will still find the need to adjust to the specifics of their family over time. While much of the focus of work-life fit programs focuses on the needs of the parents of young children, there is a growing recognition that the teenage years offer an entirely different set of challenges for working parents. Some parents find themselves requiring more flexibility in hours during the teen years when they find it is more important than ever to be present in the afterschool hours, whether for sports activities or just general supervision. While the needs of your family will always come first, it's important to understand that those needs will change over time. The more choices and options you have created for yourself, the easier it will be to adjust your professional life to align with your family's shifting needs.

Lindsay finds herself informally counseling many young women at work during their pregnancies, women who are apprehensive about how they will (or won't) manage career-life fit after having children. The one piece of advice she gives consistently is this:

> Do all the things that you think you should do. Seek high-quality child care. Talk to other parents—ones that work outside the home and ones that are stay-at-home parents. Educate yourself on work-family programs available through your employer. Think about how much time you can afford to take off work. Consider what kind of changes you want to make in your career and set the groundwork for that now. But after that, let the anxieties go, and trust that as a parent, you will always do what you need to do in order to make sure your child is properly cared for. You just

will. That may mean you keep working, because you want to, or because you need the income or benefits to care for a special needs child; or it may mean that you actually stop work, because you believe your family is best served with you at home. Families may wrestle with these decisions, but when parents make them in the best interests of themselves and their families, they rarely experience regret.

How She Does It

Tips, Tricks, and Advice for Making It Work

Women who are successful at balancing a career and their "life" typically have a long list of tips and tricks. If you are interested, ask them. While few are likely to say they have it all worked out, all are likely to offer some very tangible, tactical advice and examples for how they have made it work. In this section, we provide some highlights of key points identified in our conversations with women and in our own experiences.

Lindsay's Tips and Tricks for Working Parents

- Outsource with a purpose
- Be reasonable about what you can do
- Establish support
- Make a backup plan
- Be ready to adjust
- Ask, talk, share, and learn

Outsource with a Purpose

All of us "outsource" activities in some way. There are always tasks that due to the effort or skill required, force us to pay someone else to do. For example, it's not that hard to change the oil in your car, but most of us outsource the changing of our oil because of the hassle and time required to prepare for it, change it, and clean up afterward. For families with two working parents, if your family finances allow for it, outsourcing some activities enables you to spend more time on the activities that are most important to you. Outsourcing with a purpose means that you consciously identify which household jobs drain you of the most time or energy and consider outsourcing those in order to enable you to focus on the priorities in your personal life and limit your household activities to those that you least mind (or even enjoy) doing. Consider what household tasks seem to take the most time and which ones you don't like doing. If something rises to the top of both lists, it is a candidate for outsourcing. Lindsay received advice at one point in her career to buy an hour of time each week for each promotion received. Taking advantage of this advice has enabled Lindsay to focus on building her career while prioritizing her family and community commitments.

Be Reasonable about What You Can Do

If you don't get home each day until 5:00 p.m., don't sign your son up for a 5:15 p.m. swimming class; it won't be fun for anyone. If you or your spouse travel most of the week, minimize your weekend commitments so that you have an opportunity to relax and catch up. Seek activities that fit into your families' schedule instead of constantly fighting against the clock. For example, in signing her daughter up for a local soccer team, Lindsay requested she be placed on a team with the latest practice time. Part of work-life balance is developing realistic expectations for what you can do at work and at home and then making decisions that align to those decisions. If you constantly feel as if you are running late, overcommitted, and/or are hurrying your children out the door, you are probably being unreasonable about what you can get done in a single day. Give yourself a break and slow down. Align your expectations with your reality.

Establish Support

Working parents need help to care for their children and possibly their home. If you live near family who are able to help out, they can be an incredible resource. Close friends can also be extremely helpful for child care, carpooling, or letting a service person into your home. If you aren't near family and friends, then you need to secure more paid supports. That understanding can be important to factor in to decisions about where to live. One of the women we interviewed told a story about how her family moved from New York City to the Midwest with the hopes of slowing their pace of life and taking advantage of a new job opportunity. However, while the cost of living was lower, the schools were seemingly better, and her commute reduced in half, the relocation ended up causing more angst and stress for their family because they had no family or friend supports in place.

Make a Backup Plan

Family life is predictably unpredictable. Children get sick. Schools close unexpectedly. Service persons run late for scheduled appointments. You and your spouse both need to be out of town for business travel on the same night. These changes in schedules are always a little stressful—but this stress can be managed when you already have a backup plan in place. Line up several options for sick child care prior to the start of the school year and ask for the "OK" to call on them for help at the last minute or early in the morning. Have a conversation with your boss about expectations for work when schools close for bad weather—are you able to work from home in these cases? The key is to have the conversation ahead of time to reduce the stress on you and your family when these unexpected situations occur. Figuring out you have no one to ask for help at 6:30 a.m. when you have a sick baby and a presentation scheduled at 9 a.m. is pretty much the definition of work-life conflict; and is painful enough to make any parent cry uncle.

Be Ready to Adjust

You will likely hit a rhythm with your work and your family, and things will feel good (almost like you are having it all); and then, your child decides to quit taking a nap at day care and go to bed as soon as you bring him home for the night, leaving no time for play together; or (and this has happened to almost all of us), your perfect child care provider gives notice, leaving you to find a new child care arrangement in just weeks, while months-long waiting lists abound. The point is that children grow and change, and the demands of your career may ebb and flow; and well, things just happen that you can't predict. At a minimum, one must learn to recognize these changes as inevitable, and be ready to "go with the flow." However, a better mindset is one that recognizes these changes may lead to an even better alternative. If the day care Lindsay chose for her first child hadn't been full when she returned to work, she would have never met the wonderful caregiver who has cared for Lindsay's children.

Ask, Talk, Share, and Learn

Networking isn't just good for growing your career options—it's great for learning how other working parents are juggling child care and work. Ask other parents what they do to balance work and family; learn about the child care options available in your community, and find support in knowing that just about everyone is struggling with similar issues. Another working mom told Lindsay about a terrific day program available at the local YMCA for school-age children when school is closed; Lindsay went from feeling guilty about squeezing in work on school holidays while her daughter watched too much TV to enjoying the catch-up time at work while her daughter bounded off with a smile for a day of adventure with friends.

Figuring Out What's Right for You and Your Family

Choice is often a word that enters the work-life conversation in the context of whether or a not a mother has the "choice" to stay home; but in fact, even moms who may feel they have no choice but to work, will find they indeed do have a choice when it comes to how they experience life as a working mom. Here are some final suggestions for embracing work-life fit:

- *Stop trying to be perfect*: Anna Quindlen's powerful essay, "Being Perfect,"[19] speaks to many mothers when, she writes, that "being perfect became like carrying a backpack filled with bricks every single day." Focusing on the joy of everyday life rather than a constant requirement to keep everything organized and "just right" offers all parents the freedom to fully appreciate the gift of parenthood.
- *Let go of the guilt*: Lindsay read a terrific book called *Mommy Guilt* before she returned to work following the birth of her first child. She copied these rules and stuck them in her planner as a constant reminder:

The Seven Principles of the Mommy Guilt-Free Philosophy by Julie Bort, Aviva Pflock, and Devra Renner in their book *Mommy Guilt*

1. You must be willing to let some things go.
2. Parenting is not a competitive sport.
3. Look toward the future and at the big picture. Don't become overly hung up on the here and now.
4. Learn when and how to live in the moment.
5. Get used to saying yes more often and being able to defend your no.
6. Laugh a lot, especially with your children.
7. Make sure you set aside specific time to have fun as a family.

- *Figure out what you need "not to quit"*: There will be days, weeks, or months when you find that it is very hard to balance work with the demands of your family. When you hit one of these valleys, when you feel just short of quitting your job, stop; figure out what you need "not to quit" and go ask for it. It may mean asking your spouse for more help at home, spending money in a different way, or asking your employer for a reduced schedule. You'll be no worse off than you were before—and you'll likely even find that eventually, you are much better.

- *Nothing is forever*: It is very likely that during pregnancy, women spend more time worrying about whether or not to return to work more than any other aspect of becoming a parent; the decision is weighed, tabulated, considered, and discussed as if it's a once-and-done decision, when in fact, it's simply not. It is a decision that is reasonably easy to change. A woman can certainly always quit her job; and most women, given enough energy, time, and a little luck, can return to work after being at home full time. The next chapter offers some suggestions for both options.

Recap

We opened this book by offering the perspective that there is often very little "choice" involved when a woman heads to work each day. However, we hope that our readers recognize that you do indeed have many choices around defining what work-life fit means for you and how to approach it. Considering both the strategic aspects of work-life fit, such as the needs of your family and your own personal goals, as well the tactical realities like quality child care and planning for the unexpected, will prepare you to find your own personal work-life balance.

Recommended Reading

How She Really Does It: Secrets of Successful Stay-at-Work Moms by Wendy Sachs

The Working Mother's Guide to Life: Strategies, Secrets and Solutions by Linda Mason

Mommy Guilt: Learn to Worry Less, Focus on What Matters Most, and Raise Happier Kids by Julie Bort, Aviva Pflock, and Devra Renner

Midlife Crisis at 30: How the Stakes Have Changed for a New Generation— And What to Do about It by Lia Macko and Kerry Rubin

What Happy Working Mothers Know by Cathy Greenberg and Barrett Avigdor

Getting to 50/50: How Working Couples Can Have It All by Sharing It All by Sharon Meers and Joanna Strober

CHAPTER 9

Consider...Career-Path Navigation

Leslie puts Matty down for a nap on Monday afternoon while she straightens up after hosting playgroup with her moms club. She spends 30 minutes responding to emails and gearing up for the next day, which is the first day of her three-day workweek. She is hoping to get dinner on the table and laundry done before Matty wakes.

Amanda gets in the car at 5:00 p.m. to drive home, participating in a team meeting via her mobile phone during her drive. She enjoys dinner with her family and puts her children to bed. Then she fires up her computer at 8:30 p.m. and starts working; she has three documents to be reviewed and is hoping to get at least six hours of sleep tonight.

Alyssa drops Elise off at her neighbor's house. Alyssa is wearing a new suit; it's her first job interview since college and it's been four years since she left her job as the financial manager at a large nonprofit organization. She hopes she can remember all the new health care requirements she reviewed the night before.

In the previous chapter on work-life fit, we discussed the concept of choices in how women approach work-life fit. That theme of choices continues in this chapter. For many women, particularly highly educated women, it's not simply a choice between working or not working; instead, women face numerous options regarding how much they work, where they work, when they work, and what they do. It's important to understand the trade-offs among these choices and what you can do to maximize options and choices throughout your career.

The Issue

The traditional career model—where one takes a job at age 22 and continues working full time until retirement—does not describe the realities of the workforce for women or men today. More likely, and particularly for women, today's workers find that there are career changes, lateral moves across or within industries, periods of reduced or increased hours, and periods of non-working time (by choice or otherwise), which mean that each person's career path can be quite varied even within the same organization or industry.

A 2004 survey sponsored by the Center for Work Life Policy (now the Center for Talent Innovation) found that 37 percent of highly qualified women reported having left work voluntarily at some point in their careers; among women with children, it's 43 percent.[1] Additionally, women—particularly mothers—are likely to have worked part time at some point in their career. According to the US Department of Labor, in 2012, 57 percent of mothers with a child under six years of age worked; 29 percent of them held a part-time job.[2]

Yet, despite the reality that women are shifting in and out of the workforce, often in response to childbirth and childrearing, many women aren't finding easy ways to manage the ins and outs. Only 74 percent of women who attempt to rejoin the workforce are able to do so, and only 40 percent return to full-time, professional jobs.[3] The impact of that time out may have far-reaching effects; data from the Center for Talent Innovation shows that although the average period of time women do not work (dubbed "off-ramp" by the Center for Talent Innovation) is only 2.2 years, women lose an average of 18 percent of their earning power as a result of the off-ramp.

Making It Work

Given the richness and variety of work options available, women must approach their career paths armed with knowledge of the short- and long-term impact of these options. There are many steps women can take to prepare themselves for the realities of a career path that is likely to produce twists and turns instead of a straightforward climb to the top. In this chapter, we discuss the various options for career models, the impact of each, and offer suggestions for how you can best prepare to forge your own personal career path.

Career Paths and Models

Ladders and Lattices

The 2007 *Wall Street Journal* best seller *Mass Career Customization*, by Cathy Benko and Anne Weisberg, gave a name to the new career path taken by an increasing number of women and men: the *Lattice*. The concept of a lattice as a metaphor for modern careers is so powerful for both men and women, across all types of organizations, that Benko further explored this concept in the 2010 book *The Corporate Lattice*. Benko and Anderson write,

The lattice depicts employees' career paths as multidirectional, with moves across and down as well as up. The lattice metaphor does not offer a universal view of career success but rather a multiplicity of ways to get ahead...the metaphor also describes the changes in work as virtual, dynamic, and project based.[4]

As described in the data we presented earlier, women in particular are likely to follow a nonlinear career path that may include periods of time when they are not working or working part time. Additionally, at certain periods in their lives women may prefer to hold the line on a promotion due to the increased responsibility or time associated with it. Alternatively, women may seek a lateral opportunity in order to continue their career development through a new experience without increased demands for their time at work. These scenarios, and many more like them, illustrate how an individual's career journey can more appropriately be modeled after a lattice instead of a ladder. The lattice is a more flexible model than ladder, and it is an apt descriptor of the modern career path of both men and women.

The lattice model is also helpful from an organizational perspective. Organizations seeking to align their workplace to the needs of the modern workforce find that offering career models that fit into a lattice—versus just a ladder—enable them to provide more options for their workforce.

Career Path Options

One of the advantages to a lattice metaphor for one's career versus a ladder model is that the lattice not only enables you to move—up or over—but also offers many choices on the approach to achieve your goal. Various options for how that journey might be navigated include

- extended time off;
- flexible work arrangement;
- part-time employment;
- entrepreneurship; and
- a new career.

Extended Time Off

Extended time off is used when an employee needs time off from work (including paid and unpaid) for a period of weeks or even years but wants to be able to return to her previous position. The most commonly cited need for extended time off is due to new children or the employee's own health issue or that of a close family member.

Extended time off may include some paid time off; particularly if the employee has paid vacation, sick time, or short-term disability that can be used. Some employers also offer paid parental leave over and above what is provided via short-term disability. One of the most common forms of extended time is "Family and Medical Leave Act (FMLA) leave," which refers to the requirement that employers with more than 50 employees offer up to 12 weeks of leave (unpaid or paid) and job protection for qualified family and medical reasons. Most new mothers take advantage of some type of leave; although only 50 percent receive at least some of that time in the form of paid leave.[5] For the most part, even if an employer offers extended time off longer than what is required by FMLA, women typically only take advantage of it as a tool for recuperation from childbirth or an illness, or for a few weeks or month to care for a new child. Extended time off is generally therefore a relatively brief interruption in an employee's work history, and not a longer-term option for one's career path.

There are, however, some notable exceptions. A few organizations offer extended leaves of absence to enable an employee to pursue travel, education, family, or other pursuits. While these leaves of absence are rarely paid, they do offer an employee to essentially hit the "pause" button on her career for longer periods of time.

While most of these programs are open to men and women, men are less likely to use extended leave programs. In fact, in a 2011 survey of new dads, over 75 percent took just one week or less of leave.[6] Clearly, economic reasons are likely one of the drivers for such short leave, considering that only half of the mothers are receiving any pay for their leave following childbirth; however, men also report a stigma attached to the use of extended leave following the birth of a child. Men who indicate they would have liked to have taken more time off with their new child are often concerned that taking advantage of extended leave means they will be viewed as less committed to their employer.

Flexible Work Arrangement

Flexible work arrangements, however, are increasingly used by both women and men and continue to be an important option for navigating the corporate lattice. In the same study previously noted where dads reported taking just a week or less of leave after the birth of a child, it was also noted that of that same group, 75 percent reported taking advantage of some kind of flexible work arrangement (informal and formal).[7] The most typical forms of flexible work arrangements are described in table 9.1.[8] Note that a flexible work arrangement can be in place for an employee with a full- or part-time schedule.

Many—if not most—flexible work arrangements are informal ones, in part due to the changes in technology that have continued to blur the lines between work and nonwork time. The Sloan Center on Aging and Work

Table 9.1 Flexible work arrangement options

Description of flexible work arrangement	Advantages	Disadvantages
Flextime: Start/end the workday earlier or later than usual.	Enables employee to align work hours with other commitments including child care or school schedules.	Unless paired with other arrangements, still requires daily in-office time; while employees are allowed to choose their start and end times, they may not typically deviate from that schedule.
Work from home: Work from home for all or part of the workweek.	Reduces time spent on commuting. May allow an employee to provide support to a dependent for limited periods during the day.	Employees may not feel as connected or integrated into the organization, particularly if the rest of their coworkers are physically colocated.
Compressed work week: Work fewer (or no) hours some days and longer on other days.	Allows for longer periods of time during the week when the employee is not required to work.	Productivity may decrease on particularly long days; it may be difficult to engage the employee in ongoing efforts due to missed meetings, and so on.

Note: There are three major types of flexible work arrangements, each of which offers different advantages and disadvantages.

at Boston College cites research done that shows how prevalent informal flexible work arrangements are in practice. For example, at Bristol Myers Squibb, only 4 percent of employees were on a formal flexible work arrangement; but 67 percent of the remaining employees reported having an informal flexible work arrangement in place.[9] The same survey data also captured how important it was to women in management—84 percent indicated that informal flexible work arrangement is what helps keep them at the company.

Part-Time Employment

Part-time employment is a commonly used tool for women; in fact, a third of working mothers with young children are working part time.[10] And many of those working full time would prefer to work fewer hours given the opportunity to do so. Some initial research demonstrates that part-time work may be particularly advantageous for women. Part-time working mothers report less work-family conflict than full-time working mothers do, and in a 2011 study published in the *Journal of Family Psychology*, data showed that part-time working mothers, compared to stay-at-home mothers "were less depressed, had better health, were more sensitive to their children and were better able to provide them with learning opportunities." The impact of part-time work has not been studied as extensively as full-time work. Given the emphasis on other models, it's possible that women are missing out on the potential benefits to themselves and their families that part-time work may offer. From a career trajectory perspective, there are also numerous advantages to part-time work when compared to quitting work altogether, as will be discussed later in this chapter.

Additionally, part-time work is often combined with a flexible work arrangement. One woman we talked to technically had both a part-time schedule and a flexible work arrangement: she worked four days a week in the office, and then Friday mornings at home, with the afternoon off each Friday. She negotiated a 90 percent schedule, which meant she received 90 percent of her full-time pay. While somewhat of an unusual arrangement for "part-time," for her it provided just that little extra time she needed to take care of things at home and run her children to appointments on Friday afternoons.

Entrepreneurship
Although women are still less likely to be self-employed (only 5.5 %, compared to 8.3% of men), women-owned businesses are growing. Census Bureau data indicates that the number of women-owned businesses grew by 20 percent between 2002 and 2007, compared to 5.5 percent for men-owned firms; as of 2007, almost 30 percent of nonfarm businesses in the United States were owned by women.[11] While not all of these women-owned businesses are owned by mothers, there has certainly been a rise in the number of mothers who choose to start their own businesses partly in response to drive their own schedules and direct their own career path. This phenomenon is so prevalent that there is even a new word for it: "Momtrepreneur." Websites and blogs now abound with businesses created and fueled by women who have the energy and drive to build a new business but want to balance their desire for flexibility and to be present for their school-age children.

A New Career
Starting your own businesses is not the only way to get more control over your schedule and work life. Many women and men find that a career change—even when they are "midcareer"—offers a schedule more suitable with other obligations. Consider Heidi's story:

I was in advertising for 15 years before my son was born. I liked what I did, and tried to return to work on a reduced schedule, but it just didn't work for us. Work needed more from me and I felt like we just rushed around at home on the weekends trying to catch up on errands. I quit and went back to school to become an accountant. I started out working with individual clients when I could squeeze them in, and now, seven years later, I'm a partner in a robust tax practice. I definitely work more than full-time, but I have more control over my schedule and I still like what I do.

Heidi found that becoming an accountant gave her the flexibility to work less when her son was young, but still offered the opportunity for longer-term career growth, something she knew she would want as he got older, and she was able to increase the time she could spend working. Today, career changes are common for men and women; the upside to this trend is that it can offer women an opportunity to pursue their "dream" career in a way that aligns with their personal commitments.

Making It Work

Women and men clearly have many more options today when it comes to how they get their work done. The challenge often becomes how to piece the right options together to develop a model that works for you. The 2007 book by Cathy Benko and Anne Weisberg, *Mass Career Customization*, a precursor to *The Corporate Lattice*, offers a framework to do exactly that. Benko and Weisberg write, "Mass Career Customization does for careers what mass product customization has done for the consumer products industry: replace a one-size-fits-all approach with a bevy of customized product offerings."[12] Using the Mass Career Customization framework, individuals and organizations are able to consider options along the four dimensions of pace, workload, location/schedule, and role. "Dialing up" or "dialing down" on each of these dimensions has transparent trade-offs: for example, on the "role" dimension, choosing to stay as an individual contributor for a longer period of time—and hence passing up leadership opportunities to direct a larger team—may mean that an individual delays a promotion. By applying the Mass Career Customization framework to your own career, you can better understand the trade-offs made across various alternatives and begin to chart out a career path that works for you and those around you.

However, one can fully understand the impact of changes in these four dimensions only by considering how the use of any of the options discussed here would impact both you and your employer. It's important, therefore, to understand the options available to you at your organization as well as the formal and informal processes for putting them in place. In either model, clear communication with those around you is critical. Typically, in larger organizations that offer formal extended leave (including FMLA) and flexible work arrangements, human resources staff is available to help you understand your options and develop a proposal for your request.

If you decide to initiate a conversation with your employer about a formal change to your work schedule (such as the use of extended leave, a flexible work arrangement, or part-time work), while you must understand the

Table 9.2   Sample conversation flow when requesting a flexible work arrangement

Tips for the conversation	Sample conversation
Start by explaining why you like your job	As I believe you know, serving as the agency's business manager has given me an opportunity to be involved in all aspects of our operations.
Offer a reminder of your value to the organization	I am very proud that in just the last two years we've reduced our overhead costs, replaced our technology infrastructure, and served 10 percent more people.
Clearly explain your proposal	I would like us to discuss how it might work for me to reduce my hours in the summer months.
Mention that you've done your homework	I have talked to Gina and Sarah about how they have been able to establish successful flexible work arrangements and I have some specific ideas about how my arrangement could work.
Anticipate concerns	I went back and studied our operations last summer and I believe that I can reduce my hours in a way that will have minimal impact on the agency.
Mention an upside for the organization	In fact, given that we generally experience a 20 percent reduction in program usage during the summer months, it makes sense to reduce our staffing in some cases; and the savings will help address the gap in our operating budget.
Don't ask for an immediate "yes" or "no" to your proposal—offer a different question that enables them to say "yes"	Can you think about my idea and let me know what questions you have? I think we could then set aside some time next week to talk through your questions and figure out how this might work.
Close with a positive statement	Thank you for considering this. I really enjoy working here and believe that I have a lot to contribute.

Note: While there is no formula for this tough discussion, it's important to keep it positive, specific, and direct.

potential impact on you, in your initial conversation, focus on the impact on the employer. Considering the techniques discussed in the negotiation chapter, articulate your proposal in a way that offers benefits for both you and your employer. One approach that has worked well for many women is to request the change for a defined period of time (say, three months), which makes it easier for both of you to commit to the arrangement. Before you sit down with your supervisor to discuss your request, reach out to other people in your office who are on flexible work arrangements to find out what has worked well. Some tips and a sample conversation for making the proposal to your supervisor are offered in table 9.2.

When it comes to informal flexible work arrangements, the key is to clarify expectations between you and your supervisor. For example, if your supervisor has indicated that you may leave the office early on the days your husband is out of town, clarify whether you are going to seek permission each time or whether the supervisor expects you to manage it and just give her a head's up. It's also good to clarify the expectations regarding your availability—are you asking to be offline for a few hours in the afternoon to watch your son's soccer game, and then planning to pick back up at night—or are you OK with being called back into office during the game if something urgent comes up? As a supervisor, Lindsay has had more trouble managing informal flexible work arrangements than formal ones, typically due to misunderstandings about the frequency and nature of the flexibility needed by the employee.

In fact, there are some other important considerations for all of the career options we have introduced. In the next section, we focus on potential impacts of particular moves across the lattice.

Impact of Career Path Decisions

Introduction

Most agree that the availability of career path choices to an increasing number of workers is good for individuals and families. However, all of the options have downsides, some of which are more quantifiable than others. The downsides of the traditional career ladder are clear: it's rigid, assumes an "all or nothing" mentality, and requires constant movement forward to higher positions. The upsides, however, for the most part, are also clear. If you put the time in at each step and work hard to get to the next level, you are rewarded with increased responsibility and compensation.

The reality is that the upsides and downsides are murkier when it comes to shifts in one's career path. Sylvia Ann Hewlett's quantitative approach to evaluating women's career paths has demonstrated that there is an economic impact to stepping off the corporate ladder, particularly for extended periods of nonworking time. In fact, one of the key attributes of the Mass Career Customization model is not that it reduces the trade-offs required—but that it makes them more transparent. Finally, while a shift in your career path may be driven because of a desire or requirement to spend more time caring for your family, the reality is that it can introduce new complexities to relationships with your spouse and family, as it may lead to shifts in expectations around financial independence and household duties.

Economic Impacts

During the period of economic prosperity in the early 2000s, news outlets began to run more articles featuring stories about a new wave of highly educated and successful women (typically mothers) who were dropping out of the workforce. The issues discussed in the articles often eschewed the traditional topics that had dominated the working mother landscape (high-quality child care, family friendly workplaces, and glass ceilings) in favor of topics that struck to the heart of traditional feminism such as women's ambition and definitions of success. Article after article documented stories of highly educated women who left partnership-path careers at law firms and producer positions at media powerhouses in order to stay at home and care for their children either full or part time.

Eventually, economists, journalists, and social scientists began to dig into this reported "trend" to learn more about it. Sylvia Ann Hewlett, founder of the Center for Talent Innovation, set out to study these reports in a more systematic way. What she found was that most women do take an "off-ramp" at some point on their career highway, due to a variety of, what they dub, "pull factors" (the need to care for a child or parent) as well as "push" factors (problems in the workplace that led women to leave).

One of the most valuable aspects of Hewlett's work has been her study of "reentry." Most women who leave the workforce plan to return to it (93% in a 2004 study); yet they don't always realize how challenging it may be to do so. Hewlett's study indicated that women off-ramp for 2.2 years, on an average, but they lose an average of 18 percent of their earning power when they take an off-ramp; the penalty is higher in business at 28 percent. They found that "across sectors, women lose a staggering 37% of their earning power when they spend three or more years out of the workforce."

The particular challenge for women is that they tend to off-ramp right during a critical "building" phase of their career. The late twenties to early thirties phase of a career tends to be when extra investment—in the form of longer hours, stretch assignments, and certification/training programs—pays off down the road in terms of high-paying and more senior positions. Given that this time period corresponds to childbearing years, the alternatives are tough. Examples abound of women who tried to beat the clock—rushing through the career-building phase of their adulthood to try to squeeze in pregnancy and childbirth before it was too late. When it works, it's not a bad strategy. But ask any woman who has struggled with expensive and emotionally draining fertility treatments and you may find that it's a strategy you aren't comfortable counting on.

One particularly insightful book on this topic—and targeted at Generation X and Y (Gen X/Y)—is *Midlife Crisis at 30* by Liz Macko and Kerry Rubin. Macko and Rubin interviewed over 100 twenty-/thirtysomething women as part of their quest to understand how other women were struggling (or not) with the career and personal pressures Macko and Rubin faced.

> While working women have always struggled to navigate the emotional minefields of love and power, career and family, daughters of Baby Boomers are experiencing the conflict differently. For a generation that came of age at a time defined by options and opportunities rather than brick walls and glass ceilings, the juggling act has changed. Our mothers described the stress of balancing work and kids as a slow, steady burn; in contrast, the 17 million women of Generation X are reaching boiling points very early in their careers…and the 35 million women of Generation Y…, are being set up to experience the same scenario.[13]

Macko and Rubin illustrate that the new timetables for marriage, motherhood, and career building are in conflict in a way that previous generations never experienced. Women of Gen X and Y were raised knowing they would have choices and options when it came to career and family; what they weren't prepared for was the fact that these two would crash head-on so early in their adult lives.

Career Trajectory Impacts

In addition to the pure economic impact of taking time out or shifting gears in one's career pace, there can be an impact on a woman's long-term career growth. Taking extended parental leave or working part time for a few years, depending on the nature of the work, is likely to be a "pause" in a women's career from the perspective of upward mobility. Or using the lattice metaphor, it may involve a lateral move. We are not talking about discrimination here. Employers are not allowed to discriminate against employees who, for example, exercise FMLA. The issue is one of performance and experience. When a woman reduces the amount of time she spends working, it is likely that she may not check off the requirements for the next level as quickly as she otherwise would.

For many women, that's OK with them—in fact, a 2006 study of the Association of Executive Search Consultants, cited in *Mass Career Customization*,[14] found that "more than half of senior executives polled would go so far as to turn down a promotion if it meant losing more control over their schedule." This is also where that complicated discussion of ambition comes into play. For women who are trying to achieve their version of "having it all," it may mean a slower rise to the top or choosing a fulfilling career path that doesn't lead to the top of the organization. In fact, in Hewlett's study, only 15 percent of highly qualified women identified "a powerful position" as an important career goal.

Personal and Family Impacts

The type of career path a woman follows has a profound impact not only on her but also on those around her. The benefits to one's family in terms of increased presence and attention are inherent; one way or another it's those perceived benefits that often lead women to take a nonlinear career path. However, there can still be challenges at home. Women who work part time, for example, may feel that with reduced income they can't justify paid household help, and end up spending too much of their precious nonworking time on household chores; additionally, it can be challenging to find part-time day care, leading some families to pay for full-time care they don't need, despite the reduction in salary.

Flexible work arrangements that involve longer days can be extremely exhausting, especially when a commute is factored in; and it can be hard to shake the feeling that you need to be in touch with the office on your nonworking days—the result can mean a woman feels like she isn't doing enough at home or at work. Additionally, any change that leads to a reduction in pay, may lead to a sense that a woman has lost some financial independence, which can be a complicating factor in a relationship.

Making It Work

Do you feel like the choices, decisions, and trade-offs are cloudier than ever when it comes to navigating your own career path? We hope not—but if you do, that's OK. Making decisions about you, your family, and your work gets to the very heart of what is most important to you. It takes time to figure out what works, and as your needs or your family's needs change, you'll find you will circle back through the decision process repeatedly. The upside is that you live in a time and place where there are many options for how you approach the path of your career; in the closing section, we offer some ideas on how to increase those options.

Preparing for the Journey

Given the shift in career routes being taken by so many women, preparation for the journey is essential. The traditional model in which you graduate from college, get your first job, and then pick up skills on the job as you move up the ladder isn't enough to prepare you for the twists and turns along the way. There are steps that you can take early in your careers—and along the way—to provide more tools in your career toolbox. Benko and Anderson discuss this concept in *The Corporate Lattice*, dubbing them "Option-Creating Strategies." We propose to describe some of these tools here.

Pursue as Much Training as You Can

We have said it before and we will say it again—take advantage of every training and education opportunity available to you. Of particular priority should be trainings and certifications that are recognized outside your organization. Not only is this a good idea generally, but it can give you an edge in negotiating a change in your work schedule. An organization will be more willing to work with you on a part-time basis or flexible work arrangement if you bring a skill or credential that is important and limited in the industry.

Build Your Network

A wide internal and external network is critical to supporting a change in your career model. A broad network offers options, opportunities, and contacts. A strong internal network opens up lateral opportunities that may give you both the challenge you need and the work-life balance you are seeking. When your network is narrow, your choices feel limited and binary: work or leave the workforce; part-time or full-time. However, a rich network offers a wealth of opportunities. At any given point in your life, there is probably an opportunity out there that aligns to what you need—it's just a case of identifying it.

A strong network also helps you assess the current marketplace and make an informed decision. For a woman who decides to strike out on her own— for example, starting her own consulting business—the strength of her existing network is absolutely critical to the short- and long-term success of her business. For a woman considering a lateral move to a new organization, perhaps one that she feels is more conducive to long-term work-life balance, it's not just that her network may lead her to the position; but the information gleaned from the relationships in her network will help her make a better decision about whether the move to the new organization is a likely fit for her goals.

Build Capital

Along your career journey, you may need to ask for some help—a "lift" along the way. That lift could be in the form of taking a pass on a project that requires a lot of extra hours, taking unplanned time off because your child's summer camp fell through; or working from home part time because you want to be nearby while your teen is going through a rough time at school. When you build capital it is easier to make the "ask"; and when you do ask, you are more likely to get a yes. One woman we interviewed spent ten years working extremely hard in her organization, and then in a flurry of activity in her late thirties, underwent medical treatments, the birth of three children, and back surgery. Through all those changes in her personal life, you can imagine that she made a lot of "asks" at work—both formal and informal—and she said she doesn't recall a single one being turned down. She said that when she made the asks she knew she was banking on a strong track record of performance and commitment to the organization; and at the same time, her supervisors knew that if they gave her the flexibility she needed, they would retain a top-performing employee.

Consider Timing

Women and men often talk about the decision to delay a promotion until a certain milestone in their personal life (a child reaches first grade, a husband finishes medical school, a parent moves nearby easing care logistics). However, women should also consider the inverse—when there might be a good time to accelerate their career. Gillian is a good example. She returned to her work as a sales representative for a pharmaceutical company following the birth of her second child. At that time, her mother was living with her family and her husband had started his own small business, working out of the home. As a result, she realized she had an opportunity to do more travel and put in some extra hours on some national assignments because she was very comfortable with her child care situation. She knew however, that it would not stay that way forever—but she asked for a stretch role and got it. The role helped her get promoted. Obviously, some of the most important issues in life can't be planned or "timed"—but be aware and open to opportunities to both decelerate and accelerate your career.

Limit Financial Commitments

Financial decisions you make early in your career can have long-term effects on your willingness to take career risks or even temporarily reduce your earnings. Clearly, if you have a big mortgage payment, choosing to reduce your income will be problematic. But there are other considerations. For example, when making a decision to attend graduate school, it's critical to understand what repayment of loans will look like after graduation compared to your earning potential. One married woman we spoke with had her daughter at the age of 39 but couldn't reduce her hours or take much time off because her nonprofit legal position paid a modest salary and she was still paying back a large law school loan from attending a prestigious school. Should she have forgone attending the best school in her field? Not necessarily; but she did regret not realizing the way she had limited her options through a series of decisions.

If you see yourself as someone who might want to reduce your hours (and hence earnings) during your thirties, then you should aggressively pay student loans and save for retirement in your twenties, concurrent to the initial "building" phase of your career. Doing so will decrease the negative impact to your retirement savings and your monthly budget should you decide to reduce your earnings in your thirties. Don't think about paying loans and saving for retirement as if you are already locked into the financial constraints of family life—instead focus on the flexibility you'll have in the future—not just for children if you choose, but also for travel, a dream house, or the ability to take a long sabbatical just to do what you want! If it turns out that you don't reduce your earnings in your thirties—then all you did was set yourself up for even better long-term financial success.

Seek the Right Employer for You

Employers vary widely with regard to whether they support workplace flexibility and lattice-style thinking. It's important to do your homework both about the employer and about the nature of the industry and career as you are making decisions about where to begin your career. Certainly, organizations that offer more career path options and generous benefits are a great place to start; although sometimes smaller organizations may be able to offer more flexibility in exchange for less generous benefits. When you are considering employment with an organization, don't just focus on the experiences of the entry-level staff. Ask questions about career progression and speak with all the individuals you meet about their experiences and careers with the organization.

Recap

Navigating your career path is likely to present some of the toughest decisions you'll face on your career journey. For many adults, their careers are at least part of what defines them as individuals. It's what people *do*. It's how they support themselves and their families. Making tough decisions will no doubt lead to second-guessing and wishful thinking at points in your career; however, the only thing worse would be if, like so many of the women before, you didn't have any decisions to make, because you had so few choices. Create as many opportunities and alternatives as you can, consider your options, and make the best decision you can—who knows where it might take you!

Recommended Reading

Mass Career Customization: Aligning the Workplace with Today's Nontraditional Workforce by Cathleen Benko and Anne Weisberg

The Corporate Lattice: Achieving High Performance in the Changing World of Work by Cathleen Benko and Molly Anderson

"Off-Ramps and On-ramps: Keeping Talented Women on the Road to Success," *Harvard Business Review*, March 2005, by Sylvia Ann Hewlett and Carolyn Buck Luce

CHAPTER 10

Consider...Working in a Global Environment

Diedre finds herself simultaneously elated and filled with dread. She found out today that she has been offered a year long rotation in her company's Brussels office. This is the kind of opportunity that as a teenager, sitting through all those French classes, she had dreamed about—but is there any chance it will work to take her husband and son with her for the assignment? Even with a monthly trip home, she doesn't think she could possibly leave them behind in the United States for that long,

It's 8:30 p.m. and Kimberly is still in the office waiting for documents from a teammate from a country halfway around the world. She looks at the clock. At this rate, she may be able to get an almost full night's sleep if she wakes up and does her first call of the day from home. Her international team is virtual so they agreed on a call twice a day. However, they are spread across so many different time zones that the first call is at 5:00 a.m. for Kimberly. It wouldn't be so bad if everyone was on time. The document finally arrives in her inbox. Kimberly looks at it and finds half a dozen errors halfway into the first page. "I don't know why he never does what I ask him to," she thinks, frustrated.

Joanne looks around at the attendees of the reception; the room is filled with a mix of US employees (all male except for her) working abroad and their spouses as well as local employees and their spouses. She strikes up her third conversation of the evening with one of the local male employees of her company, and for the third time, after some small talk, is asked a variation of the polite question typically asked of the female spouses of her male expat colleagues, "Now, what are you doing with your time while you are here?" She smiles and explains that she leads the design of new products for their multinational company.

Thomas L. Friedman's book *The World Is Flat*[1] captured the incredible changes underway across the world. One of the key messages of the book is that globalization impacts everyone, even if one never steps foot in another country. The world has seen explosive change and has become increasingly interconnected over the last 30 years. The products we use—clothes, cars, tools, appliances, airplanes, and computers—arrive from a multitude of countries. Many products are assembled from parts made in multiple countries. Contact among the people of the world is accelerating through technology. The interconnectedness of the world has led to enormous employment opportunities for those who understand how to work with different cultures. While globalization has led to significant economic opportunities and new innovations, the increased contact between cultures creates significant challenges in how people work with one another. A person who recognizes these opportunities and can balance her knowledge with the ability to work with people from other cultures will be an asset to any organization with a global presence.

The Issue

In the last 20 years of the twenty-first century, a series of changes occurred very rapidly:

- *International travel has increased:*
  - International air travel has gone from 465.5 million passengers in 1990 to 2.75 billion passengers in 2011.[2]
  - The numbers of students who have moved to another country to study have increased greatly. Currently, there are nearly 720,000 international students coming to the United States alone. In 2009, 3.43 million students moved from their home country to another to study. The United States is the number one destination for students, followed by the United Kingdom.[3]
- *Political changes led to increased trade:*
  - The fall of the Berlin wall on November 9, 1989, and German reunification a year later added over 16 million people to Germany's total population. The Union of the Soviet Socialist Republics dissolved in 1991 and 15 new countries were created that previously were part of the Union of the Soviet Socialist Republics. Countries went from closed societies to open societies. Among them were Bulgaria, Czechoslovakia, Romania, and Poland.[4]

- *New markets opened up for consumer and other goods:*
  - Brazil, Russia, India, and China, the BRIC countries, went from relatively closed markets to open markets. Manmohan Singh led India to significant changes in the country's political and economic structure. Singh was named finance minister of India in 1991 and led the economy to one that was more open and increased trade. Singh became prime minister in 2004 and changes in India accelerated. The GDP in India went from $323.51 billion in 1994 to $721.57 billion in 2004.[5] Brazil also made significant economic and political changes. Cardozo, with his Real Plan, which opened the economy and expanded trade, became president in 1994 and was reelected in 1998. Luiz Inácio Lula da Silva continued the peaceful transition to an open economy in 2002 and was reelected in 2006. Brazil's GDP went from $546.2 billion in 1994 to $2.5 trillion in 2011. In Russia, Boris Yeltsin became President in 1991. Russia's GDP went from $509.4 billion in 1991 to $1.5 trillion in 2010. Privatization began and is continuing today. China changed their political and economic structure in 1978, and their GDP has grown from $148.2 billion in 1978 to $7.3 trillion in 2011.[6]
  - The European Union went from 12 member countries in 1990 to its current 27 members with 500 million people.[7] The European Union's GDP in 2011 was $17.6 trillion, making it the largest economy in the world.[8] The euro was instituted as a common currency in 2002. In addition to the common currency, there was free movement of the population to follow higher paying or more interesting jobs in all 27 countries. Many experts believe that the issues that are being faced right now in the European Union have to do more with cultural differences than economic policy.
  - In the Western hemisphere NAFTA, the North American Free Trade Agreement, was signed in 1993 to enhance trade between Mexico, the United States, and Canada.[9] CAFTA, Central American Free Trade Agreement, was signed in 2005 and increase in trade occurred.[10]
- *Trade and manufacturing became truly global enterprises as companies started selling and producing goods in other countries:*
  - The largest selling car in China is a Buick.[11] The largest selling car in the United States is a Toyota Camry, made in Kentucky.[12] Worldwide auto-manufacturing companies have relocated tens of thousands of people to places where their cars are being sold, requiring their employees to live and work in entirely new cultures.
  - Burberry, Michael Kors, and Louis Vuitton are companies selling their products internationally with their products made and sold throughout the world. Selling products throughout the world requires

Some jobs, which were part of a team effort, required everyone to be present in the office at the same time, working together. Other jobs, where people worked individually, could have flexible hours. Universalists think that everyone should start at the same time whether it is necessary or not. The universalist orientation is also less likely to be shared by the French and Italians.

If the management had known that the Americans and the British were typically nonemotional and the Germans were very nonemotional compared to the Italians and the French, they would have had known better how to deal with heated discussions about specific issues. They would have understood that the French, the Germans, and the British ascribe status based on where one attended university. The Americans would have been more successful if they had informed the French and the Germans about the credentials held by key members of the management team—especially the women.

The team would have known that the Germans wanted a strict work relationship, with very little social relationships compared to the southern Europeans and the Americans. They could have improved their working relationships if they would have started with more formal nonwork meetings and moved on to informal ones.

Picking up, moving, and living in an entirely new culture is complicated; it's also very hard to successfully develop and sustain teams comprising individuals from multiple countries. Senior human resources staff report that one of the most difficult assignments they have is to recruit an international manager. There is a great demand for people who are willing to learn about other cultures and work successfully within them.

Women as International Managers

Yochanan Altman and Susan Shortland had interesting observations about women's progress in obtaining international positions in their article "Women and International Assignments: Taking Stock—A 25-Year Review."[21] They reported that in the 1970s and 1980s, very few women were offered or accepted international assignments. However, in the 1990s, more and more women were working for international companies and relocating to accept international assignments. After 2000, the number of women who asked for and accepted international assignments increased. Altman and Shortland's work indicates that discrimination is typically more problematic in countries other than the woman's home country, and if so, the discrimination needs to be managed by the organization. They also report that some women may have an advantage working internationally because of their relational skills, empathy, and their ability to be more sensitive to social cues, which are helpful skills when working in different cultures.

Making It Work

Even if a manager never leaves her own country, it is likely that she will be supervising people from other cultures and will need to develop skills to manage employees with very diverse attitudes and ways of approaching work. As globalization continues to accelerate, it is essential to have individuals with international knowledge and experience in key positions. The need for experienced internationalists has become so critical and the supply so low that if you are willing to seek an international position, your chances of obtaining one are high. What can you do to best position yourself for one of these assignments?

Key Traits for Success on an International Assignment

- Curiosity
- Comfort in different surroundings and unknown situations
- Sense of humor
- Easygoing manner—not easily offended
- Knowledge about other countries—language, culture, history, and knowledge of world geography
- Perseverance
- Self-confidence
- Enthusiasm

If you studied abroad or lived in several places growing up (not even necessarily international locations), you are likely able to adapt to different locations and cultures. In terms of being selected for international assignments, women had this advice to give:

- Focus on what is in front of you. Do excellent work on your assignments now.
- Value other people's perspectives, which may be different from yours.
- Be willing to go. Your organization may not find many people willing to pack up and move to a different country. If your personal situation allows you to do so, go for it. In fact, more organizations are offering international assignments earlier in careers when both men and women are less likely to have family commitments that would make an international assignment difficult.
- And most importantly, make sure your organization knows that you want an international assignment.

If you're willing to relocate internationally, you may be hired with less experience than is typically preferred for the job because the organization cannot find anyone else who is willing to relocate to another country.

Once you start traveling, hold on! The experience of working internationally will often get you on a fast track. More and more companies are requiring international assignments to reach senior management. Globalization continues to increase and understanding cultural differences and how to interact, lead, and manage people with different backgrounds and from different countries is essential in today's world. The willingness to accept an international assignment also allows you to be in a position that might not otherwise have been open to you at this point in your career.

Understanding Different Cultures

Definition

An international assignment requires a deep awareness of your own culture and that of the country where you go to work. Culture is "the sum total of ways of living built up by a group of human beings, which is transmitted from one generation to another."[22] This is true enough, but with the acceleration of the changes occurring in immigration, as well as the interaction and contact with people from different cultures, a more comprehensive and inclusive definition is needed. The complexity of the following definition should indicate to you how difficult it is to understand the concept of culture and how difficult it is to understand another culture.

In *Mirror for Man*,[23] Clyde Kluckhohn, an often-cited anthropologist, defines culture as

> "the total way of life of a people; the social legacy the individual acquires from his group; a way of thinking, feeling, and believing; an abstraction from behavior; a theory on the part of the anthropologist about the way in which a group of people in fact behave; a storehouse of pooled learning; a set of standardized orientations to recurrent problems; learned behavior; a mechanism for the normative regulation of behavior; a set of techniques for adjusting both to the external environment and to other men; a precipitate of history"; and as a map, as a sieve, and as a matrix.

When someone says, "we need to change the culture around here" or "you need to understand how the culture around here is different," think of Kluckhohn's definition and you'll know how difficult it can be to put your finger on the intricacies of culture. Kluckhohn's perspective points out how much effort it is to get people from different cultures to work together.

Women are often skillful at establishing rapport, listening to people, and being able to see how cultural components impact an organization, which are important skills when working in other cultures.

Intersection of Organizations and Culture

Edgar Schein, a professor at the Sloan School at the Massachusetts Institute of Technology, explains how culture should be understood from a more practical and organizational level. Schein was a key consultant at a Massachusetts computer company in the late 1970s. Schein's book, *Organization, Culture, and Leadership*, is one of the most influential management books in history. Schein's view is that an organization's culture and leaders are intertwined; an effective leader must understand the organizational culture and how it can be managed, which leads to the achievement of organizational goals.[24] Schein believes that a key responsibility of leadership is to create a productive, positive, organizational culture.

Schein views culture as dynamic—it is learned, passed on, and changed. Schein says, "In fact, there is a possibility—underemphasized in leadership research—that the *only thing of real importance that leaders do is to create and manage culture* and that the unique talent of leaders is their ability to work with culture."[25]

Understanding Culture

To successfully work in another culture, it's vital to establish a framework. Even though culture is exceedingly complex, there are useful guidelines and concepts that you can use to help you learn about different cultures and how to work in cultures that are not your own. Recognizing that a culture is complex, enigmatic, and puzzling is critical to building a foundation of cultural understanding. We highlight two frameworks for international management in the following sections that will help you approach cultural roadblocks: "Project GLOBE" and the work of "Fons Trompenaars."

Global Learning and Observation to Benefit the Environment (Project GLOBE) Project GLOBE was founded in 1997 by Robert House, a professor at the University of Pennsylvania. Project GLOBE's focus is on global leadership and organizational behavior effectiveness. One hundred and fifty researchers have worked together for many years to gather information about the cultural practices and leadership characteristics necessary to function in multicultural environments that became a foundation of Project GLOBE.[26]

In addition to dividing societies into cultural clusters, the Project GLOBE researchers also identified nine cultural attributes and related how their significance—high/low, for example—lead to cultural variables.

Germany, Austria, France, Japan, Italy, and other countries. Trompenaars's seminar evoked a lot of laughter about cultural differences (remember our point earlier about the importance of having a good sense of humor in international assignments?). His point was that you should not take your culture so seriously—and if you are just a little offended, let it go. Lindsay was once with a group of international colleagues who mocked the seven-page dress code issued by the US human resources staff. She thought the document was descriptive and helpful for employees, but her international colleagues saw it as evidence that Americans have trouble figuring out how to dress appropriately. Despite Lindsay's defense of the approach, they all had a good laugh. Trompenaars teaches that all cultures should be treated with respect, but at the same time we should have a sense of humor about some of our individual culture's idiosyncrasies.

A key concept learned from Trompenaars is that creative solutions need to be identified that meet the needs of both parties rather than splitting the difference and finding a midpoint that does not solve anyone's problem. In order to arrive at a productive outcome, Trompenaars's suggestion is to award teams for creativity but to reward individuals for teamwork. Everyone becomes very competitive regarding how one can best cooperate when one is rewarded for teamwork. Understanding cultures allows a manager to identify cultural motivators. A closer look at this research is essential for anyone supervising employees from a different culture.

Jim's experience with a joint venture in Tennessee with American and Japanese employees demonstrated firsthand the need for the cultural awareness promoted by Trompenaars. For example, when the Americans wanted to make a change to the operations of the plant, they would have a discussion with the Japanese, and the Japanese appeared to agree. The effort would initiate and the Americans would discover that the Japanese did not actually agree with the idea. If the participants in the Tennessee plant had read Trompenaars's book and known that the Japanese are typically less assertive and Americans are typically the most assertive culture, they might have learned that Japanese are less direct than Americans are. They would have allowed for time to talk about alternatives and to slowly come to a consensus rather than being told about a solution. In another situation, a plan that relied on individual awards to increase productivity at the plant failed. It did little to engage the Japanese who were more motivated by group awards. To use Trompenaars's terms, the Japanese were collectivists and the Americans were individualistic.

Understanding motivators within particular cultures is also critical for identifying points of commonalties. For example, when it comes to performance orientation, the Japanese are ranked right next to the Americans, and they would have known that both cultures were interested in a high-performing plant.

Trompenaars studied and gathered data from a large number of companies and developed information from thousands of individual participants. The empirical results are a part of the information presented in his seminar and his book. He points out, like Schein, that culture is an important piece of how people solve problems. Different cultures solve problems differently. Businesses and organizations spend a significant amount of time identifying solutions to problems. It seems obvious that if organizations can't collectively solve problems, they are headed toward an uncertain future. Trompenaars separates problem solving into three parts:

- Problems that arise from our relationships
- Problems that concern the concept of time
- Problems that relate to the environment[29]

He then lists seven fundamentals of culture—five relate to relationships, one to time, and one to the environment—and demonstrates how each one is essential in solving the problems of the organization in order to have a successful organization (see table 10.1).

Table 10.1 Trompenaars's seven fundamentals of culture

Relationships

Universalism vs. particularism	A universalist believes, "What is good and right can be defined and always applies," while a particularist gives "attention to the obligations of relationships and unique circumstances." In a universalist culture, such as the English, a person under oath would likely tell the truth about another individual even if he were saying something negative about a family member. In a particularist culture, such as the Greek, a family member or a member of a social club is treated differently than someone with no personal connection. The Marwari culture in India traditionally has only hired family members in their businesses because they trust them. They rarely, if ever, are senior managers outside of their group.
Individualism vs. collectivism	Do people regard themselves as individuals or primarily as part of a group? Americans are rugged individualists. They like to work by themselves, and they like to have one person in charge. The Japanese are collectivists. They travel together and they work together.

continued

Table 10.1 Continued

Relationships

Neutral vs. emotional	Should the nature of interactions be objective and detached, or is expressing emotion acceptable? Italians and most southern Europeans seem to be very emotional; for example, they use animation when they talk. The Germans and the Danes are not. You can't tell with a quick look what they are feeling or thinking.
Specific vs. diffuse	In a specific culture, the only relationship you have is a business one. A diffuse orientation means that the whole person is involved in a business relationship; there is a real and personal contact instead of the specific relationship predescribed by the business relationship.
Ascription vs. achievement	Ascription refers to having status attributed to you by birth, kinship, gender, or age. For example, the French ascribe their competence based on the school that they went to. If one went to one of the top French universities, they are thought to be smart. If they didn't, they might not get the job. An achievement orientation means you are judged on your record and what you have recently accomplished. Americans are more achievement oriented.

Time

Sequential vs. synchronic	A sequential view of time refers to a series of passing events. Things happen one after another. A synchronic view of time means that past, present, and future are all intertwined. The past is the predictor of the future. The present is based on the past and the future will happen because of what we have always done.

Environment

Attitudes to the environment	A controlling nature perspective leads to a sense that forces affecting one's environment reside within the person. Individuals can affect the environment. They can build big bridges, big dams, and keep back the tide. For example, the Dutch live under sea level. They control their environment. An outer control perspective is a sense that the world is more powerful than the individual is.[30]

Table 10.2 Individualism versus collectivism

Individualism	Collectivism
More frequent use of "I" form.	More frequent use of "we" form.
Decisions made on the spot by representatives.	Decisions referred back by delegate to organization.
People ideally achieve alone and assume personal responsibility.	People ideally achieve in groups, which assume joint responsibility.
Vacations taken in pairs, even alone.	Vacations in organized groups with extended family.

Recognizing the differences between individualism and collectivism is particularly important because it has such an impact on team dynamics in the work place. It's important to understand how a culture or individual's orientation to one over the other could drive interaction (see table 10.2).

Understanding these differences and adapting to them can help both women and men be successful international managers.

Women as International Managers

Introduction

Both men and women need to understand the cultural issues we discussed in order to successfully work in a global environment. However, there are international travel and business issues that are specific to women. Two resource books exploring this topic are *Do's and Taboos around the World for Women in Business* by Axtell, Briggs, Corcoran, and Lamb[30] as well as *International Business: A Basic Guide for Women* by Tracey Wilen.[31]

The following specific issues are pertinent for women:

- Work-life balance
- Discrimination
- Sexual harassment

Work-Life Balance

Talk with any woman who works internationally and the issue of work-life balance typically comes up very quickly in two contexts:

- *Spouses and Children*: A 2006 survey by Mercer, and quoted in an article by Expatica, indicated that 74 percent of male expats had partners prior to their assignment but only 25 percent of females did so.[32] Additionally, as we mentioned earlier, in the same survey over half of male expats are typically accompanied by a partner (and presumably children if they have them) but only 16 percent of female expats are accompanied by a partner. Too often, as in one of the examples we used to open the chapter, women working abroad are often assumed to be the spouse of a male expatriate.[33] Women (as do men) must decide whether to take their children and spouse with them on their assignment or leave them at home with plans for trips home as frequently and reasonably as possible. Both are tough decisions. The reality is that, even today, most female expats don't have children.[34] And the ones we met often cited being childfree as one of the reasons they felt they were able to work abroad. Successful working women are often married to successful working men, and it can be a difficult decision for any spouse—male or female—to find a job in a new country or to decide to stop working. If one spouse does stop working, in which case a social support system in the assigned country becomes critical.

- *Ability to maintain relationships at home and develop new ones abroad*: The women we talked with said it can be lonely to work abroad. Women whose jobs involved frequent back and forth travel between the United States and other countries cited challenges in engaging in any kind of regular community commitment and being available to join friends for social activities. As one woman put it, "People always think I'm out of the country, so they don't invite me to join them." For women, particularly single ones, who were living abroad, they also indicated challenges in joining social activities with other expats, which are often focused on families, spouses and children.

Companies are increasingly addressing some of the barriers that have contributed to lower numbers of women taking international assignments. One of the ways they are doing this is by offering international assignments to both men and women earlier in their careers, which offers women the option of obtaining international experience potentially prior to marriage and/or children. Another possibility is providing employment support for the "trailing spouse" to help him obtain work in the location of the assignment.

If you think you would be interested in an international assignment and are concerned that family may present challenges for you midcareer, consider pursuing an international assignment early in your career. And of course, if the opportunity comes when in fact you do find yourself married and/or with children, don't say no without considering the possibilities! You and your spouse may find that an international assignment offers your entire family an opportunity for growth, learning, travel, and new experiences.

Discrimination

Louise Arbour, United Nations High Commissioner for Human Rights from 2004–2008, said as part of 2008 International Women's Day, "Almost every country in the world still has laws that discriminate against women."[35] Globally, women are likely to have lower-skilled, lower-paying jobs than men[36] and more likely to be victims of violence.[37] And of course, in some countries, discrimination against women is a cultural norm, reinforced through laws and customs. It is important that you understand the potential challenges you may encounter around discrimination and consider ahead of time how you will address them. Most large, international companies have strict policies against discrimination in any country; nonetheless, depending on your location around the world, you are likely to experience it one way or another.

The best way to address the more subtle discrimination that still permeates some cultures is to either "credential" yourself in your introduction or be sure one of your colleagues does it. In other words, be sure that your international colleagues know your level, background, and expertise early in your interaction. Being sure people with whom you are working know who you are, is good advice for women working anywhere in the world. Doing so establishes your credibility and makes it clear to everyone that you are there to get a job done. Finally, should you experience overt or significant discrimination during your assignment, immediately raise the issue with your boss and your organization's human resource department.

Sexual Harassment

Depending on the counties one is visiting, women may experience sexual harassment when working in an international setting. There are many guides available to educate women about this topic prior to travel; in fact, a number of colleges offer online reading materials and training sessions for women prior to study abroad to help prepare them for such potential experiences. Ranging from inappropriate touching in crowded public transportation to comments on your appearance to questions at the office about your perssonal life—or even worse, to violence—managing and addressing sexual harassment abroad can be very challenging for American women who are less likely nowadays to experience overt sexual harassment in United States workplace.

Certainly, as with the issue of discrimination, you should engage your company's leadership and human resources department to understand the company's approach to addressing sexual harassment in other counties. At a minimum, prior to your departure you should educate yourself on potential risks for harassment in the designated country and determine ahead of time strategies for addressing it. You should also understand potential risks to your personal safety and what protocol and support your employer has should you experience concerns about your safety. Finally, when in doubt, rely on your intuition and common sense.

Recap

International assignments continue to be one area where women are making progress, albeit slow. The reasons driving the slower trajectory for women are often focused around family issues. While companies are taking steps to provide the proper support structure for women international mangers, it is important you consider your options for an international assignment.

Recommended Reading

Riding the Waves of Culture: Understanding Diversity in Global Business by Fons Trompenaars and Charles Hampden-Turner

CHAPTER 11

Do...Put It All Together

We wrote this book because we found that women weren't being exposed to these important topics early enough in their careers. It's easier to establish a new habit than to correct an existing one, particularly when it comes to personal attributes such as communication, work-life fit, and leadership, just to name a few. As you were reading the book, you may have realized that you want to change the way you are doing something or start focusing on an area to which you hadn't previously devoted much thought. Given that you may not have even landed in your chosen career field yet, it may feel overwhelming when you consider all the pieces of your career and the factors involved in putting those pieces into place. It doesn't need to feel that way, and to that end, we offer several thoughts on your next steps in applying the concepts in this book to your career.

If You Only Take One Thing Away from This Book, It Should Be...

Build your board. Surrounding yourself with people who want you to be successful is one of the best steps you can take to position yourself for long-term success. A good mentor is worth a pile of books on any subject. A sponsor can help you navigate the complexities of organizational politics and help pull you through challenges, especially on the days when it might seem easier to scale back career ambitions (and you will certainly have those days!). A good sponsor is clearly a career booster; and in some particularly challenging careers where women are consistently underrepresented, it is a necessity for success.

When You Are Yourself, Everything Is a Little Bit Easier

Thank goodness that the days are gone when women felt like they needed to "act like a man" in order to be a leader. The expectation that we have for authenticity in our interactions with each other ultimately means that you'll be most successful when you are able to simply be yourself. The concept of authenticity can be challenging for women early in their careers, because they are just starting to develop a self-image of themselves as working women. At times, perhaps when you start dressing more formally, or when you find yourself leading a team meeting for the first time, you may find that you feel like you are faking it a bit, and that's OK. Transitioning into a new or different role, especially one with more responsibility and visibility, may initially feel like a stretch. That kind of discomfort is natural, because it's a direct result of both personal and career growth. Eventually, it will feel normal.

Being yourself at work—the phrase that is often used is "bringing your whole self to work"—means that your identity as a woman doesn't have to be left at the door when you walk in the office each day. Men and women are more successful and more satisfied at work when there is an alignment between their personal and professional lives. When there is misalignment, the pressure and fatigue that originates from putting on a mask of a "different person" at work can be overwhelming. One sign that it may be time to leave an organization or make a career change is if you consistently find yourself struggling to have that alignment. In those cases, it may be time to shift to a career or an organization that is more aligned with your priorities and passions as well as your true character.

Awareness Gets You At Least Halfway There

We pointed out considerable research in this book that helps explain gender differences in the workplace. And we made some suggestions about how you might use that knowledge to influence your behavior and build a successful career. It might seem overwhelming if you look back at the chapters in this book and pull out all the "to-do's" and "you shoulds." Don't let it be. One of the most important aspects of being successful is being aware of yourself and your environment. You may not always know what to do, or even be able to do it, but simply having an understanding of the situation will enable you to respond in a way that makes the most sense for your career. This concept is particularly applicable when we consider ambition. You are always going to be faced with decisions around your career, whether to take a promotion, a new position, reduce hours, or even stop working for a period. There is clearly no one right answer. But being informed by what we have learned about women and ambition will enable you to sift through the noise, maybe push back a little on some preconceived notions, and make the decision that is best aligned with your goals.

Focus on One or Two Things at a Time

If you read this book cover to cover, it might feel like it's New Years Day and you have a list of resolutions a mile long. Stop apologizing at work. Ramp up a work wardrobe. Take on roles that offer more visibility. Join a local nonprofit board. The list surely goes on. Remember that just by being aware of many of these issues you'll make progress without even trying. After that, choose one or two activities at a time as your focus. Perhaps you want to strengthen your brand in a field where you have been working for a short time; identify specific steps you can take to build your brand and focus on those.

Different aspects of this book will resonate with you at different times in your career. What you focus on when you start a new job is very different from what you may focus on when you are a few years into a position and seeking a promotion. When you focus on a few things at a time, you'll be able to recognize your success and likely see better results from your efforts.

Keeping Reading...Other People's Books

Successful people don't just learn from their own experiences—they learn from others' too. Throughout this book, we referenced a number of other books that offer you the opportunity to delve deeper into a particular subject. In the months before Lindsay returned to work from her first maternity leave, she ordered a stack of books on working motherhood; the preparation helped her navigate those first few months back. We designed this book as an overview of the key elements for a successful career but encourage you to seek out more in-depth information as you need it.

Closing Words

We wrote this book because of the energy and engagement we witnessed in young women during classroom and informal discussions on these topics. We hope that as you read, it created in you a sense of excitement, possibility, and potential for the career ahead. Our best wishes to you for a successful career and life.

Additional Resources

The following organizations are good resources for working women:

- *Catalyst*: An organization that works with businesses to increase opportunities specifically for women.

- *Forte Foundation*: A group made up of top companies and business schools that helps to educate talented women in working toward becoming successful leaders.
- *9to5: National Association of Working Women*: An organization dedicated to helping strengthen the capabilities of women for work in economic justice.
- *American Medical Women's Association*: An organization that works to encourage women to become leaders in health care.
- *American Society of Women Accountants*: A group dedicated to enhancing women's opportunities in the accounting and finance fields.
- *National Association for Female Executives (NAFE)*: One of the largest organizations for businesswomen, this organization works on giving women the proper tools and resources needed to succeed in the business world.
- *Women in Government Relations (WGA)*: This nonprofit group empowers women and offers mentoring, networking, and leadership opportunities in all careers pertaining to government relations.
- *The Women's Business Development Center (WBDC)*: WBDC assists women business owners to achieve economic independence through entrepreneurship.
- *The Center for Talent Innovation (CTI, formally Center for Work-Life Policy) founded by Sylvia Ann Hewlett*: CTI is a nonprofit "think tank" with a focus on diversity and talent management.

The organizations listed above are just a few of the organizations devoted to support of women's careers. In addition to national organizations, virtually every city has various networking and professional development organizations focused on women.

Notes

1 Introduction

1. Joanna Barsh and Lareina Yee, "Unlocking the Full Potential of Women in the US Economy," report by McKinsey, April 2011. http://www.mckinsey.com/Client_Service/Organization/Latest_thinking/Unlocking_the_full_potential.aspx (accessed December 23, 2012).
2. "Table 616: Employed Civilians by Occupation, Sex, Race and Hispanic Origin: 2010," US Census Bureau. http://www.census.gov/compendia/statab/2012/tables/12s0616.pdf (accessed December 27, 2012).
3. Josh Mitchell, "Women Notch Progress: Women Now Constitute One-Third of Nationals Doctors and Lawyers," *The Wall Street Journal*, December 4, 2012. http://online.wsj.com/article/SB10001424127887323717004578159433220839020.html (accessed December 27, 2012).
4. Catalyst, *Catalyst Census Fortune 500 Women Executive Officers and Top Earners*, 2012. http://www.catalyst.org/knowledge/2012-catalyst-census-fortune-500-women-executive-officers-and-top-earners (accessed December 23, 2013).
5. "From Gen Y Women to Employers: What They Want in the Workplace and Why It Matters for Business," Business and Professional Women's Foundation, October 2011. http://www.bpwfoundation.org/documents/uploads/YC_SummaryReport_Final_Web.pdf (accessed December 27, 2012).
6. Stephanie Coontz, "The Myth of Male Decline," *The New York Times*, September 29, 2012. http://www.nytimes.com/2012/09/30/opinion/sunday/the-myth-of-male-decline.html?pagewanted=all (accessed December 23, 2012).

2 Build Your . . . Board

1. "The White House Project Report: Benchmarking Women's Leadership, 2009," The White House Project. http://thewhitehouseproject.org/wp-content/uploads/2012/03/benchmark_wom_leadership.pdf (accessed November 21, 2012).
2. Catalyst, *Knowledge Center: U.S. Women in Business*. Last modified December 11, 2012. http://www.catalyst.org/publication/132/us-women-in-business (accessed December 28, 2012).

3. Terry Morehead Dowrkin, Virginia Maurer, and Cindy Schipani, "Career Mentoring for Women: New Horizons/Expanded Methods," *Business Horizons* 55, no. 4 (2012): 363–372.

4. Nancy Carter and Christine Silva, *Mentoring: Necessary but Insufficient for Advancement*, Catalyst, 2010. http://www.catalyst.org/file/415/mentoring _necessary_but_insufficient_for_advancement_final_120610.pdf (accessed November 21, 2012).

5. Priscilla Claman, "Employ a Personal Board of Directors," in *The Harvard Business Review Guide to Getting the Mentoring You Need, Harvard Business Review*, 2011.

6. Jill Flynn, Kathryn Heath, and Mary Davis Holt, *Break Your Own Rules: How to Change the Patterns of Thinking That Block Women's Paths to Power* (San Francisco: Jossey-Bass, 2011).

7. *Coaching and Mentoring: How to Develop Top Talent and Achieve Stronger Performance* (Boston, MA: Harvard Business School Press, 2004).

8. *Oxford English Dictionary.* http://oxforddictionaries.com/definition/english /mentor (accessed November 21, 2012).

9. Sylvia Ann Hewlett, *The Sponsor Effect: Breaking through the Last Glass Ceiling* (Center for Talent Innovation, Harvard Business Review Research Report, 2011).

10. Sylvia Ann Hewlett, Lauren Leader-Chivee, and Karen Sumberg, *Sponsor Effect: UK* (New York, NY: Center for Talent Innovation, 2012).

11. Kathy E. Kram, "Phases of the Mentor Relationship," *Academy of Management Journal* 26, no. 4 (1983): 608–625.

12. S. S. Pisimisi and M. G. Ioannides, "Developing Mentoring Relationships to Support the Careers of Women in Electrical Engineering and Computer Technologies: An Analysis on Mentors' Competencies," *European Journal of Engineering Education* 30, no. 4 (2005): 477–486.

13. Marci McDonald, "The Mentor Gap," *U.S. News and World Report*, November 3, 2003.

14. Ronald J. Burke and Carol A. McKeen, "Do Managerial Women Prefer Women Mentors?" *Psychological Reports* 76 (1995): 688–690.

15. Adam Bryant, "Xerox's New Chief Tries to Redefine Its Culture," *The New York Times*, February 21, 2010.

16. "Centering on Mentoring: A Training Program for Mentors and Mentees," American Psychological Association. http://www.apa.org/education/grad /mentoring-training.pdf (accessed November 19, 2012).

3 Build Your . . . Brand

1. Kristie Tamsevicius, "Branding on the Net." http://www.brandingonthenet. com/products/topbrands.pdf (accessed November 20, 2012).

2. Marc de Swaan Arons, "How Brands Were Born: A Brief History of Modern Marketing," *The Atlantic.* http://www.theatlantic.com/business/print/2011/10 /how-brands-were-born-a-brief-history-of-modern-marketing/246012 / (accessed November 20, 2012).

3. "Target Finds Success in Designer Brands," Foxnews.com, August 10, 2002. http://www.foxnews.com/story/0,2933,60075,00.html (accessed November 21, 2012).

4. "Arthur Andersen," *Wikipedia, the Free Encyclopedia.* http://en.wikipedia.org/w/index.php?title=Arthur_Andersen&oldid=522880162 (accessed November 21, 2012).

5. "Execunet Stats," Ruby Media Group, 2010. http://blog.rubymediagroup.com/personal-branding-faqs/ (accessed November 21, 2012).

6. David McNally and Karl D. Speak, *Be Your Own Brand: A Breakthrough Formula for Standing out from the Crowd* (San Francisco: Berrett-Koehler Publishers, 2003), pp. 13–14.

7. Catherine Kaputa, *You Are a Brand!: How Smart People Brand Themselves for Business Success* (Boston, MA: Nicholas Brealey Publishing, 2010).

8. Hubert Rampersad, *Authentic Personal Branding: A New Blueprint for Building and Aligning a Powerful Leadership Brand* (Charlotte, NC: Information Age Publishing, 2009).

9. Lois P. Frankel, *Nice Girls Don't Get the Corner Office: 101 Unconscious Mistakes Women Make That Sabotage Their Careers* (New York: Business Plus, 2010).

10. Daniel Freedman, "Do Women Need to Act Like Men on Wall Street?" *Forbes,* March 16, 2011. http://www.forbes.com/sites/danielfreedman/2011/03/16/do-women-need-to-act-like-men-on-wall-street/print/ (accessed November 20, 2012).

11. McNally and Speak, *Be Your Own Brand: A Breakthrough Formula*, p. 46.

12. "Facebook's Zuckerberg Says the Age of Privacy Is Over," Readwrite.com, January 9, 2010. http://readwrite.com/2010/01/09/facebooks_zuckerberg_says _the_age_of_privacy_is_ov (accessed December 30, 2012).

13. Maria Bartiromo, "Inside the Mind of Google," CNBC.com, December 4, 2009. http://www.cnbc.com/id/33831099 (accessed November 20, 2012).

14. Rampersad, *Authentic Personal Branding.*p.80.

15. Charles Scott of CTS Consulting Group LLC, *Interviewing Skills Workshop*, delivered at Gettysburg College, October 2012.

4 Build Your . . . Communication Skills

1. Ronald Riggio, PhD, "The Five Most Common Ways Bosses Screw Up," *Psychology Today*, September 24, 2010.

2. Anna Fels, "Do Women Lack Ambition?" *Harvard Business Review*, April 2004.

3. Jill Flynn, Kathryn Heath, and Mary Davis Holt, *Break Your Own Rules: How to Change the Patterns of Thinking That Block Women's Paths to Power* (San Francisco: Jossey-Bass, 2011), p. 66.

4. Sandi Mann, "Politics and Power in Organizations: Why Women Lose Out," *Leadership and Organizational Development Journal* 16, no. 2 (1995): 9–15.

5. Deborah Tannen, "The Power of Talk: Who Gets Heard and Why," *Harvard Business Review* 73, no. 5 (September–October 1995): 138–148.

6. Deborah Tannen, *Talking from 9 to 5: Women and Men at Work* (New York: Harper Collins, 2001).

7. Tannen, "The Power of Talk."
8. Karina Schumann and Michael Ross, "Why Women Apologize More Than Men: Gender Differences in Thresholds for Perceiving Offensive Behavior," *Psychological Science*, September 20, 2010.
9. Tannen, "The Power of Talk."
10. Nancy Bonvillain, *Language, Culture, and Communication* (Upper Saddle River, NJ: Prentice Hall, 2007).
11. Pamela Hobbs, "The Medium Is the Message: Politeness Strategies in Men's and Women's Voice Mail Messages," *Journal of Pragmatics* 35 (2003): 243–262.
12. Carol Gilligan, Nona Lyons, and Trudy Hanmer, eds., *Making Connections: The Relational Worlds of Adolescent Girls at Emma Willard School* (Cambridge, MA: Harvard University Press, 1990), p. 10.
13. Peggy Klaus, *Brag! The Art of Tooting Your Own Horn without Blowing It* (New York: Warner Business Books, 2003).
14. Michael Argyle, *Bodily Communication* (New York: International Universities Press, 1975), p. 251.
15. Amy Cuddy, "The Psyche on Automatic," *Harvard Magazine*, November–December 2010. http://harvardmagazine.com/2010/11/the-psyche-on-automatic (accessed December 30, 2012).
16. Lois P. Frankel, *Nice Girls Don't Get the Corner Office: 101 Unconscious Mistakes Women Make That Sabotage Their Careers* (New York: Business Plus, 2010), pp. 188, 202, and 206.

5 Build Your . . . Negotiation Skills

1. Robin Pinkley and Gregory Northcraft, *Get Paid What You Are Worth* (New York: St. Martin's Press, 2000), p. 6.
2. A. C. Sherman, G. E. Higgs, and R. L. Williams, "Gender Differences in the Locus of Control Construct," *Psychology and Health* 12, no. 2, pp. 239–248.
3. Mika Brzezinski, *Knowing Your Value: Women, Money, and Getting What You Are Worth* (New York: Weinstein Books 2010), p. 42.
4. Ibid., p. 45.
5. Linda Babcock and Sara Laschever, *Women Don't Ask: Negotiation and the Gender Divide* (Princeton, NJ, and Oxford, UK: Princeton University Press, 2003), p. 132.
6. Deborah Kolb and Judith Williams, "Listening to Women: New Perspectives on Negotiation," *Women's Media* (blog), October 4, 2009. http://www.womensmedia.com/lead/188-listening-to-women-new-perspectives-on-negotiation.html (accessed November 25, 2012).
7. Babcock and Laschever, *Women Don't Ask*.
8. Deborah Kolb and Judith Williams, *Shadow Negotiation: How Women Can Master the Hidden Agendas That Determine Bargaining Success* (New York: Simon and Schuster, 2000), p. 11.
9. Babcock and Laschever, *Women Don't Ask*.
10. Ibid., p. 64.

11. Alice H. Eagly and Linda L. Carli, *Through the Labyrinth: The Truth about How Women Become Leaders* (Boston, MA: Harvard Business School Press, 2007), p. 96.
12. Kolb and Williams, *Shadow Negotiation*, p. 11.
13. Kolb and Williams, "Listening to Women."

6 Consider . . . Ambition

1. "Ambition," *Wikipedia, the Free Encyclopedia.* Last modified November 4, 2012. http://en.wikipedia.org/wiki/Ambition (accessed December 28, 2012).
2. Catalyst, *Women MBAs.* Last modified July 2012. http://www.catalyst.org /publication/250/women-mbas (accessed December 28, 2012).
3. Jane Leber Herr and Catherine Wolfram, "'Opt-Out' Rates at Motherhood across High-Education Career Paths: Selection versus Work Environment," January 2009. http://faculty.haas.berkeley.edu/wolfram/Papers/OptOut_Final _Jan09.pdf (accessed December 28, 2012).
4. Catalyst, *Knowledge Center: U.S. Women in Business.* Last modified December 11, 2012. http://www.catalyst.org/publication/132/us-women-in-business (accessed December 28, 2012).
5. Carol Gilligan, Nora Lyons, and Trudy Hammer, eds., *Making Connections: The Relational Worlds of Adolescent Girls at Emma Willard School* (Cambridge, MA: Harvard University Press, 1990).
6. Anna Fels, *Necessary Dreams: Ambition in Women's Changing Lives* (New York: Anchor Books, 2004).
7. Jerome Kagan and Howard Moss, *From Birth to Maturity* (New Haven, CT: Yale University Press, 1983).
8. "Young, Underemployed, and Optimistic: Coming of Age, Slowly, in a Tough Economy," Pew Research Center. Last modified February 9, 2012. http:// www.pewsocialtrends.org/2012/02/09/young-underemployed-and-optimistic/ (accessed December 28, 2012).
9. Jennifer L. Lawless and Richard L. Fox, "Men Rule: The Continued Under-Representation of Women in U.S. Politics," Women and Politics Institute, American University School of Public Affairs, January 2012. http:// www.american.edu/spa/wpi/upload/2012-Men-Rule-Report-web.pdf (accessed December 28, 2012).
10. Leslie Bennetts, *The Feminine Mistake: Are We Giving up Too Much?* (New York: Hyperion, 2007), p. 46.
11. "Transcript and Video of Speech by Sheryl Sandberg, Chief Operating Officer, Facebook," Barnard College. Last modified May 18, 2011. http://barnard.edu /headlines/transcript-and-video-speech-sheryl-sandberg-chief-operating-officer -facebook (accessed December 28, 2012).
12. Fels, Anna. "Do Women Lack Ambition?" *Harvard Business Review*, April 2004, Volume 82, Issue 4, pages 50–60.
13. Fels, Anna. "Do Women Lack Ambition?" *Harvard Business Review*, April 2004, Volume 82, Issue 4, pages 50–60.

14. A. C. Sherman, G. E. Higgs, and R. L. Williams, "Gender Differences in the Locus of Control Construct," *Psychology and Health* 12, no. 2, pp. 239–248.
15. Katherine Graham, *Personal History* (New York: Alfred A. Knopf, 1997).
16. Alice H. Eagly and Linda L. Carli, *Through the Labyrinth: The Truth about How Women Become Leaders* (Boston, MA: Harvard Business School Press, 2007).
17. Sandi Mann, "Politics and Power in Organizations: Why Women Lose Out," *Leadership and Organizational Development Journal* 16, no. 2 (1995): 9–15.
18. Charles F. Carver and Michael F. Scheier, *On the Self-Regulation of Behavior* (New York: Cambridge University Press, 2001).
19. Albert Bandura and Robert Wood, "Effect of Perceived Controllability and Performance Standards on Self Regulation of Complex Decision-Making," *Journal of Personality and Social Psychology* 56, no. 5 (1989): 805–814.
20. "Ambition and Gender at Work," Institute of Leadership and Management, 2011. http://www.i-l-m.com/downloads/resources/centres/communications-and-marketing/ILM_Ambition_and_Gender_report_0211.pdf (accessed December 28, 2012).
21. James B. Stewart, "A C.E.O.'s Support System, a k a Husband," *The New York Times*, November 4, 2011. http://www.nytimes.com/2011/11/05/business/a-ceos-support-system-a-k-a-husband.html?pagewanted=all (accessed December 28, 2012).
22. Sylvia Rimm, Sara Rimm-Kaufman, and Ilonna Rimm, *See Jane Win: The Rimm Report on How 1,000 Girls Became Successful Women* (New York, NY: Three Rivers Press, 2000).

7   Consider . . . Leadership

1. Alice H. Eagly and S. Karau, "Role Congruity Theory of Prejudice toward Female Leaders," *Psychological Review* 109, no. 3 (2002): 573–598.
2. Shankar Vedantam, "The Myth of the Iron Lady," *The Washington Post*, November 12, 2007. http://www.washingtonpost.com/wp-dyn/content/article/2007/11/11/AR2007111101204.html (accessed December 22, 2007).
3. Todd L. Pittinsky, Laura M. Bacon, and Brian Welle, "The Great Woman Theory of Leadership?—Perils of Positive Stereotypes and Precarious Pedestals," in *Women and Leadership: The State of Play and Strategies for Change*, Barbara Kellerman and Deborah L. Rhode, eds. (San Francisco: Jossey-Bass, 2007), p. 95.
4. Ibid., p. 96.
5. Virginia E. Schein, "Women in Management: Reflections and Projections," *Women in Management Review* 22, no. 1 (2007): 6–19.
6. Ibid.
7. Moe Grzelakowski, *Mother Leads Best: 50 Women Who Are Changing the Way Organizations Define Leadership* (Chicago: Dearborn Trade Publishing, 2005).
8. Alice H. Eagly and Linda L. Carli, *Through the Labyrinth: The Truth about How Women Become Leaders* (Boston, MA: Harvard Business School Press, 2007), p. 121.

9. Ibid., p. 123.

10. Alice H. Eagly and Linda L. Carli, "Women and the Labyrinth of Leadership," *Harvard Business Review*, September 2007. http://hbr.org/2007/09/women-and -the-labyrinth-of-leadership/ar/1 (accessed November 25, 2012).

11. James Burns McGregor, *Leadership* (New York: Harper and Row, 1978).

12. Robert Reiss, "How Ritz-Carlton Stays at the Top," *Forbes*, October 30, 2009. http://www.forbes.com/2009/10/30/simon-cooper-ritz-leadership-ceon etwork-hotels.html (accessed March 2, 2013)

13. Richard E. Walton, "From Control to Commitment in the Workplace," *Harvard Business Review*, March 1985. http://hbr.org/1985/03/from -control-to-commitment-in-the-workplace/ar/4 (accessed November 25, 2012).

14. Ibid.

15. Michael Porter, "Formulating Strategy," *Harvard Business Review*, November 1, 1996. http://hbr.org/product/what-is-strategy/an/96608-PDF-ENG (accessed November 25, 2012).

16. Ibid.

17. Edgar Schein, "Coming to a New Awareness of Organizational Culture," *Sloan Management Review*, Winter 1984, p. 63.

18. Ibid., p. 9.

19. Laura Morgan Roberts, "Chapter 12—Bringing Your Whole Self to Work— Lessons in Authentic Engagement from Women Leaders," in *Women and Leadership: The State of Play and Strategies for Change*, Barbara Kellerman and Deborah L. Rhode, eds. (San Francisco: Jossey-Bass, 2007), p. 330.

20. Abraham Zaleznik and Manfred F. R. Kets De Vries, *Power and the Corporate Mind* (Boston, MA: Houghton Mifflin, 1975), p. 63.

21. Evangelina Holvina, "Chapter 13—Women and Power: New Perspectives on Old Challenges," in *Women and Leadership: The State of Play and Strategies for Change*, Barbara Kellerman and Deborah L. Rhode, eds. (San Francisco: Jossey-Bass, 2007), p. 362.

22. Rosabeth Moss Kanter, *Men and Women of the Corporation* (New York: Basic Books, 1977), p. 177.

23. Leslie Kwoh, "Bosses Get Low Marks," *The Wall Street Journal*, July 11, 2012. http://online.wsj.com/article/SB200014240527023032922045775190504233 13624.html (accessed December 22, 2012).

8   Consider . . . Work-Life Fit

1. Hilda L. Solis and Keith Hall, "Women in the Labor Force: A Databook," US Bureau of Labor Statistics. Last modified December 2011. http://www.bls.gov /cps/wlf-databook-2011.pdf (accessed December 28, 2012).

2. K. Aumann, E. Galinsky, and K. Matos, *The New Male Mystique* (New York: Families and Work Institute, 2011).

3. "The Harried Life of the Working Mother," Pew Research Center, October 1, 2009. http://www.pewsocialtrends.org/2009/10/01/the-harried-life-of-the -working-mother/ (accessed December 28, 2012).

4. Chiung-Ya Tang and Shelley MacDermid Wadsworth, "Time and Workplace Flexibility," Families and Work Institute. http://familiesandwork.org/site/research/reports/time_work_flex.pdf (accessed December 28, 2012).
5. Eileen Boris and Carolyn Herbst Lewis, "Caregiving and Wage-Earning: A Historical Perspective on Work and Family," in *The Work and Family Handbook*, Marcie Pitt-Catsouphes, Ellen Ernst Kossek, and Stephen Sweet, eds. (Mahwah, NJ: Psychology Press, 2006).
6. "The Harried Life of the Working Mother," Pew Research Center.
7. Aumann, Galinsky, and Matos, *The New Male Mystique*.
8. Jeffrey Rosenberg and W. Bradford Wilcox, "The Importance of Fathers in the Healthy Development of Children," US Department of Health and Human Services. Last modified 2006. http://www.childwelfare.gov/pubs/usermanuals/fatherhood/fatherhood.pdf (accessed December 28, 2012).
9. "Do US Men Value Fatherhood over Their Careers?" *Science Daily*, October 12, 2011. http://www.sciencedaily.com/releases/2011/10/111013113816.htm (accessed December 28, 2012).
10. Prof. Brad Harrington, Fred Van Deusen, and Iyar Mazar, "The New Dad: Right at Home," Boston College Center for Work and Family. Last modified 2012. http://www.bc.edu/content/dam/files/centers/cwf/pdf/The%20New%20Dad%20Right%20at%20Home%20BCCWF%202012.pdf (accessed December 28, 2012).
11. Prof. Brad Harrington, Fred Van Deusen, and Iyar Mazar, "The New Dad: Caring, Committed and Conflicted," Boston College Center for Work and Family. Last modified 2011. http://www.bc.edu/content/dam/files/centers/cwf/pdf/FH-Study-Web-2.pdf (accessed December 28, 2012).
12. "Charting Parenthood: A Statistical Portrait of Fathers and Mothers in America," US Department of Health and Human Services. http://fatherhood.hhs.gov/charting02/introduction.htm (accessed December 28, 2012).
13. "Table 5: Employment status of the population by sex, marital status, and presence and age of own children under 18, 2010–2011 annual averages," in "Employment Characteristics of Families," Bureau of Labor Statistics, 2012. http://www.bls.gov/news.release/famee.t05.htm (accessed December 28, 2012)
14. Laura Vanderkam, "What Moms Can Learn from Dads," blog updated based on a June 2008 article for *USA Today*. http://lauravanderkam.com/2009/06/what-moms-can-learn-from-dads/ (accessed December 28, 2012).
15. Gretchen Livingston and D'Vera Cohn, "Childlessness Up among All Women; Down among Women with Advanced Degrees," June 25, 2010. http://pewresearch.org/pubs/1642/more-women-without-children (accessed December 28, 2012).
16. "Childfree," *Wikipedia, the Free Encyclopedia*. http://en.wikipedia.org/wiki/Childfree (accessed December 28, 2012).
17. Ajay Chaudry, Juan Manuel Pedroza, Heather Sandstrom, Anna Danziger, Michel Grosz, Molly Scott, and Sarah Ting, "Child Care Choices of Low-Income Working Families," Urban Institute, January 2011. http://www.urban.org/UploadedPDF/412343-Child-Care-Choices.pdf (accessed December 28, 2012).

18. Joan C. Williams and Penelope Huang, "Improving Work-Life Fit in Hourly Jobs: An Underutilized Cost-Cutting Strategy in a Globalized World," The Center for Work Life Law, 2011. http://www.worklifelaw.org/pubs /ImprovingWork-LifeFit.pdf (accessed December 28, 2012), p. 3.
19. Anna Quindlen, *Being Perfect* (New York: Random House, 2005).

9   Consider . . . Career-Path Navigation

1. Sylvia Ann Hewlett and Carolyn Buck Luce, "Off-Ramps and On-Ramps: Keeping Talented Women on the Road to Success," *Harvard Business Review* 83, no. 3 (March 2005): 43–54.
2. "Women's Employment during the Recovery," US Department of Labor, May 3, 2011. http://www.dol.gov/_sec/media/reports/FemaleLaborForce /FemaleLaborForce.pdf (accessed December 28, 2012).
3. Hewlett and Luce, "Off-Ramps and On-Ramps."
4. Cathy Benko and Molly Anderson, *The Corporate Lattice: Achieving High Performance in the Changing World of Work* (Boston, MA: Harvard Business Review Press, 2010), p. 5.
5. "Maternity Leave and Employment Patterns of First-Time Mothers: 1961– 2008," US Bureau of Labor Statistics. Last modified October 2011. http:// www.census.gov/prod/2011pubs/p70–128.pdf (accessed December 28, 2012).
6. Prof. Brad Harrington, Fred Van Deusen, and Iyar Mazar, "The New Dad: Caring, Committed and Conflicted," Boston College Center for Work and Family. Last modified 2011. http://www.bc.edu/content/dam/files/centers/cwf /pdf/FH-Study-Web-2.pdf (accessed December 28, 2012).
7. Ibid.
8. Kyra L. Sutton and Raymond A. Noe, "Family-Friendly Programs and Work-Life Integration: More Myth than Magic?" in *Work and life Integration: Organizational, Cultural and Individual Perspectives*, Ellen Ernst Kossek and Susan J. Lambert, eds. (Mahwah, NJ: Lawrence Erlbaum Associates, 2005), pp. 151–171.
9. "Business Impacts for Flexibility: An Imperative for Expansion," Corporate Voices for Working Families. Last modified 2005. http://www.cvworkingfami-lies.org/downloads/Business%20Impacts%20of%20Flexibility.pdf (accessed December 28, 2012).
10. "Women's Employment during the Recovery," US Department of Labor.
11. Ibid.
12. Cathy Benko and Anne Weisberg, *Mass Career Customization: Aligning the Workplace with Today's Nontraditional Workforce* (Boston, MA: Harvard Business School Press, 2007), p. 5.
13. Liz Macko and Kerry Rubin, *Midlife Crisis at 30: How the Stakes Have Changed for a New Generation—and What to Do about It* (New York: Plume, 2005), p. 2.
14. Benko and Weisberg, *Mass Career Customization*.

10 Consider . . . Working in a Global Environment

1. Thomas L. Friedman, *The World Is Flat: A Brief History of the Twenty-First Century* (New York: Farrar, Straus and Giroux, 2006).
2. "Passenger Numbers to Reach 2.75 Billion by 2011," IATA. Last modified October 24, 2007. http://www.iata.org/pressroom/pr/pages/2007–24–10–01.aspx (accessed June 26, 2012).
3. "Record Numbers of International Students Worldwide!" *Student Abroad Magazine*. Last modified March 10, 2011. http://studentabroadmagazine.wordpress.com/2011/03/10/record-numbers-of-international-students-worldwide/ (accessed June 26, 2012).
4. "New Countries of the World: The 34 New Countries Created since 1990," About.com. Last modified 2012. http://geography.about.com/cs/countries/a/newcountries.htm (accessed June 20, 2012).
5. "GDP (current US$)," The World Bank. Last modified 2012. http://data.worldbank.org/indicator/NY.GDP.MKTP.CD (accessed June 21, 2012).
6. Ibid.
7. Ibid.
8. "European Union," European Union. Last modified 2009. http://www.encyclopedia.com/topic/European_Union.aspx (accessed June 20, 2012).
9. "This Day in History," History. Last modified 2012. http://www.history.com/this-day-in-history/nafta-signed-into-law (accessed June 21, 2012).
10. "CAFTA-DR (Dominican Republic-Central America FTA)," Office of the United States Trade Representative. Last modified 2012. http://www.encyclopedia.com/topic/European_Union.aspx (accessed June 21, 2012).
11. "Buick Excelle Is China's Best Selling Car in 2011," *AutoGuide*. Last modified January 25. http://www.autoguide.com/auto-news/2012/01/buick-excelle-is-chinas-best-selling-car-in-2011.html (accessed June 22, 2012).
12. "The Best-Selling Cars of 2011," *Forbes*. Last modified November 2, 2011. http://www.forbes.com/sites/joannmuller/2011/11/02/the-best-selling-cars-of-2011/ (accessed June 22, 2012).
13. "Honda Worldwide," Honda. Last modified 2012. http://world.honda.com/index.html (accessed June 22, 2012).
14. "KIA Motors Corporation," KIA. Last modified 2012. http://www1.kia.eu/Company/Kia-Motors-Corporation/ (accessed June 22, 2012).
15. "60 Minutes," CBS, October 28, 2012.
16. Jared Shelly, "Where Are All the Expat Women?" *Human Resource Executive Online*, February 7, 2011. http://www.hreonline.com/HRE/view/story.jhtml?id=533329676 (accessed December 2, 2012).
17. Mierlla Visser, "Women Expatriates: What Do You Do All Day?" reprinted from *XPat Journal* 7 (Spring 2005). http://www.expatica.com/hr/story/women-expatriates-what-do-you-do-all-day-21648.html (accessed December 2, 2012).
18. "Record Number of Female Expats," Expatica, October 17, 2006. http://www.expatica.com/nl/essentials_moving_to/essentials/record-number-of-female-expats-33780_8462.html (accessed December 2, 2012).

19. Paul M. Caligiuri and Rosalie L. Tun, "Comparing the Success of Male and Female Expatriates from a US-Based Multinational Company," *The International Journal of Human Resource Management* 10, no. 5 (October 1999): 763–782.

20. Paul Caligiuri and Wayne F. Cascio, "Sending Women on Global Assignments: Challenges, Myths and Solutions," *WorldatWork Journal* (Second Quarter 2000): 34–41.

21. Yochanan Altman and Susan Shortland, "Women and International Assignments: Taking Stock—A 25-Year Review," *Human Resource Management* 47, no. 2 (2008): 199–216. doi: 10.1002/hrm.20208.

22. "Definitions for Culture," Definitions. Last modified 2012. http://www.definitions.net/definition/culture (accessed June 18, 2012).

23. Clyde Kluckhohn, *Mirror For Man* (New York: Whittlesey House, a division of the McGraw Hill Book Company, 1949), pp. 17–39.

24. Edgar H. Schein, *Organizational Culture and Leadership* (San Francisco: Jossey-Bass Publishers, 1988), p. 171.

25. Ibid., p. 171.

26. Mansour Javidan and Robert J. House, "Cultural Acumen for the Global Manager: Lessons from Project GLOBE," *Organizational Dynamics* 29, no. 4 (2001): 289–305.

27. Ibid.

28. Alfons Trompenaars and Charles Hampden-Turner, *Riding the Waves of Culture: Understanding Diversity in Global Business* (New York: McGraw Hill, 2012).

29. Ibid.

30. Roger E. Axtell, Tami Briggs, Margaret Corcoran, and Mary Beth Lamb, *Do's and Taboos around the World for Women in Business* (New York: John Wiley and Sons, 1977).

31. Tracey Wilen, *International Business: A Basic Guide for Women* (Bloomington, IN: Xlibris Corporation, 2000).

32. "Record Number of Female Expats," Expatica.

33. Visser, "Women Expatriates."

34. Shelly, "Where Are All the Expat Women."

35. "Women Still Face Discrimination Worldwide, Says UN Rights Chief," United Nations, March 7, 2008. http://www.un.org/apps/news/story.asp?NewsID =25893 (accessed December 2, 2012).

36. "Women, Poverty, and Economics." United Nations Women. http://www.unifem.org/gender_issues/women_poverty_economics/ (Accessed March 2, 2013)

37. Facts and Figures on Women Worldwide." United Nations Secretary-General's Campaign to End Violence Against Women. Last modified November 2011. http://www.un.org/en/women/endviolence/pdf/pressmaterials/unite_the_situation_en.pdf (Accessed March 2, 2013

38. Trompenaars and Hampden-Turner, *Riding the Waves of Culture*, pp. 8–10.

Bibliography

"2011 Working Mother 100 Best Companies." Working Mother. Last modified 2011. http://www.workingmother.com/best-company-list/116542 (Accessed November 6, 2012).

"60 Minutes." CBS. October 28, 2012.

Altman, Yochanan, and Susan Shortland. "Women and International Assignments: Taking Stock—A 25-Year Review." *Human Resource Management* 47, no. 2 (2008): 199–216. doi: 10.1002/hrm.20208 (Accessed December 28, 2012).

"Ambition." *Wikipedia , the Free Encyclopedia* . Last modified November 4, 2012. http://en.wikipedia.org/wiki/Ambition (Accessed December 28, 2012).

"Ambition and Gender at Work." Institute of Leadership and Management. http://www.i-l m.com/downloads/resources/centres/communications-and-marketing /ILM_Ambition_and_Gender_report_0211.pdf (Accessed December 28, 2012).

Argyle, Michael. *Bodily Communication.* New York: International Universities Press, 1975.

Arroba, Tanya, and Kim James. "Are Politics Palatable to Women Managers? How Women Can Make Wise Moves at Work." *Women in Management Review* 3, no. 3 (1988): 123–130.

"Arthur Andersen." *Wikipedia, the Free Encyclopedia.* http://en.wikipedia.org/w /index.php?title=Arthur_Andersen&oldid=522880162 (Accessed November 21, 2012).

Aumann, Kerstin, Ellen Galinsky, and Kenneth Matos. *The New Male Mystique.* New York: Families and Work Institute, 2011.

Axtell, Roger E., Tami Briggs, and Margaret Corcoran. *Do's and Taboos around the World for Women in Business.* New York: John Wiley and Sons, 1977.

Babcock, Linda, and Sara Laschever. *Ask for It: How Women Can Use the Power of Negotiation to Get What They Really Want.* New York: Bantam Books, 2008.

———. *Women Don't Ask: Negotiation and the Gender Divide.* Princeton, NJ, and Oxford, UK: Princeton University Press, 2003.

Bandura, Albert, and Robert Wood. "Effect of Perceived Controllability and Performance Standards on Self Regulation of Complex Decision-Making." *Journal of Personality and Social Psychology* 56, no. 5 (1989): 805–814.

Barsh, Joanna, and Yee Lareina. "Unlocking the Full Potential of Women in the US Economy." Report by McKinsey, April 2011. http://www.mckinsey.com /Client_Service/Organization/Latest_thinking/Unlocking_the_full_potential. aspx (Accessed December 23, 2012).

Bartiromo, Maria. "Inside the Mind of Google." CNBC.com. Last modified December 4, 2009. http://www.cnbc.com/id/33831099 (Accessed November 20, 2012).

Benko, Cathy, and Anne Weisberg. *Mass Career Customization: Aligning the Workplace with Today's Nontraditional Workforce.* Boston, MA: Harvard Business School Press, 2007.

Benko, Cathy, and Molly Anderson. *The Corporate Lattice: Achieving High Performance in the Changing World of Work.* Boston, MA: Harvard Business Review Press, 2010.

Bennetts, Leslie. *The Feminine Mistake: Are We Giving up Too Much?* New York: Hyperion, 2007.

"Best Benefits Work Life Balance." CNN Money. Last modified February 2011. http://money.cnn.com/magazines/fortune/bestcompanies/2011/benefits/work _life.html (Accessed November 6, 2012).

"The Best-Selling Cars of 2011." *Forbes.* Last modified November 2, 2011. http:// www.forbes.com/sites/joannmuller/2011/11/02/the-best-selling-cars-of-2011 / (Accessed June 22, 2012).

Bonvillain, Nancy. *Language, Culture, and Communication.* Upper Saddle River, NJ: Prentice Hall, 2007.

Boris, Eileen, and Carolyn Herbst Lewis. "Caregiving and Wage-Earning: A Historical Perspective on Work and Family." In *The Work and Family Handbook.* Marcie Pitt-Catsouphes, Ellen Ernst Kossek, and Stephen Sweet, eds. Mahwah, NJ: Psychology Press, 2006, 73–93.

Bort, Julie. Aviva Pflock, and Devra Renner. *Mommy Guilt: Learn to Worry Less, Focus on What Matters Most, and Raise Happier Kids.* New York, NY:Amacom, 2005.

Bryant, Adam. "Xerox's New Chief Tries to Redefine Its Culture." *The New York Times,* February 21, 2010.

Brzezinski, Mika. *Knowing Your Value: Women, Money, and Getting What You Are Worth.* New York: Weinstein Books, 2010.

"Buick Excelle Is China's Best Selling Car in 2011." *AutoGuide.* Last modified January 25, 2012. http://www.autoguide.com/auto-news/2012/01/buick-excelle-is -chinas-best-selling-car-in-2011.html (Accessed June 22, 2012).

Burke, Ronald J., and Carol A. McKeen. "Do Managerial Women Prefer Women Mentors?" *Psychological Reports* 76 (1995): 688–690.

"Business Impacts for Flexibility: An Imperative for Expansion." Corporate Voices for Working Families . Last modified 2005. http://www.cvworkingfamilies .org/system/files/Business%20Impacts%20of%20Flexibility.pdf (Accessed December 28, 2012).

"CAFTA-DR (Dominican Republic-Central America FTA)." Office of the United States Trade Representative. Last modified 2012. http://www.encyclopedia.com /topic/European_Union.aspx (Accessed June 21, 2012).

Caligiuri, Paul, and Wayne F. Cascio. "Sending Women on Global Assignments: Challenges, Myths and Solutions." *WorldatWork Journal* (Second Quarter 2000): 34–41.

Caligiuri, Paul M., and Rosalie L. Tun. "Comparing the Success of Male and Female Expatriates from a US-Based Multinational Company." *The International Journal of Human Resource Management* 10, no. 5 (October 1999): 763–782.

Carter, Nancy, and Christine Silva. "Mentoring: Necessary but Insufficient for Advancement." 2010. Catalyst. http://www.catalyst.org/file/415/mentoring _necessary_but_insufficient_for_advancement_final_120610.pdf (Accessed November 21, 2012).

Carver, Charles F., and Michael F. Scheier. *On the Self-Regulation of Behavior*. New York: Cambridge University Press, 2001.

Catalyst. *Catalyst Census Fortune 500 Women Executive Officers and Top Earners*. Last modified December 11, 2012. http://www.catalyst.org/knowledge/2012 -catalyst-census-fortune-500-women-executive-officers-and-top-earners (Accessed December 23, 2012).

———. *Knowledge Center: U.S. Women in Business*. Last modified December 11, 2012. http://www.catalyst.org/knowledge/us-women-business-0 (Accessed December 28, 2012).

———. *Women MBAs*. Last modified July 2012. http://www.catalyst.org /publication/250/women-mbas (Accessed December 28, 2012).

"Centering on Mentoring: A Training Program for Mentors and Mentees." American Psychological Association. http://www.apa.org/education/grad /mentoring-training.pdf (Accessed November 19, 2012).

"Charting Parenthood: A Statistical Portrait of Fathers and Mothers in America." US Department of Health and Human Services. http://fatherhood.hhs.gov /charting02/introduction.htm (Accessed December 28, 2012).

Chaudry, Ajay, Juan Manuel Pedroza, Heather Sandstrom, Anna Danziger, Michel Grosz, Molly Scott, and Sarah Ting. "Child Care Choices of Low-Income Working Families." Urban Institute. January 2011. http://www.urban.org/Uploa dedPDF/412343-Child-Care-Choices.pdf (Accessed December 28, 2012).

"Childfree." *Wikipedia, the Free Encyclopedia*. http://en.wikipedia.org/wiki /Childfree (Accessed December 28, 2012).

Claman, Priscilla. "Employ a Personal Board of Directors." In *The Harvard Business Review Guide to Getting the Mentoring You Need* (blog), October 20, 2010. *Harvard Business Review*, 2011.

Coaching and Mentoring: How to Develop Top Talent and Achieve Stronger Performance. Boston, MA: Harvard Business School Press. 2004.

Coontz, Stephanie. "The Myth of Male Decline." *The New York Times*, September 29, 2012. http://www.nytimes.com/2012/09/30/opinion/sunday/the-myth-of-male -decline.html?pagewanted=all (Accessed December 23, 2012).

"Countries." European Union. Last modified 2012. http://europa.eu/about-eu /countries/index_en.htm (Accessed June 20, 2012).

Covert, Bryce. "Why Can't Women Have It All? It's Not You—It's Discrimination." *The Nation*, June 21, 2012. http://www.thenation.com/blog (Accessed December 28, 2012).

Cuddy, Amy. "The Psyche on Automatic." *Harvard Magazine*, November–December 2010. http://harvardmagazine.com/2010/11/the-psyche-on-automatic (Accessed December 30, 2012).

Darling, Diane. *The Networking Survival Guide: Practical Advice to Help You Gain Confidence, Approach People, and Get the Success You Want.* New York: McGraw-Hill, 2010.

de Swaan Arons, Marc. "How Brands Were Born: A Brief History of Modern Marking." *The Atlantic.* http://www.theatlantic.com/business/print/2011/10/how-brands-were-born-a-brief-history-of-modern-marketing/246012/ (Accessed November 20, 2012).

"Definitions for Culture." Definitions. Last modified 2012. http://www.definitions.net/definition/culture (Accessed June 18, 2012).

"Do US Men Value Fatherhood over Their Careers?" *Science Daily*, October 12, 2011. http://www.sciencedaily.com/releases/2011/10/111013113816.htm (Accessed December 28, 2012).

Dowrkin, Terry Morehead, Virginia Maurer, and Cindy Schipani. "Career Mentoring for Women: New Horizons/Expanded Methods." *Business Horizons* 55, no. 4 (2012): 363–372.

Eagly, Alice H., and Linda L. Carli. *Through the Labyrinth: The Truth about How Women Become Leaders.* Boston, MA: Harvard Business School Press, 2007.

———., "Women and the Labyrinth of Leadership." *Harvard Business Review*, September 2007. http://hbr.org/2007/09/women-and-the-labyrinth-of-leadership/ar/1 (Accessed November 25, 2012).

Eagly, Alice H., and S. Karau. "Role Congruity Theory of Prejudice toward Female Leaders." *Psychological Review* 109, no. 3 (2002): 573–598.

Ehrlich, Paul. *Human Natures.* Washington, DC: Island Press, 2000.

"Employment Characteristics of Families." Bureau of Labor Statistics. 2012. http://www.bls.gov/news.release/famee.t05.htm (Accessed December 28, 2012).

Ensher, Ellen A., and Susan Elaine Murphy. *Power Mentoring: How Successful Mentors and Protégés Get the Most Out of Their Relationships.* San Francisco: Jossey-Bass, 2005.

"Execunet Stats." Ruby Media Group. http://blog.rubymediagroup.com/personal-branding-faqs/ (Accessed November 21, 2012).

"European Union." European Union. Last modified 2009. http://www.encyclopedia.com/topic/European_Union.aspx (Accessed June 20, 2012).

"Facebook's Zuckerberg Says the Age of Privacy Is Over." Readwrite.com. January 9, 2010. http://readwrite.com/2010/01/09/facebooks_zuckerberg_says_the_age_of_privacy_is_ov (Accessed December 30, 2012).

"Facts and Figures on Women Worldwide." United Nations Secretary-General's Campaign to End Violence Against Women. Last modified November 2011. http://www.un.org/en/women/endviolence/pdf/pressmaterials/unite_the_situation_en.pdf (Accessed March 2, 2013).

Fels, Anna. "Do Women Lack Ambition?" *Harvard Business Review* 82, no. 4 (April 2004): 50–60.

———. *Necessary Dreams: Ambition in Women's Changing Lives.* New York: Anchor Books, 2004.

Fiorina, Carly. *Tough Choices: A Memoir.* New York: Penguin Group, 2006.

Fisher, Roger, William Ury, and Bruce Patt. *Getting to Yes: Negotiating Agreement without Giving In.* New York: Penguin Books, 2011.

Flynn, Jill, Kathryn Heath, and Mary Davis Holt. *Break Your Own Rules: How to Change the Patterns of Thinking That Block Women's Paths to Power.* San Francisco: Jossey-Bass, 2011.

Frankel, Lois P. *Nice Girls Don't Get the Corner Office: 101 Unconscious Mistakes Women Make That Sabotage Their Careers.* New York: Business Plus, 2010.

Freedman, Daniel. "Do Women Need to Act Like Men on Wall Street?" *Forbes,* March 16, 2011. http://www.forbes.com/sites/danielfreedman/2011/03/16 /do-women-need-to-act-like-men-on-wall-street/print/ (Accessed November 20, 2012).

Friedman, Thomas L. *The World Is Flat: A Brief History of the Twenty-First Century.* New York: Farrar, Straus and Giroux, 2006.

"From Gen Y Women to Employers: What They Want in the Workplace and Why It Matters for Business." Business and Professional Women's Foundation . October 2011. http://www.bpwfoundation.org/documents/uploads/YC_SummaryReport _Final_Web.pdf (Accessed December 27, 2012).

"GDP (Current US$)." The World Bank. Last modified 2012. http://data.worldbank .org/indicator/NY.GDP.MKTP.CD (Accessed June 21, 2012).

Gilligan, Carol. *In a Different Voice: Psyhcological Theory and Women's Development.* Cambridge, MA: Harvard University Press, 1998.

Gilligan, Carol, Nora Lyons, and Trudy Hammer, eds. *Making Connections: The Relational Worlds of Adolescent Girls at Emma Willard School.* Cambridge, MA: Harvard University Press, 1990.

Graham, Katharine. *Personal History.* New York: Alfred A. Knopf, 1997.

Greenberg, Cathy L., and Barratt S. Avigdor. *What Happy Working Mothers Know.* Hoboken, NJ: John Wiley and Sons, 2009.

Grzelakowski, Moe. *Mother Leads Best: 50 Women Who Are Changing the Way Organizations Define Leadership.* Chicago: Dearborn Trade Publishing, 2005.

Halle, Tamara, PhD. "Charting Parenthood: A Statistical Portrait of Fathers and Mothers in America." *Child Trends.* 2006. http://fatherhood.hhs.gov/charting02 /introduction.htm (Accessed December 28, 2012).

"The Harried Life of the Working Mother." Pew Research Center . Last modified October 1, 2009. http://www.pewsocialtrends.org/2009/10/01/the-harried-life-of -the-working-mother/ (Accessed December 28, 2012).

Harrington, Prof. Brad, Fred Van Deusen, and Iyar Mazar. "The New Dad: Caring, Committed and Conflicted." Boston College Center for Work and Family. Last modified 2011. http://www.bc.edu/content/dam/files/centers/cwf/pdf/The New Dad Right at Home BCCWF 2012.pdf (Accessed December 28, 2012).

———. "The New Dad: Right at Home." Boston College Center for Work and Family. Last modified 2012. http://www.bc.edu/content/dam/files/centers/cwf /pdf/The%20New%20Dad%20Right%20at%20Home%20BCCWF%202012 .pdf (Accessed December 28, 2012).

Harvard Business Review on Work and Life Balance. Boston, MA: Harvard Business School Press, 2000.

Herr, Jane Leber, and Catherine Wolfram. "'Opt-Out' Rates at Motherhood across High-Education Career Paths: Selection versus Work Environment." January 2009. http://faculty.haas.berkeley.edu/wolfram/Papers/OptOut_Final_Jan09 .pdf (Accessed December 28, 2012).

Hewlett, Sylvia Ann. *The Sponsor Effect: Breaking through the Last Glass Ceiling.* Boston: Center for Talent Innovation. Harvard Business Review Research Report, 2011.

Hewlett, Sylvia Ann, and Carolyn Buck Luce. "Off-Ramps and On-Ramps: Keeping Talented Women on the Road to Success." *Harvard Business Review* 83, no. 3 (March 2005): 43–54.

Hewlett, Sylvia Ann, Lauren Leader-Chivee, and Karen Sumberg. *Sponsor Effect: UK.* New York, NY: Center for Talent Innovation, 2012.

Hobbs, Pamela. "The Medium Is the Message: Politeness Strategies in Men's and Women's Voice Mail Messages." *Journal of Pragmatics* 35 (2003): 243–262.

Holvina, Evangelina. "Chapter 13—Women and Power: New Perspectives on Old Challenges." In *Women and Leadership: The State of Play and Strategies for Change.* Barbara Kellerman and Deborah L. Rhode, eds. San Francisco: Jossey-Bass, 2007, p. 362.

"Honda Worldwide." Honda. Last modified 2012. http://world.honda.com/index .html (Accessed June 22, 2012).

"International Tourism Receipts Surpass US$1 trillion in 2011." World Tourism Organization. Last modified May 7, 2012. http://media.unwto.org/en /press-release/2012–05–07/international-tourism-receipts-surpass-us-1-trillion-2011 (Accessed June 20, 2012).

Javidan, Mansour, and Robert J. House. "Cultural Acumen for the Global Manager: Lessons from Project GLOBE." *Organizational Dynamics* 29, no. 4 (2001): 289–305.

Kagan, Jerome, and Howard Moss. *From Birth to Maturity.* New Haven, CT: Yale University Press, 1983.

Kanter, Rosabeth Moss. *Men and Women of the Corporation.* New York: Basic Books, 1977.

Kaputa, Catherine. *You Are a Brand!: How Smart People Brand Themselves for Business Success.* Boston, MA: Nicholas Brealey Publishing, 2010.

Kellerman, Barbara, and Deborah L. Rhode. *Women and Leadership: The State of Play and Strategies for Change.* San Francisco: Jossey-Bass, 2007.

"KIA Motors Corporation." KIA. Last modified 2012. http://www1.kia.eu /Company/Kia-Motors-Corporation/ (Accessed June 22, 2012).

Klaus, Peggy. *Brag! The Art of Tooting Your Own Horn without Blowing It.* New York: Warner Business Books, 2003.

Kluckhohn, Clyde. *Mirror for Man.* New York: Whittlesey House, a division of the McGraw Hill Book Company, 1949.

Kolb, Deborah, and Judith Williams. "Listening to Women: New Perspectives on Negotiation." *Women's Media* (blog), October 04, 2009. http://www.womensmedia .com/lead/188-listening-to-women-new-perspectives-on-negotiation.html (Accessed November 25, 2012).

———. *Shadow Negotiation: How Women Can Master the Hidden Agendas That Determine Bargaining Success*. New York: Simon and Schuster, 2000.

Kolb, Deborah, Judith Williams, and Carol Frohlinger. *Her Place at the Table: A Woman's Guide to Negotiating Five Key Challenges to Leadership Success*. New York: Simon and Schuster, 2010.

Kossek, Ellen Ernst, and Susan J. Lambert. *Work and Life Integration: Organizational, Culture and Individual Perspectives*. Mahwah, NJ: Lawrence Erlbaum Associates, 2005.

Kram, Kathy E. "Phases of the Mentor Relationship." *Academy of Management Journal* 26, no. 4 (1983): 608–625.

Kwoh, Leslie. "Bosses Get Low Marks." *The Wall Street Journal*, July 11, 2012. http://online.wsj.com/article/SB20001424052702303292204577519050423313 624.html (Accessed December 22, 2012).

Lawless, Jennifer L., and Richard L. Fox. "Men Rule: The Continued Under-Representation of Women in U.S. Politics," Women and Politics Institute, American University School of Public Affairs. January 2012. http://www.american .edu/spa/wpi/upload/2012-Men-Rule-Report-web.pdf (Accessed December 28, 2012).

Livingston, Gretchen, and D'Vera Cohn. "Childlessness Up among All Women; Down among Women with Advanced Degrees." June 25, 2010. http://pewresearch .org/pubs/1642/more-women-without-children (Accessed December 28, 2012).

———. "More Women without Children." Pew Research Center. Last modified June 25, 2012. http://pewresearch.org/pubs/1642/more-women-without-children (Accessed December 28, 2012).

Macko, Liz, and Kerry Rubin. *Midlife Crisis at 30: How the Stakes Have Changed for a New Generation—and What to Do about It*. New York: Plume, 2005.

Malhotra, Deepak, and Max H. Bazerman. *Negotiation Genius: How to Overcome Obstacles and Achieve Brilliant Results at the Bargaining Table and Beyond*. New York: Bantam Books, 2008.

Mann, Sandi. "Politics and Power in Organizations: Why Women Lose Out." *Leadership and Organizational Development Journal* 16, no. 2 (1995): 9–15.

Mason, Linda. *The Working Mother's Guide to Life: Strategies, Secrets, and Solutions*. New York: Three Rivers Press, 2002.

"Maternity Leave and Employment Patterns of First-Time Mothers: 1961–2008." US Bureau of Labor Statistics. Last modified October 2011. http://www.census .gov/prod/2011pubs/p70–128.pdf (Accessed December 28, 2012).

McDonald, Marci. "The Mentor Gap." *U.S. News and World Report*, November 3, 2003.

McGregor Burns, James. *Leadership*. New York: Harper and Row, 1978.

McNally, David, and Karl D. Speak. *Be Your Own Brand: A Breakthrough Formula for Standing out from the Crowd*. San Francisco: Berrett-Koehler Publishers, 2003.

———. *Be Your Own Brand: Achieve More of What You Want by Being More of Who You Are*. San Francisco: Berrett-Koehler Publishers, 2011.

Meers, Sharon, and Joanne Strober. *Getting to 50/50: How Working Couples Can Have It All by Sharing It All*. New York: Bantam Books, 2009.

Mitchell, Josh. "Women Notch Progress: Women Now Constitute One-Third of Nationals Doctors and Lawyers." *The Wall Street Journal*, December 4, 2012. http://online.wsj.com/article/SB10001424127887323717004578159433220839020.html (Accessed December 27, 2012).

Morgan, Abi. *The Iron Lady*. Distributed by 20th Century Fox, The Weinstein Company US, Pathé International. 2011. DVD.

"New Countries of the World: The 34 New Countries Created since 1990." About.com.Lastmodified2012.http://geography.about.com/cs/countries/a/newcountries.htm (Accessed June 20, 2012).

Nohria, Nitin, and Rakesh Khurana, eds. *Handbook of Leadership Theory and Practice: An HBS Centennial Colloquium on Advancing Leadership*. Boston, MA: Harvard Business Press, 2010.

"Passenger Numbers to Reach 2.75 billion by 2011." IATA. Last modified October 24, 2007. http://www.iata.org/pressroom/pr/pages/2007–24–10–01.aspx (Accessed June 26, 2012).

Pinkley, Robin, and Gregory Northcraft. *Get Paid What You Are Worth*. New York: St. Martin's Press, 2000.

Pisimisi, S. S., and M. G. Ioannides. "Developing Mentoring Relationships to Support the Careers of Women in Electrical Engineering and Computer Technologies: An Analysis on Mentors' Competencies." *European Journal of Engineering Education* 30, no. 4 (2005): 477–486.

Pitt-Catsouphes, Marcie, Ellen Ernst Kossek, and Stephen Sweet, eds. *The Work and Family Handbook: Multi-Disciplinary Perspectives and Approaches*. New York: Psychology Press, 2006.

Pittinsky, Todd L., Laura M. Bacon, and Brian Welle. "The Great Woman Theory of Leadership?—Perils of Positive Stereotypes and Precarious Pedestals." In *Women and Leadership: The State of Play and Strategies for Change*, Barbara Kellerman and Deborah L. Rhode, eds. San Francisco: Jossey-Bass, 2007, p. 95.

Porter, Michael. "Formulating Strategy." *Harvard Business Review*, November 1, 1996. http://hbr.org/product/what-is-strategy/an/96608-PDF-ENG (Accessed November 25, 2012).

Quindlen, Anna. *Being Perfect*. New York: Random House, 2005.

Rampersad, Hubert. *Authentic Personal Branding: A New Blueprint for Building and Aligning a Powerful Leadership Brand*. Charlotte, NC: Information Age Publishing, 2009.

"Record Number of Female Expats." Expatica. October 17, 2006. http://www.expatica.com/nl/essentials_moving_to/essentials/record-number-of-female-expats-33780_8462.html (Accessed December 2, 2012).

"Record Numbers of International Students Worldwide!" *Student Abroad Magazine*. Last modified March 10, 2011. http://studentabroadmagazine.wordpress.com/2011/03/10/record-numbers-of-international-students-worldwide/ (Accessed June 26, 2012).

Riggio, Ronald, PhD. "The Five Most Common Ways Bosses Screw Up." *Psychology Today*, September 24, 2010. http://www.psychologytoday.com/blog/cutting-edge-leadership/201009/the-five-most-common-ways-bosses-screw (Accessed December 28, 2012); http://www.nytimes.com/2011/11/05/business

/a-ceos-support-system-a-k-a-husband.html?pagewanted=all (Accessed December 28, 2012).

Rimm, Sylvia, Sara Rimm-Kaufman, and Ilonna Rimm. *See Jane Win: The Rimm Report on How 1,000 Girls Became Successful Women.* New York, NY: Three Rivers Press, 2000.

Roberts, Laura Morgan. "Chapter 12—Bringing Your Whole Self to Work—Lessons in Authentic Engagement from Women Leaders." In *Women and Leadership: The State of Play and Strategies for Change.* Barbara Kellerman and Deborah L. Rhode, eds. San Francisco: Jossey-Bass: 2007,p. 330.

Rosenberg, Jeffrey, and W. Bradford Wilcox. "The Importance of Fathers in the Healthy Development of Children." US Department of Health and Human Services. Last modified 2006. http://www.childwelfare.gov/pubs/usermanuals /fatherhood/fatherhood.pdf (Accessed December 28, 2012).

Sachs, Wendy. *How She Really Does It: Secrets of Successful Stay-at-Work Moms.* Cambridge, MA: Perseus Books, 2005.

"A Safe Trip Abroad." Travel.State.Gov: A Service of the Bureau of Consular Affairs. Last modified 2012. http://travel.state.gov/travel/tips/safety/safety_1747.html (Accessed June 26, 2012).

Sandberg, Sheryl. *Lean in: Women, Work and the Will to Lead.* New York, NY: Knopf, 2013.

Schein, Edgar H. "Coming to a New Awareness of Organizational Culture." *Sloan Management Review* (Winter 1984), pp. 9 and 63.

———. *Organizational Culture and Leadership.* San Francisco: Jossey-Bass Publishers, 1988.

Schein, Virginia E. "Women in Management: Reflections and Projections." *Women in Management Review* 22, no. 1 (2007): 6–19.

Schumann, Karina, and Michael Ross. "Why Women Apologize More Than Men: Gender Differences in Thresholds for Perceiving Offensive Behavior." *Psychological Science,* September 20, 2010.

Scott, Charles, of CTS Consulting Group LLC. *Interviewing Skills Workshop.* Delivered at Gettysburg College. October 2012.

Shelly, Jared. "Where Are All the Expat Women." *Human Resource Executive Online.* February 7, 2011. http://www.hreonline.com/HRE/view/story .jhtml?id=533329676 (Accessed December 2, 2012).

Sherman, A. C., G. E. Higgs, and R. L. Williams. "Gender Differences in the Locus of Control Construct." *Psychology and Health* 12, no. 2, pp. 239–248.

Solis, Hilda L., and Keith Hall. "Women in the Labor Force: A Databook." US Bureau of Labor Statistics. Last modified December 2011. http://www.bls.gov /cps/wlf-databook-2011.pdf (Accessed December 28, 2012).

Stewart, James B. "A C.E.O.'s Support System, a k a Husband," *The New York Times,* November 4, 2011. http://www.nytimes.com/2011/11/05/business/a-ceos -support-system-a-k-a-husband.html?pagewanted=all (Accessed December 28, 2012).

"Strategy." *Oxford English Dictionary Compact Edition.* New York: Oxford University Press, 1971. http://oxforddictionaries.com/definition/english/strategy (Accessed November 25, 2012).

Sutton, Kyra L., and Raymond A. Noe. "Family-Friendly Programs and Work-Life Integration: More Myth than Magic?" In *Work and Life Integration: Organizational, Cultural and Individual Perspectives.* Ellen Ernst Kossek and Susan J. Lambert, eds. Mahwah, NJ: Lawrence Erlbaum Associates, 2005, pp. 151–171.

"Tactics." *Oxford English Dictionary Compact Edition.* New York: Oxford University Press, 1971. http://oxforddictionaries.com/definition/american_english/tactic?region=us&q=tactics (Accessed November 25, 2012).

Tamsevicius, Kristie. "Branding on the Net." http://www.brandingonthenet.com/products/topbrands.pdf (Accessed November 20, 2012).

Tang, Chiung-Ya, and Shelley MacDermid Wadsworth. "Time and Workplace Flexibility." Families and Work Institute. http://familiesandwork.org/site/research/reports/time_work_flex.pdf (Accessed December 28, 2012).

Tannen, Deborah. "The Power of Talk: Who Gets Heard and Why." *Harvard Business Review* 73, no. 5 (September–October 1995): 138–148.

———. *Talking from 9 to 5: Women and Men at Work.* New York: Harper Collins, 2001.

"Target Finds Success in Designer Brands." Foxnews.com . http://www.foxnews.com/story/0,2933,60075,00.html (Accessed November 21, 2012).

"This Day in History." History. Last modified 2012. http://www.history.com/this-day-in-history/nafta-signed-into-law (Accessed June 21, 2012).

Thompson, Leigh. *The Mind and Heart of the Negotiator.* Upper Saddle River, NJ: Prentice Hall, 2011.

"Transcript and Video of Speech by Sheryl Sandberg, Chief Operating Officer, Facebook." Barnard College. Last Modified May 18, 2011. http://barnard.edu/headlines/transcript-and-video-speech-sheryl-sandberg-chief-operating-officer-facebook (Accessed December 28, 2012).

Trompenaars, Alfons, and Charles Hampden-Turner. *Riding the Waves of Culture: Understanding Diversity in Global Business.* New York: McGraw Hill, 2012.

Vanderkam, Laura. "What Moms Can Learn from Dads." Blog updated based on a June 2008 article for *USA Today.* http://lauravanderkam.com/2009/06/what-moms-can-learn-from-dads (Accessed December 28, 2012).

Vedantam, Shankar. "The Myth of the Iron Lady." *The Washington Post*, November 12, 2007. http://www.washingtonpost.com/wp-dyn/content/article/2007/11/11/AR2007111101204.html (Accessed December 22, 2007).

Visser, Mierlla. "Women Expatriates: What Do You Do All Day?" *XPat Journal* 7 (Spring 2005). http://www.expatica.com/hr/story/women-expatriates-what-do-you-do-all-day-21648.html (Accessed December 2, 2012).

Walton, Richard E. "From Control to Commitment in the Workplace." *Harvard Business Review*, March 1985. http://hbr.org/1985/03/from-control-to-commitment-in-the-workplace/ar/4 (Accessed November 25, 2012).

Wellington, Sheila, Marcia Brumit Kropf, and Paulette R. Gerkovich. "What's Holding Women Back?" *Harvard Business Review*, June 2003. http://hbr.org/2003/06/whats-holding-women-back/ar/2 (Accessed December 28, 2012).

"The White House Project Report: Benchmarking Women's Leadership, 2009." The White House Project. http://thewhitehouseproject.org/wp-content/uploads/2012/03/benchmark_wom_leadership.pdf (Accessed November 21, 2012).

Wilen, Tracey. *International Business: A Basic Guide for Women*. Bloomington, IN: Xlibris Corporation, 2000.

Williams, Joan C., and Penelope Huang. "Improving Work-Life Fit in Hourly Jobs: An Underutilized Cost-Cutting Strategy in a Globalized World." The Center for Work Life Law. 2011. http://www.worklifelaw.org/pubs/ImprovingWork-LifeFit.pdf (Accessed December 28, 2012).

Wolfe, Lahle. "Corporations Sued for Gender Discrimination against Women and Men: Gender Discrimination More Common against Women, but It Happens to Men, Too." About.com. http://womeninbusiness.about.com/od/sexual-discrimination/a/Corporations-Sued-For-Gender-Discrimination-Against-Women-And-Men.htm (Accessed December 28, 2012).

"Women Still Face Discrimination Worldwide, Says UN Rights Chief." United Nations. March 7, 2008. http://www.un.org/apps/news/story.asp?NewsID=25893 (Accessed December 2, 2012).

"Women, Poverty, and Economics." United Nations Women. http://www.unifem.org/gender_issues/women_poverty_economics/ (Accessed March 2, 2013).

"Women's Employment during the Recovery." US Department of Labor. May 3, 2011. http://www.dol.gov/_sec/media/reports/FemaleLaborForce/FemaleLaborForce.pdf (Accessed December 28, 2012).

"Young, Underemployed, and Optimistic: Coming of Age, Slowly, in a Tough Economy." Pew Research Center (online forum message). February 09, 2012. http://www.pewsocialtrends.org/2012/02/09/young-underemployed-and-optimistic/ (Accessed December 28, 2012).

Zaleznik, Abraham, and Manfred F. R. Kets De Vries. *Power and the Corporate Mind*. Boston, MA: Houghton Mifflin, 1975.

Index

360-degree feedback 18

advisor 7, 8
Altman, Yochanan 162
ambition 46, 89–101
apology 49, 51
appearance 62
Arbour, Louis 173
Argyle, Michael 59–60
Arthur Andersen 29
asking advantage 69

Babcock, Linda 68–69
Bandura, Albert 98–99
BATNA 75
behavior theory 105
Benko, Cathy 142, 147
Bennetts, Leslie 93
board of advisors 7–12
Bonvillain, Nancy 54
Boris, Eileen 127
bragging 55
brand
    alignment 26
    building 30
    gaps 35
    personal 27
    product 28, 29
    students 31
    SWOT analysis 32, 33, 34
Brzezinski, Mika 68
Burns, James McGregor 108
Burns, Ursula 17

career change 146–147
career path 141

Carli, Linda 70, 98, 106–107
Center for Talent Innovation 10, 142, 150
chief executive officers 90
child care 134
child-free 132–133
childhood play 92
Claman, Priscilla 9
Clifton StrengthsFinder 17, 71
confidence 98
Congressional membership and gender 90, 92
communication
    direct 55
    indirect 55
corporate lattice 142–143, 153
Cuddy, Amy 60–62
cultural awareness 167–171
cultural differences 167–171
culture, organizational 117

De Vries, Manfred 119
decisiveness 112
deficit model 106
Dyson 114

Eagly, Alice 70, 98, 106–107
elevator speech 58
employee empowerment 108
employee involvement 108, 118
entrepreneur 35, 146
ex-patriots 160, 162
eye contact 61

Facebook 36
Family Medical Leave Act 144, 148
feedback 50
Fels, Anna 46, 48, 92, 95

femininity 95
flexible work arrangement 144
Flynn Heath Holt 9, 16, 96
Fox, Richard 93
Frankel, Lois 35, 61
Freud, Sigmund 91
Friedman, Thomas 158
Frohlinger, Carol 69

Gallup's StrengthsFinder 17, 71
gestures 61
Gettysburg College, Garthwait Leadership
    Center 12
Gilligan, Carol 55, 68, 91
globalization 164
Graham, Katherine 97
great man theory 105, 106
great woman theory 105
Grzelakowski, Moe 106
guilt-free parenting 139

Hennessee, E. Lee 35
Hewlitt, Syliva Ann 150
Hobbs, Pamela 54
House, Robert 165
household economy 128–129

informational interviewing 42
international assignments 163–164
    discrimination 173
    safety 174
    sexual harassment 173
    work-life balance 171–172
interviews
    asking questions during 41
    behavioral interviews 41
    conducting 40
    phone interviews 40
    preparation 39

Kagan, Jerome 92
Kanter, Rosabeth 94, 120
Kaputa, Catherine 33
Keegan, John 119
Klaus, Peggy 55
Kluckhohn, Clyde 164
Kohlberg, Lawrence 91
Kolb, Deborah 69
Kram, Kathy 13

laissez-faire leadership style 108–09
Laschever, Sara 68–69
Lawless, Jennifer 93
leadership 103–123
    gender gap 1, 8
Lewis, Carolyn Herbst 127
linguistic style 47
LinkedIn 20, 23, 40, 41
locus of control 66–67, 96–97

Macko, Liz 151
Mann, Sandi 46
mass career customization 142, 147
MBAs 90
McNally, David 31, 36
mentor 7–10
mentoring 13
    feedback 17
    formal 15
    gender 16–17
    informal 14
    for men 8
    peer mentoring 9, 11
    phases of mentoring 13
Moss, Howard 92
Myers-Briggs Type Indicator 17

negotiation 65–85
    approach 73–77
    salary 79
    shadow 69–70
network 19, 153
    composition of 23
    maintenance of 23
    value of 19
nonverbal communication 59
Northcraft, Gregory 66

Off-Ramps 150–151
organizational culture 117
organizational politics 98
outsourcing 136–137

part-time work 142, 145–146
personal brand, see brand
Piaget, Jean 91
Pinkley, Robin 66
politeness 54
Porter, Michael 113

posture 61
power 119
presence 117
Project GLOBE 165–167

Rampersad, Hubert 33, 38
Reagan, Ronald 199
recognition 92
returning to work 150
Rimm, Ilonna 100
Rimm, Sylvia 100
Rimm Report 100
Rimm-Kaufman, Sara 100
ritual opposition 50, 53
Ritz Carlton 109
Rometty, Virginia 99
Ross, Michael 51
Rubin, Kerry (*Midlife Crisis at 30*) 151
Rutter, Julia 95

salary negotiation, *see* negotiation
Sandberg, Sheryl 93–94
Scheier, Michael 98
Schein, Edward (*Organization, Culture and Leadership*) 117, 165
Schein, Virginia 105
Schmidt, Eric 26
Schroeder, Pat 132
Schuman, Karina 51
SCORE 16
sex-typing 105
Seymour, Lesley Jane 58
shadow negotiation 69, 70
Shortland, Susan 162
situational leadership style 105
Slaughter, Ann-Marie 133
Sloan Center on Aging and Work 144
social cognition theory 98
social media 29, 35, 36
Southwest Airlines 113–114
Speak, Karl D. 31, 36

sponsor 8–12
stay-at-home dads 131
Stone, Pamela 93
strategic planning 114–116
strategy 112–113
StrengthsFinder 17, 71
supports for working parents 137–138
SWOT analysis 32, 33, 34

taking credit 96
Tannen, Deborah 47, 48
team concept 108
time off 143
total quality management 108
Toyota 113
trait theory 105
transactional leadership style 108, 112
transformative leadership style 108–109, 114
Trompenaars, Fons 161, 165, 169–171

universalist 162

Walton, Richard E. 110
Weisberg, Anne 142, 147
Williams, Judith 69
Wood, Robert 98–99
work-life balance, *see* work-life fit
work-life conflict 133, 146
work-life fit 125–140
    conflict 126
    gender 130–131
    history of 128
    international assignments 171–172
    men 126, 131
work-life integration, *see* work-lift fit

ZOPA 74, 75
Zaleznik, Abraham (*Power and the Corporate Mind*) 119
Zuckerberg, Mark 36

CPSIA information can be obtained at www.ICGtesting.com
Printed in the USA
BVOW02s1913190314

348181BV00005B/15/P